A Home
from Home

From Immigrant Boy
to English Man

GEORGE ALAGIAH

ABACUS

ABACUS

First published in Great Britain in 2006 by Little, Brown
This paperback edition published in 2007 by Abacus

9 10

A CIP catalogue record for this book
is available from the British Library.

ISBN 978-0-349-11911-3

Typeset in Palatino by M Rules
Printed and bound in Great Britain by
Clays Ltd, St Ives plc

Papers used by Abacus are from well-managed forests
and other responsible sources.

MIX
Paper from
responsible sources
FSC® C104740

Abacus
An imprint of
Little, Brown Book Group
Carmelite House
50 Victoria Embankment
London EC4Y 0DZ

An Hachette UK Company
www.hachette.co.uk

www.littlebrown.co.uk

To my parents, Donald and Therese. You took the risk and I and my sisters – Mari, Rachel, Christine and Jenny – we have all reaped the benefits. We thank you.

To the millions who have left the land of their birth for the promise of a better life in a strange place. You know – and I understand – that the toughest frontier to cross is the one that lies between two questions: 'Should I go?' and 'Shall I stay?' Between them lies the challenge of migration; it's like a great mountain range between the past and the future. When you meet the challenge, when you climb the mountain, you can see where you came from and where you have yet to go. You can link them together and make your journey whole.

Contents

Contents

Acknowledgements

Above all this book is an attempt to compare my own 'sink or swim' experience as an immigrant child with that of thousands of immigrant children today who find their contact with Britain is limited – sometimes by preference, sometimes by circumstance. Childhood memories and conversations with friends and family helped me to conjure up the anxieties and challenges of growing up away from my parents in a largely white school.

When it came to trying to show what life is like for those who grow up in immigrant enclaves today I had to rely on the kindness and guidance of others. In Bradford Angie Kotler was unstinting in the time and effort she devoted to ensure that I met a cross section of people. I salute the way she helped me so ably and fully despite having reservations about some of my conclusions.

In Tower Hamlets, London, Sister Christine Frost virtually held my hand as we walked from one estate to another. I will always remember the way this demure, slight woman would be greeted on the streets by all manner of people regardless of their colour or religion. Like a latter-day missionary she encouraged tolerance by example.

Plenty of other people have helped and, mostly, I have tried to acknowledge my debt to them in the text. There are some, however, whom I want to acknowledge here.

Like me, Dhananjayan Sriskandarajah is a product of the Sri Lankan Tamil diaspora – the Australian end of it. That, coupled with a professional interest in migration, made him an astute judge of parts of this book.

In reading the final text Humphrey Keenleyside adroitly combined the roles of being a very old friend and a diligent critic.

Katie Joice's research was invaluable. It was made possible by the generosity of Elaine and David Potter.

At the BBC Mark Damazer, Peter Horrocks and Amanda Farnsworth have all been supportive.

Richard Beswick, my editor at Little, Brown, showed immense patience as he waited for the words I first promised him at a lunch in what now feels like another era. He's overseen the whole process with a light touch but clear vision. Jane Selley teased out all the little but irritating mistakes in the text while Iain Hunt coped admirably with a succession of revisions.

My agent, Margaret Hanbury, has been at hand with good advice whenever I needed it.

All of them have left this book better than it deserved to be when it first came off my printer. The remaining shortcomings are down to me and me alone.

Finally, it is my family – Frances, Adam and Matt – who have had to put up with a husband and father who was semi-detached for long periods of time – and almost always when there was something important that needed doing around the home! Thank you.

Preface

Halfway through writing this book, on a beautiful summer morning in July 2005, I got a call from Amanda Farnsworth, my editor
at the *Six O'Clock News*. Her voice was taut, her instruction simple:
'Get in as soon as you can. It looks like there are attacks on the
Underground.' In the aftermath of the London terrorist atrocities
in which 52 innocent people were killed – the first suicide bombings in Europe – one central question preoccupied all those who
were trying to find some explanation for what had happened. In
pubs and cafés, at dinner parties and community halls, in
churches and mosques, in the House of Commons and in the
homes where the terrorists had once lived, people wanted to
know how British-born lads could do this in their own land. How
could the sons of Pakistani immigrants who had decided to settle
here – the fathers of one of them even owned that quintessen-
tially English institution, a fish and chip shop – end up with such
ambivalence for the lives of their fellow countrymen and women?
Virtually every newspaper, radio and TV station addressed the
issue; one stands out in my memory. On Radio 4's *Today* programme on 18 July 2005, Professor Michael Clark of King's
College in London put it like this (with hindsight we can disre-
gard his caution in attributing blame):

> If these four young men were genuine suicide bombers aris-
> ing out of our society in ways that could not have been

detected before and didn't have a profile that made them look like suicide bombers . . . what is surprising and shocking is that this might have arisen from young men in our own society who gave no previous indication that they were prepared to do this.

Professor Clarke could not have known at the time that the name of one of the men, Mohammed Siddiq Khan, had previously cropped up on the periphery of a separate security service investigation. His surprise and shock flows from the assumption that Mohammed Siddiq Khan and his cohorts, Hasib Hussain, Shehzad Tanweer and Germaine Lindsay, shared the values and traditions of 'our society'.

That assumption is no longer credible – at least not in certain communities or sections within them. I had suspected as much, and that is why I first decided to write a book that would look at what we mean when we talk about multicultural Britain. At the time my aim was simply to explore the difference between my own experiences as an immigrant – what you might loosely call an integrationist approach – and the experiences of more recent immigrants, some of whom seem to live in parallel communities. The events of July 2005 have heightened my concerns in ways which I could never have imagined when I set out on this book.

'There is a form of separate development in Britain,' I told my publisher, Richard Beswick, back in 2003. The term 'separate development', with its echoes of apartheid in South Africa, was provocative but I thought it was apt in one important sense – I believed then, and still do now, that separation is partly the product of successive governments pursuing a race relations policy based on multiculturalism. Whatever we meant by multiculturalism, surely encouraging people to live separately was not part of the package. Or was it? Multiculturalism has given us – immigrants – the right to be different but failed to provide sufficient incentives to integrate. As I ask later on in this book: has institutionalised tolerance for diversity led to institutional indifference to separation?

Of course segregation, on its own, is not always problematic. Many of the Punjabis of Southall in west London, the Gujaratis of Leicester, and the Jews of north London, to give just three examples, live in largely distinct communities, but it would be difficult to argue that they have been unsuccessful or resentful immigrants. On the contrary, they have contributed significantly to their communities. And despite what was said by some commentators at the time of the attacks, it isn't true that Muslims have a special problem with patriotism. The vast majority of Muslims want to integrate even if the process, for them, has been more challenging. But where custom, religion – in this case Islam – and poverty overlap, there is a version of segregation that is totally at odds with the diverse but united nation that most people want.

Some of what I found in Bradford in west Yorkshire and Tower Hamlets in London while researching this book alarmed me. On one estate in Tower Hamlets I met young people who had had so few dealings with white people that, years later, they could still count them off. I spent a morning with a first-generation West Indian woman, Helen, who looked back with affection at a time before multiculturalism, when her council estate had 'all sorts'. Today she is among a handful of English-speaking tenants in a block dominated by Bangladeshis. In Bradford the separation has become so acute that the council is spending tax-payers' money to bring white and Asian children together through 'linking projects'. I don't question the commitment or vision of the people who organise these things, but I do worry about a race relations policy that has made their work necessary.

Of course I'm not saying that I or anyone else might have predicted, let alone imagined, the murderous consequences that flowed from the alienation from British society that one assumes the suicide bombers felt. My aim when I set out to write this book was to show that there are thousands of young immigrant boys and girls who cannot aspire to the achievements and sense of belonging that I and my sisters have acquired since we first came here in the sixties. I was worried that there is a generation of immigrants who will be forever locked into an ethnic ghetto, unable fully to exploit everything that Britain has to offer. After July 2005, it seems the stakes are much higher. We need to look beyond the welfare of the immigrants, it is the state of our nation that is now being called into question.

The bombers may have had British passports, they may have had Yorkshire accents and worn the street garb of all urban youth, but just how British did they feel? More importantly, did we, in Britain, set any sort of standard, demand any sort of behaviour, offer any form of encouragement that might have enticed them away from the savage influences of those who persuaded them to turn the capital's trains and buses into charnel houses?

Londoners were only just beginning to come to terms with what had happened when another group of would-be terrorists failed in their attempt to bomb the city. I was at a memorial service, waiting to interview the mother of one of the victims of the 7 July bombings, when I heard the tell-tale scream of police sirens. Exactly two weeks after the first attacks, three more trains and a bus had been targeted. This time the alleged terrorists failed – their devices didn't explode and the men were on the run.

By the time they were all captured, it was clear that the extremist interpretation of Islam that had infected sections of Britain's Pakistani community had also worked its way into the hearts and minds of immigrants from the Horn of Africa. The first fugitive suspect to be captured was a Somali, Yassin Hassan Omar.

It turned out that Yassin Hassan Omar had come to this country as an unaccompanied minor, a refugee, in 1992. He was eleven at the time, and had sought sanctuary from a situation I knew only too well. In the year he came to Britain, I had made several trips to Somalia to cover the civil war and the famine that it caused. In my book *A Passage to Africa*, I called it a 'year of living dangerously'. In feeding centres I had seen young children take their last breath, in hospitals I'd seen boys and girls who had been caught up in the indiscriminate conflict between warlords; and on the streets I'd watched fearfully as young men strutted around with AK-47 rifles slung over their shoulders, looking for someone to fight. Tens of thousands of children perished.

So Yassin Hassan Omar was one of the lucky few. He got away. He got the chance to start a new life. Night after night, as I wrote up the day's events on my computer screen at the *Six O'Clock News* desk, I simply couldn't fathom or accept how the Somali community in London had allowed this young man to forget just how fortunate he was. So often, and in private, I had railed against populist and infectious attacks on asylum seekers, but in the aftermath of that failed attack on London, I too was plagued by doubts and tempted by those same ungenerous sentiments. One newspaper headline put it in typically blunt but telling fashion: 'The benefit bombers who repaid help with hatred'. For those who had always objected to an open, tolerant Britain ready to accept its share of the world's refugee burden, the CCTV images of dark-skinned young men accused of plotting mass murder seemed to prove their point.

And that is why we need to re-examine multiculturalism, the policy that has underpinned race relations policy in Britain for the best part of forty years. We need to accept that a part of the way in which it has been implemented may have delivered something we never envisaged or intended. To ignore the lessons of July 2005 is to risk a backlash that might unhinge everything that has been achieved since modern immigration to Britain began in the mid to late fifties. In Chapter 3, for example, I look at how the pendulum is swinging away from the liberal and inclusive immigration policies that made Holland and Denmark so unique.

After the events of July 2005, the political class in Britain began to question multiculturalism in a way it had never done before. Speaking in the month after the attacks, the Prime Minister, Tony Blair, said he never knew 'quite what people mean when they talk about multiculturalism', though in the same breath he admitted to having used the term himself 'occasionally'. Later that August the outgoing Leader of the Opposition, Michael Howard, chose the *Guardian* to raise his own doubts about the policy.

'Perhaps one of the mistakes we have made in recent years,' he wrote, 'is a tendency to place emphasis on the need to encourage the retention of attachment to other traditions, and not enough on the British identity we all share.'

As they always do, the politicians made it sound as if their various pronouncements on the subject of multiculturalism were breaking new ground. If this book achieves anything at all, I hope it shows that what the politicians debate in the public realm is only a belated version of the private battle immigrants have been dealing with in their day-to-day lives from the minute they set foot on these shores.

I want to personalise the debate about multiculturalism, about immigration and about identity because that is where its subtlety is revealed most poignantly and accurately. I want to give names to the numbers, character to the statistics and emotions to the theories.

The language of race and identity is strewn with pitfalls for the uninitiated. The term 'assimilation', for example, carries with it a huge amount of baggage, virtually a dirty word in some circles. They imbue it with the characteristics of an Uncle Tom or a 'coconut' – dark on the outside but white underneath. I'm not sure that I accept this. Where I have used the term in this book it simply refers to the process of acquiring English habits but without making any judgement about the person involved. 'Integration' is another of these watchwords. In general I use it to refer to the process through which whole groups, as opposed to individuals, join the mainstream.

I am also mindful that being British is not the same as being English. I am a British citizen with the rights, responsibilities and duties that that confers, but I am English by inclination and culture.

In researching this book, I have discovered how much has already been written on these subjects. Many others, often people far better qualified to make judgements, have tackled the issues. But I hope I bring something new. I have applied my craft, my ability to tell a story, to issues that are all too often obscured in either politically correct language or academic impenetrability. Above all, I have tried to make my point through the experiences of people on the ground. So, to take immigration as an example, I hope that whether you agree with my views or not, you will at least come to respect the honest endeavours of the individuals I have talked to.

This book is emphatically not an attack on multiculturalism as a whole. I and millions of others have benefited from a policy that has sought to ensure that immigrants – especially those from the 'visible' minorities – enjoy the same opportunities as everyone else. No one can seriously doubt the enormous progress that has been made in fighting the racism that stained the lives of so many hard-working people.

Here's one example from my family's own experience. In the seventies my parents spent a couple of years in Britain while my father did some postgraduate studies. Money was tight and my mother went out to look for work. She was offered a back room job with a major supermarket chain, but the manager who interviewed her said she would not be able to wear her sari to work. My mother, knowing what a difference the weekly pay cheque would mean, agreed to the condition. That was not how my father saw things when my mother gave him what she thought was good news. No wife of his was going to be told what she could or could not wear. So it was back to the classified ads in the *Evening Standard*. If my father felt insulted, I felt embarrassed. Why couldn't my mum dress like all the other mums?

Today no supermarket chain is able to impose that kind of culturally specific condition on its workers. Indeed, many take pride in being sensitive to their employees' various needs. And today few immigrant children would be embarrassed by their parents' clothing, at least no more than all children are always embarrassed by the state of their parents' attire! In fact, the 'Indian' look can be quite a fashion statement. So if I'm critical of multiculturalism, it's not because I want to ditch it but because I want to make it better.

As I say, I was already some way into writing this book when those attacks on London took place. It was a conversation with the broadcaster Jonathan Dimbleby, back in 2002, that first got me thinking about how Britain's various communities relate to each other. Jonathan is president of the development agency Voluntary Service Overseas (VSO), and he told me how the organisation hoped to publish a series of essays on what he called 'cultural exchange'. From its beginnings, VSO had stressed that the cross-border friendships between its volunteers and those they tried to help in poor countries were just as important as the work itself. Jonathan said VSO wanted to find out whether those kinds of relationships were developing here at home between people of different backgrounds, races and cultures. Would I, he asked, join the likes of Meera Syal, Ben Okri, Jung Chang and David Blunkett in exploring multicultural Britain?

Just a couple of years earlier my family had returned to Britain after nearly four years in Nelson Mandela's South Africa – I had been the BBC's Africa correspondent based in Johannesburg. We had watched how this fledgling democracy tried to extricate itself from the disastrous legacy of apartheid. We had marvelled at the way some of our friends managed to let go of the prejudices that had dominated their past. We were caught up in their excitement as they savoured the fruits of friendship across the once unbridgeable racial divide. But we also learned to temper our enthusiasm for this new South Africa with the knowledge that our friends were, as often as not, the exception rather than the rule. My reporting assignments had taken me to places where farm workers were still being exploited; where white parents baulked at the idea of black children sitting next to their children in the classroom; and where property developers made money out of offering fearful whites the dubious security of living in a walled community. Above all, we saw that while politics and circumstance might throw black and white together at work, they invariably spent their leisure apart. And in this black people were just as remiss as their white counterparts.

So it was with some hope that we had returned to our polyglot corner of London, itself one of the most cosmopolitan cities on the planet. Stoke Newington in the London Borough of Hackney is as ethnically mixed as you can get (at 59.4 per cent the white people make up a smaller proportion of the population than anywhere else in England and Wales). Imagine a stroll down to Clissold Park. At the fishmonger's on the high street, the Jamaicans are in early, eager to get their red snapper and kingfish. Turn left on to Church Street and you are into that gentrified world where the old hardware stores and barber's shops are giving way to coffee bars, gift shops and trendy clothing boutiques. The ubiquitous curry houses have now been joined by Turkish, Italian and 'modern European' restaurants. Where once you might have ordered a pint of best bitter, middle-class mums with space-age prams now sit down to a shot of wheatgrass and the leader column in the *Independent*. A pub that sold packets of pork scratchings in the old days will now serve a side order of black olives. On Queen Elizabeth's Walk – where that famous monarch is said to have exercised her horses – you might have to skirt around a group of Hassidim, brisk and urgent as they head for any one of the synagogues tucked into the line of Victorian terraced housing. It might be midsummer, but in their black coats and felt hats they seem oblivious to London's cloying heat. And in the park itself, Asian youth are showing that they are now just as keen on football as their fathers were on cricket. On the face of it, multicultural Britain is alive and kicking.

That was the Britain I set out to write about for the VSO essay. But as I began to jot down my thoughts, as I began to look over the garden fence and out into wider Britain, a different sort of image emerged. It was a bit like those satellite pictures that start with a single building and then zoom out till you see the whole country. The big picture looks like a mosaic, and what we were experiencing in Stoke Newington was just one little piece of it. While our little chip in the mosaic had flecks of many colours, it was surrounded by those dominated by just one. Reluctantly, I came to the conclusion that while there may indeed be many colours, many cultures in Britain, that did not necessarily mean there was any meaningful exchange between them. All too often these communities were immersed in their own traditions and, occasionally, suspicious of others.

The response to that essay, reprinted in the *Guardian* newspaper, was telling. Those on the right who hate the idea of multiculturalism saw what they wanted to see – a man of Asian origin apparently speaking their language.

But it was the comments from other black and Asian people, so-called experts on race relations, that were more surprising. They saw betrayal; they saw a successful Asian man pulling up the drawbridge once he had got across the river of prejudice and indifference that still blights the lives of too many people of colour.

Shortly after my essay was published, David Goodhart produced a very provocative piece on multiculturalism in the magazine *Prospect*. In the article he argued that diversity can sometimes make social cohesion more difficult. In his response Trevor Phillips, the chairman of the Commission for Racial Equality, acidly observed that 'nice people do racism too'. But pretty soon Trevor Phillips himself was apparently questioning the usefulness of multiculturalism as a guiding principle for race relations in Britain, arguing that it encouraged separateness. He wanted more 'common values' and lamented the way the literature of Dickens and Shakespeare had been lost on many immigrants!

What all this means is that the debate about race relations is now more volatile and polarised than at any time in recent memory – probably for a generation. Not since the period of mass migration to Britain from its far-flung colonies in the fifties, sixties and seventies have race relations presented such a challenge. It is almost impossible to open a newspaper – tabloid or broadsheet – without seeing an article on the subject. The overarching consensus on how Britain's many races should be managed – achieved through legislation, debate, precedent and familiarity – has begun to crumble. Alarmist headlines about bogus asylum seekers and benefit spongers have made it virtually impossible to have a rational debate about the issue. Questions are being asked that were unthinkable just five years ago.

There is one crucial difference in the way the debate is being conducted this time round. When our fathers and mothers were trying to define and defend their place in Britain, they were doing so as outsiders, first-generation immigrants hobbled by all the personal uncertainties of building a new life in a new country. At the back of their minds there was that nagging doubt about how far they could go in asserting their rights. Should they just keep their heads down, work hard and simply hope that somehow it would be better for their children?

I am one of those children. I, and countless others, have grown up in Britain. Unlike our parents, we have nothing to prove and nothing to lose. Nobody can take away our 'Britishness'. Some of us have scaled the heights of this hierarchical society and can speak with authority and influence. We are able to take part in the debate and not have it shaped for us by well-meaning progressives or bigoted Little Englanders.

As migrant journeys go, mine has been exceptional. The total-immersion therapy of a predominantly white boarding school is in stark contrast to the experience of many black and Asian children today. Today, school can represent a microcosm of whichever ethnic community they belong to. What will happen if plans to increase the scope and number of faith-based schools takes hold? That initiative, though well intentioned, may serve to exacerbate the trend towards ethnically concentrated schools.

While my own upbringing may have entailed an unnatural – and undesirable – dislocation from my parents' traditions, the reverse may be true for many immigrant children growing up today – an unnatural and undesirable estrangement from the culture of the country in which they will have to make their mark.

Either way, we all have to cope with the dilemma faced by migrants through the ages – we are caught between the desire to fit in and the communal admonition to remember where we started. While we build one home here (not literally, but in our minds), we think back to the home we left behind. There is assimilation on the one side and heritage on the other. For the most part immigrants become adept at juggling both halves of their lives. Even now, after all these years, I am aware that my accent will change ever so slightly when I spend a long time with my father or other Sri Lankans. In front of the camera in studio N6 at BBC Television Centre my voice is a model of Received Pronunciation. I am both those things. When England are playing cricket in an Ashes series I rejoice at every nick that sends an Aussie batsman back to the pavilion. But when the opponents are Sri Lankans I clap for every four struck by a rampant Sangakkara. I am the sum of my parts.

Modern British fiction has caught up with this most personal of conflicts. In *White Teeth*, Zadie Smith lets the two brothers, Millat and Magid, act out the alternative life paths, though in a delicious twist it is the brother who is sent back to Pakistan who ends up the most Anglophile. Among immigrant communities we all know someone who, like Chanu in Monica Ali's *Brick Lane*, believes all will be well once he gets his family 'back home', away from the corrupting influences of life in London's East End.

But where is home? I've been back to Sri Lanka just three times since 1961 when my family left the country, and on the last occasion, in December 2002, it was after a gap of nearly 30 years. I certainly didn't see that trip as a journey 'back home'. I thought I had long since resolved the question about where I belonged. At most I'd seen it as a trip down memory lane; a chance to show Frances, my English wife, and our two sons where it had all started. It turned out to be much more than that. In Sri Lanka I discovered that however English I felt, I couldn't escape the fact that I had started off somewhere else.

London
June 2006

1

Sink or Swim

Look at it from my point of view. Not the way you know me now – familiar and confident – but the way I was back in September 1967. I am eleven going on twelve. I am a child in a strange place. I am nervous. I am about to be dropped off at boarding school in Portsmouth.

I have been to Britain once before, in 1963. The family had come over for a few weeks to enrol my two elder sisters in a Catholic boarding school in Littlehampton. My abiding memory of that trip is not of the country that would one day become my home, but of the devastation in my parents' eyes on hearing President John F. Kennedy had been assassinated. It was my eighth birthday. We were in a basement flat in London's Holland Park, where I was playing with the cowboy gun I had been given as a present. But far away in the state of Texas, in the land of real cowboys with real guns and real bullets, a man had been shot dead, and with it the curtain had come down on a dream that much of the world had wanted to share. It seems utterly implausible that any American president now living or yet to come could be mourned in such a way.

So four years later, in 1967, it's my turn. Just imagine how I'm feeling as my father – choking back the emotion which he feels he cannot show me – prepares to climb back into the minicab that brought us down to the coast from London. He's trying to smile for me, but I've seen him cry before, when his brother died, so I can tell he's on the verge of doing so again. I'm going to be a brave boy. My father has told me that and I'm not going to let him down. So I too hold back the tears.

Man and boy – trapped in the need to look strong. My father, this constant and reassuring figure in my life, is about to drive out of it. I know I will not see him for the best part of a year. But still I tell myself not to cry.

Perhaps it would have been different had my mother been there. But she is far away. My parents couldn't afford the plane fare for her and the other children to come to England. So she's in Sri Lanka at the tail end of a holiday. From there she will join my father in Ghana, where the family moved to in 1961. She would not have been afraid to cry, and then, maybe, it would have been okay for me to cry too. As an even younger child, the silky folds of her sari had been like a protective skin which I wrapped around myself when I was frightened of the dark, when I heard noises in our African backyard. On this day there is no sari to clutch, no embrace to reassure me, no smile to lighten the load.

Before this I have never been away from my parents – not both at the same time. We do not understand it at the time, at least I didn't, but we will never again share the same roof as parents and child for more than a few weeks a year – seven or so weeks if we're lucky. We will be together for the long holidays, but they are strange reunions. It's not that we aren't happy to be together but that we contrive to be happier than is normal between adolescent children and their parents. We, the children, are always on best behaviour, ever mindful of the huge sacrifice (not just in money, but in love) they have made to give us a British education. And our parents, in turn, seem more grateful than they should be for the simple pleasure of being with the brood they brought into this world.

Now, on a lifeless, tarred five-a-side pitch outside Woodleigh House for first- and second-formers, we talk about how it will be when we meet up next summer. Next summer – whenever that is. You see, I've never had to worry about summer, autumn, winter and spring before. Before, there was the dry season – when the west African *hamartan* blew hard and strong – and the rainy season. Here, my sisters tell me, it rains all the time, even when it's supposed to be the dry season. That's just one of the many strange things I am about to learn as I begin my British life.

The driver of the cab gives me a pat on the shoulder and reminds me to wash behind my ears. It's a warning that only makes sense when, a few days later, that is precisely where the school matron looks to see if I have cleaned myself properly.

I watch the vehicle creep out of the car park, on the other side of the football pitch. It's a green Vauxhall. How do I remember that? It's because I have replayed the scene many times in my head. At critical moments in my life, when I have faced a challenge that I think is beyond me, when I have felt my body drained of its warmth, leaving only the cold emptiness of anxiety, I know that the first time I felt that way was the day I said goodbye to my father at boarding school. In the hours before a dangerous assignment, in the days and weeks after a relationship has ended, in the seconds before I realise our child is okay after all – every time I have known that the anxiousness springs from the same place in my mind that was exposed on that late summer day.

I can picture it all now. I am trying to pretend that it's like my father is going off to work. He is sitting in front. In the back seat is Auntie Ranee Eliathamby. She's not really my auntie, but in our culture we referred to all my parents' close friends as auntie and uncle. Auntie Ranee, her husband Jakes, and their three children – Anna, Ram and Renu – will be a sort of surrogate family. It is to their house in Streatham, south London, that I will make my way for the first half-term break and quite a few more till I make English friends who will invite me to their homes for the holidays. I can see that my father has pulled out his handkerchief. The car stops at the gate. My father waves. And then he's gone. I am alone. I'm not really alone; there are dozens of other boys around me. But I feel lonelier than I have ever felt before.

There isn't much else I remember about that day, the day I was dropped off at St John's College. I do remember my father trying to tip the house prefect – an incredibly tall sixth-former called Eilert 'Lofty' Eilertsen – and the rather stilted exchange that followed. I remember shaking hands with Brother Ignatius, trying hard not to stare at his clerical collar from which dangled two spade-like bits of plastic – vestigial remnants of an ancient religious tradition. Beyond that I cannot remember any detail, just a feeling, an overwhelming sense of displacement. Perhaps I feel like a woman who's walked into a room full of men; is everyone looking at me or am I just imagining it? I feel awkward; I feel strange. Suddenly my voice doesn't seem right, even the 'English' accent that I thought I had perfected. I feel different. Above all, I feel foreign.

As for detail, it's an event a little later on that week that sticks out in my memory because it was the moment I realised I was going to have to develop a pretty thick skin if I was going to make it in England. That morning I learned to laugh at myself – or at least to pretend to laugh at myself – and in so doing acquired one of the most important skills in the armoury of an outsider trying to fit in. We weren't allowed to shower every day so my moment of revelation – so to speak – must have come a few days into my first week at boarding school.

Shower days were allocated dormitory by dormitory. Even so there were always more boys than there were showers. The old hands knew that on shower days you couldn't hang about. As soon as the bell went, you grabbed your washbag (which you would have placed in a convenient place the night before) and ran for the shower block. In the first couple of weeks of term, it was always one of the new kids who ended up standing around, knees knocking, teeth chattering, with a towel wrapped around his waist, while the others took more than the few minutes they were allocated. Being late for your shower meant you were late for the rest of the morning. You were the last to get changed, last to make it across the yard to the refectory, which meant you ended up with the coldest and mangiest bit of toast. All of which meant you were the one who got the telling-off from Brother Ignatius, the housemaster of Woodleigh.

On the day in question I made it to the shower on time. The idea of not bathing every day was bad enough (we'd always suspected the English were not as clean as they pretended); to hang around getting cold while you waited for your twice-weekly ablution was an even worse prospect, so I shot out of my bed like a sprinter off the blocks. So far, so good.

'Can I borrow some shampoo?' one of the boys was asking the chap next to him.

'Get your own. If I can remember to bring mine, so can you.'

'Don't be a Jew.' Yes, we used to say things like that. Along with 'poof' and 'spastic' and a few others that would be unacceptable now.

'You've got loads there, the bottle's full. Go on, give us a bit.'

'No, my mum says this one's got to last me till half-term.'

'Oh diddums, we don't want to upset mummy, do we?' It was my first taste of the sarcasm that was to be a prominent feature of most boarding house arguments. You learned very quickly never to invoke your mother as a defence against anything. Mummies were for sissies. Family was something you kept in your mind, something you thought about only when it was dark and you'd pulled the blanket over your head. You learned to divide yourself. The daytime boy, all brass and bollocks, and the night-time boy, vulnerable and homesick.

The boy made a grab for the bottle of shampoo but missed it. The two of them started to struggle. It looked as if there was going to be a fight. Half the boys were hoping that was precisely what would happen, shouting 'Fight, fight!' in a *Lord of the Flies* sort of way. The other half were beginning to look terrified, imperceptibly backing away from the streams of warm water and towards the door. I was in the latter camp. I offered him some of my shampoo.

It all calmed down. And that was when my problem began. There had to be something else for everyone to talk about.

'Why haven't you got a line like this?' I realised the question was addressed to me. The boy was pointing at his waist, where he had a distinct tan-line. It was the autumn term and everyone had come back from their holidays and were nicely browned except for the bit where they wore swimming trunks. I suppose I could have sounded terribly superior and said something about mad dogs and Englishmen, but actually my mind was a complete blank. The longer I took to think of something, anything, to say, the more I became the centre of attention. And that was the last place I wanted to be.

'Don't you go swimming where you come from?' somebody else chipped in.

'Well I can't really swim,' I said, relieved to have found the right gear to get my mouth into action and desperately hoping that would be the end of the inquisition.

'What, you've never been in a pool?'

'Yes, I have.'

'Then what do you wear when you go in?'

'I wear swimming trunks.'

'Then why don't you have a line like the rest of us?' This time the boy said it with an exaggerated tone of exasperation, as if he had just been put in charge of an imbecile. He looked around. He was on a winning run and he knew it.

How could I explain that we were brought up never to hang around in the sun? How could I explain that we had no need to tan ourselves in order to feel that we looked good? How could I explain that I had never had a communal shower before and that I had never seen a tan-line before? Above all, how could I explain that I wanted all of them to stop looking at me?

'I don't know,' I said lamely. My mind, after that ever-so-brief reawakening, was going back to what seemed to be its natural state for that particular morning – dormant.

It was the chap who'd borrowed my shampoo who waded in

next. He was the boarding house joker and he sensed a punchline coming on.

'Well I know,' he shouted so everybody could hear. 'He hasn't got a tan because in bongo-bongo land they all run around with no clothes and they get brown all over!' He was proud of himself. He laughed at his own joke and everybody joined in.

And then I joined in too. I couldn't think of anything else to do. I was embarrassed but I was not angry. I was hurting but I couldn't show it. I wanted to run but I dared not. I wanted to cry but I knew that if I started I wouldn't be able to stop. So it was easier to pretend it didn't matter. I just stood there smiling, but wishing I could disappear in the steam that had by then engulfed the washroom.

Today children would be encouraged to report such an incident. At best it would been seen as an act of bullying; at worst it would be put down to racism. Back in September 1967 it would probably have been dismissed as a bit of robust – if inconsiderate – schoolboy joshing. I know one thing. I hadn't even heard of racism, so even if I had decided to talk to the housemaster, it was not a charge I would have made.

Was that boy a racist? I don't think so. Should he have been more caring? Yes. I met him many, many years later. He came up to me after I had given a public lecture. We embraced, we reminisced about the glory days. I didn't remind him about the incident in the shower and he would have been utterly embarrassed if I had. He told me how proud he was of what I had achieved. I believed him.

By the way, this tanning business has been a recurrent theme in the English phase of my life. That rare occurrence of the sun's rays coinciding with weekends or holidays has always seen me diving for cover while my English friends peel off. When the men start removing their shirts and the women start tucking their skirts into their knickers you begin to understand what lily-white really means.

A few days after that shower room incident, on my first Saturday at boarding school, I was reminded again that I was not like the other boys. This time it was not what I looked like but how I dressed that set me apart.

It was the announcement from the house prefect that we could get into 'home clothes' that turned my stomach. What home clothes? I had a trunk full of clothes but they were all school clothes. Crisp and clean. All greys and whites and blues, some still in their packaging, exactly as they had been when my father had paid for them at Knight & Lee, the school outfitter on the corner of Grove Road South and Elm Grove. No doubt somewhere on the list of things we were allowed to take to school there must have been a note about casual clothing for the weekend. If there was such a reminder my father had not noticed it.

So as the multicoloured tank-tops came out, and the faded jeans were pulled on, all I could do was slip into yet another pair of flannel trousers, another grey shirt and a sleeveless blue jumper.

These first days taught me just how much catching up I had to do. I was like a juggler who can't stop, ever. New accent, new clothes, new stories, new friends, new habits, new food, new lessons – I had to keep all the balls in the air, all the time. There was no respite. I couldn't leave it all behind at 3.45 in the afternoon. I couldn't walk out of the school gates, catch a bus home, where I could be my old self again, slip back into the old accent and wait for my mum to give me a treat – her special pancakes with the *jaggery* and coconut filling, perhaps. In a boarding school, when school's out, all that happens is that there is more of the same. You just shift location from the classroom to the dormitory. The only time you have to yourself is when you're in bed.

The list of things I had to get used to ranged from the culinary to the comical. There was food that tasted as if it had been brought to the table before the cook had had time to put a vital ingredient in it, or the loo seats that made you jump because they were so cold. For quite a while I took to lining the seat with sheets of toilet paper. It was a terribly delicate operation. Unlike the triple-ply soft-on-your-bum rolls that Labrador pups play with in the TV advertisements today the boarding house issue was thin and about as absorbent as a page from our jotters in the classroom. It used to take me so long to arrange the sheets of paper in exactly the right place that I abandoned the practice and resigned myself to the sharp shock treatment. It may even have helped things along.

I can trace my habit of taking both tea and coffee without milk back to those fight-to-be-first breakfasts on formica-topped tables. A plastic jug of milk would be placed in the middle of a table seating eight boys. By the time everyone else had had their share, I had to choose between covering my Weetabix – which to me looked and tasted like bricks made out of sawdust – or having milk in my coffee. Camouflaging the Weetabix in an inch or so of milk was the more urgent task.

In the first two years at St John's College – middle school – we had to wear shorts with long socks folded over once just below the knee. The six inches or so between the top of the socks and the bottom of the shorts were exposed to everything that the English winter could throw at us. Boys in the second year had an even larger gap to worry about. A growth spurt over the long holidays meant you came back with your shorts riding halfway up your thighs because your parents had been reluctant to invest in a new pair that would be redundant at the end of the year. For some reason even the thriftiest parents, the ones who expected their sons to squeeze into last year's shorts, were nevertheless willing to buy new blazers. But they always purchased them several sizes too big, in the hope that they might survive through till O levels in the fifth year. What this meant, of course, was that the blazers would fall well below the shorts, leaving the playground scattered with these rather strange-looking beings with voluminous torsos, fingertips where their hands should be and a couple of purple-cold knees appearing out of nowhere! And by this stage in the school career the socks would have lost their first-term elasticity and would be flopping around the ankles like an old turkey's neck.

An abiding memory of break time in the winter months is the singeing I would get on the tender skin behind my knees as I leaned back on the industrial-sized radiators that were stationed all too scarcely along the corridors. It was the job of the teacher on playground duty to shoo us out into the cold. 'Go on, Alagiah, get out there and get some fresh air.' By the end of the lunch break my brown skin would have turned dry and ashen in the chafing wind. I would look down and see how it was all parched, with a pattern like dry mud looked back home. It used to embarrass me and I would spend most of the afternoon trying to pull my shorts down or my socks up. It took many months before I realised that a squeeze of body cream would give my knees the lustre they were meant to have.

For some things, though, I had been prepared. Before being taken down to Portsmouth, my father and I had stayed with the Eliathambys, the family who accompanied me and my father when I was dropped off at St John's. They were Sri Lankans we had first met in the provincial town of Takoradi, in Ghana. Jakes Eliathamby was a doctor, a pioneer in that first wave of immigrants to be employed by the NHS. His wife Ranee looked after the home. Their children had been our playmates back in Ghana. Auntie Ranee had showed me how to make a bed. These were the days before duvets. You needed two sheets, several blankets, and a lot of tugging and pulling. In Africa we'd used a single sheet. Now I learned how to fold back the top sheet, making sure I held on to the blankets as I did so. That way you got a nice band of white sheet set against the coloured blanket. At the other end of the bed she showed me how to pleat the corners so they could be tucked under the mattress without making a lumpy mess that would spoil the line of the bedspread. It was a skill that stood me in good stead when I worked as a chambermaid (the PC days of calling it a chamberperson had yet to come) in a London hotel as a holiday job.

Looking back at that first year at boarding school, I can see that it was like a crash course in becoming English. Virtually everything I did, I was doing for the first time. I was at an age when picking up habits is easy. A child's ears and eyes are more acutely tuned to the prevailing fashions and moods than an adult's.

I had done it all once before, when my family had first moved from Sri Lanka to Ghana in 1961. I had rid myself of my Sri Lankan roots and adopted the styles and accents of west Africa. Like an actor who puts on a new costume and learns new words, I too got to grips with my new role. It frightens me now when I think back to how much I changed, how much I was expected to change, in the space of a decade or so. I went from being a rather timid, sheltered boy in Sri Lanka to becoming an independent teenager in Britain, via a diversion to Africa. By the time I was twelve I had a claim on three continents. My sense of being Sri Lankan had already been more or less buried, and over the next few years it was my attachment to Africa that would have to give way to a new identity.

Of course, you don't lose your other identity, you just smuggle it away. You hide it in a place only you know about. One day when you're feeling more confident you can bring it out again. (In my case that didn't really happen till I made my return journey to Sri Lanka nearly forty years after I'd left it.) But first you have to convince everybody around you that you are clubbable, that you're one of them.

The first part of that process was the language. In Ghana I had adopted the quasi-pidgin that we all used in the playground. We used to play 'socca' not soccer; I had 'sistahs' but no 'broddahs'; I 'arks' people to do things for me and I was always sure to show 'respec' to my teacher, Mr Frank Mason. When I was at home I spoke like my parents, with an Asian lilt. Now, in England, I got down to learning not only a new accent, but what seemed to be an arcane vocabulary as well.

I still don't know exactly what 'diddums' (remember the shower room taunt) means or where it comes from, but instinctively I caught on to what it implied and when I could use it. I thought 'plonker' was vague but useful as an all-purpose insult. I soon realised, though, that 'wanker' was an altogether more precise curse and one which spoke volumes for the way English boys talked freely about things I had always assumed were private and sometimes shameful. My parents had told me all about the currency in England; indeed, we had learned it in our school in Accra. Twelve pence made a shilling and twenty shillings made a pound. But no one had told me that 'tuppence' would get you a few boiled sweets at the newsagent around the corner from the school or that a 'tanner' would buy me a portion of chips with salt and vinegar thrown in from the 'chippy' next to the King's Theatre.

Pronunciation – as opposed to a general accent – was, perhaps, the biggest challenge. The first casualty in this department was my name. It took just a couple of morning registration sessions to realise that attempts to cling on to the Tamil way of pronouncing Alagiah were futile. The way we used to say it, the way it was meant to be said, was like this: the first 'al' is more like the beginning of Ullswater; and the g is more like an h. So phonetically you might write it so: Ullerhiya. Simple really. No, not at all. Not if you were Mr 'Wally-Whiff' Walsworth of class IW. The 'whiff' in question was the stale afterburn of a packet of Woodbine or some such a day. It seemed easier to let him mispronounce the name than to hear him mangle it in a vain and embarrassing attempt to get it right. Looking back, it was me that would get embarrassed, not him. In those days – before anyone was really talking about diversity or multiculturalism – you felt like apologising if you had a 'funny' name.

English, as spoken by the English, is full of verbal pitfalls which only the most alert and watchful foreigner avoids. There are two particular areas that gave me trouble. The first was where to put the stress in a multisyllable word. Take the word simplicity. In Ghana, if we ever used it, we would have split it in two at a convenient point and come out with simply-city, with a more or less equal stress on the two parts. At St John's that would have been greeted with howls of derision, with some joker mimicking me for the rest of the day. So I learned to place the stress where most English people put it – as in sim-PLIC-ity. I say that's the way *most* English say it, because even the English are not always agreed on exactly where the stress should be on some words. You will hear some people talk about a CONTRO-versy and others talk about a con-TROV-ersy. If the locals can't agree on how to pronounce a word, what hope was there for a twelve-year-old foreign boy?

The other difficulty was with certain letters, the main culprits being v and w, especially when they were in close proximity (another one of those stress words) to each other. Every time somebody asked me how I was getting on, I had to make a conscious effort not to say I was doing 'wery vell, thank you'. In later years my sisters and I used to love *Mind Your Language*, the sitcom in which the actor Barry Evans teaches English to a class full of sundry immigrants. If our English friends thought it was funny, we thought it was funnier. We knew, much to our private, cringe-making embarrassment, that although it was patronising, it was all true. Even now, as a presenter on the nation's most watched news programme, I am careful to rearrange my v-words and w-words lest some atavistic urge to mix them up breaks through. Imagine how I felt, back in February 2005, when I had to tell a TV audience of millions that Charles and Camilla had changed their 'Windsor wedding venue' from the castle to the town hall!

And then there is the accent as a whole. I had a choice, of course. There was the accent that I heard in the playground. St John's was a state-funded Catholic school that took its students predominantly from the city of Portsmouth and its suburbs. Though undoubtedly bright, the pupils at the school were not from privileged backgrounds and their accents reflected their station. So Pompey-twang was certainly an option. Those of us who were fee-paying boarders – about 100 out of a school roll of 800 or so – came from a more varied background. In those days our accents were far more closely related to what our parents did for a living. So Michael O'Leary, whose parents had a house in the Hampshire countryside from where his banker father would commute into London, had what one might call a middle-class accent typical of the south-east. Charlie Pask, whose father was an RAF technician stationed in Germany, owed his accent to long stints with his grandparents, who owned the Havelock Tavern in Portsmouth. Greg Insull wasn't a boarder but I knew he came from somewhere called Birmingham and it took me a great deal of time to understand him at all! And then there was the accent I heard on TV. This was long before the current vogue for regional accents on our airwaves and Received Pronunciation was the order of the day. I'm talking Richard Baker and Robert Dougall here.

So how did I end up with the accent that is now familiar to audiences around the country? It didn't come from my school-mates who, as I say, spoke with a regional accent more common on the football terraces of Fratton Park than in the drawing rooms of middle England. I know this much – I didn't choose my accent in any conscious way; instead I grew into it. It's as if, as a child immigrant, I had a built-in instinct which helped me to tune into the one accent that would ensure a ready acceptance into English society.

My sisters, too, have the same accent. I'm quite sure that my accent has opened doors that would have been shut tight to other immigrants who retained their mother accent or, if they'd picked one up here, had the 'misfortune' to settle on one that was less in tune with the British establishment. All over the world, accents offer a clue about where someone is from. I can tell a Sri Lankan from an Indian as soon as they've uttered a few sentences. In a group of Africans I can tell which is from the west and which is from the south. And, of course, we have our regional accents here in Britain. Just listen to the difference between a West Country burr and a Belfast brogue. But we also have other subtle distinctions that play a more insidious role. What I call class-talk is the mystery ingredient that eludes all but the most tuned-in immigrants.

In Britain class almost always trumps race. Let me show you

how it works. All through school and well beyond I used to travel on my Sri Lankan passport. I would use it once a year when I travelled back to Africa for summer holidays with my parents. Going out my stomach was always a-flutter with the anticipation of a family reunion; coming back it was always tight as a knot with the anticipation of the immigration queue. I used to hate the way we were separated out, British to one side and all the foreigners on another. So I was always standing with the Bangladeshis, the Indians, the Iraqis and other 'suspect' nationalities – at least that's how it seemed to me. Of course, the immigration service would have said this division was merely an administrative convenience, but while that may have dealt with the facts, it did little to erode perceptions. One queue was almost exclusively white, while the other, the one that I would be in, was predominantly brown, black and all shades in between. It was also by far the longer of the queues, which meant you had more time to worry about how you were going to be dealt with by the immigration officer.

As I approached the front of the queue, I used to try to work out which of the immigration staff looked the friendliest. By allocating roughly five minutes for each traveller I would calculate which desk I was most likely to be ushered towards. By the time I was three or four places from the front, I was close enough to get a sense of how others were being treated. When anyone was asked to step aside for a moment, I knew there was trouble brewing, something was wrong with their papers. That's when I would check my own passport and the letter from the school which I always carried. You could hear the rather stilted conversations.

'How long are you coming here for?' the immigration officer would ask in that slow, deliberate way they reserved for foreigners. The answers were much harder to pick up. Worried and confused, the travellers would tend to mumble their replies. In any case, they had their backs to me so their voices didn't carry nearly so well.

'Where will you stay?'

'How much money have you got on you?'

'Are you going to get a job?' I always thought that was a bit of a trick question. If you said 'yes' you might be accused of taking someone's job. But if you said 'no' you could be accused of being a scrounger. In those days I didn't know about work permits, quotas and the like.

'Have you got any relatives who are here already?'

'Are any members of your family going to join you here?'

And so it would go on until it was my turn. I would hand over my Sri Lankan passport in the same way a man who's been stopped on the motorway hands over his driving licence. Whether you've done anything wrong or not, you do it in a rather sheepish manner. You feel a little guilty just because you've been asked for it. Such is the power of authority.

'Now what have we here?' was the sort of opening gambit I remember.

'Hello,' I'd say in the chirpiest, most southern-counties tone I could muster. And that usually did the trick. That little word was enough. It was like a codeword, it was my 'open sesame'. One word, just five letters, and yet it conveyed a mountain of information about me. I was educated, I had the right background, I had, to put it bluntly, the right class. Faced with the choice of making an assessment according to my colour and passport, or making one on the basis of my middle-class accent, it was always the latter that was chosen. I'm not saying they would have bent the rules or ignored a missing stamp in my passport. But their attitudes did change almost instantaneously. It was the difference between being prepared to believe me and being primed to be sceptical.

That first year at St John's College was a sink-or-swim year. Being sent to boarding school is like being thrown in at the deep end. There's no shallow end in which you can practise your strokes. One day you're in Africa, the next you're in England. One day your parents are there for you, the next they are thousands of miles away. One day you're a foreigner, the next you have to learn to be English. It's all or nothing.

Some things – like accents – you can pick up pretty quickly. Others, like casual clothes for the weekends, can be bought. My elder sisters, who were boarded at a convent in Littlehampton, helped me with that during our first half-term break together in London. But other attributes of being English are harder to ascertain and more difficult to adopt. A sense of humour, for example. So much depends on innuendo, a gut feeling for what is funny and what isn't. Then there's that all-important sense of belonging. You can learn to say the right things, dress the right way, play the right games, but what you can't get – at least not right away – is a shared history. That takes time. And in any case, Britain in 1967 – the year I arrived – was itself a nation in transition. The old Britain of fixed ideas and moral certainties was giving way to one in which the lines between right and wrong, good and bad were becoming more confused. As it turned out, 1967 was something of a watershed. The post-war *bonhomie* was wearing thin. Nowhere was this more obvious than in questions of race.

The Beatles may have believed that 'All you Need Is Love' – it was the top-selling single of 1967 – but everywhere you looked during the late sixties, brotherly love was a quality that was in short supply. There was a sourness creeping into public life. Women of a certain age may have been swooning under the Anglo-Indian charms of Engelbert Humperdinck and his ballad 'Release Me', but on the fringes of the nation's political life there were people who were openly showing a visceral distaste for the very idea that people could be both Indian and English. The notion that the Commonwealth was a brotherhood forged under the British Empire and sustained by the sense of duty handed down by an imperial generation was giving way to something altogether more sinister.

You see, 1967 was also the year in which the National Front was established out of a loose coalition of fascist groups, including the British National Party and the League of Empire Loyalists.

The Front opposed the process of decolonisation that was, by then, pretty much complete, and blamed Britain's relative economic decline on the earliest signs of a racially mixed society. The non-white population then accounted for about 1.5 per cent of the population, hardly the kind of numbers that could sustain the claim that Britain's white pedigree was being besmirched by the infiltration of darker hues. Even allowing for the priapic powers attributed to black men in the febrile imagination of these bigots, it was a preposterous claim.

The Front may have been peopled by a small and bitter band of political thugs who still hankered after the days when to be born British meant you had a God-given right to rule a quarter of the world's people, but they also tapped into a more widespread shift in the mood of the nation. The previous year a survey on race relations had found that some 80 per cent of the respondents thought that too many immigrants had been allowed to settle in Britain. Apparently, the difference between the National Front and the rest of the country was that while the former was prepared to bellow their prejudices from loudspeakers, the rest of the country preferred to confine its views to the privacy of an anonymous survey.

However, when they got a chance to express their views on race at the polls, the result was chilling. Three years earlier, for the first time in the modern era, a British politician had openly used what became known as the race card. During the Smethwick by-election of 1964, supporters of the Conservative candidate, Peter Griffiths, pounded on the doors of voters with a simple, but highly effective message: 'If you want a nigger neighbour, vote Liberal or Labour.' He won the seat, and what is more, did so against the political tide which brought in a Labour government under Harold Wilson. If you were one of the country's 820,000 'coloured' population, it was becoming pretty obvious which way the wind was blowing – it was blowing hard in your face and it was ice-cold. It was time to wrap up against the change in Britain's political climate.

Race relations was only one arena in which the old consensus was breaking down. Harold Wilson had come to power in 1964 promising to drag the country into the modern age. He painted a vision of an up-to-date Britain driven by what he called 'the white heat of technology'. But as many people were frightened by the prospect as were enamoured of it.

This national dichotomy could be seen in the BBC. Even dear old Auntie, which in those days had a claim to be the unrivalled repository of the Zeitgeist, appeared to be pulling in two directions at the same time. On the one hand, in what would prove to be a commercially astute and editorially progressive move, in 1967 it launched Radio 1. At a stroke it undermined the pirate radio stations that had been increasing their audience share by appealing to the growing irreverence of the sixties generation. The DJs who had honed their rebellious credentials on the illicit airwaves couldn't resist the temptation to become national figures. With the same deft skills that saw them flick from one vinyl record to another, they eased into their new roles as national figures on the BBC's payroll. Some of them, such as Tony Blackburn, were still in the public eye decades later.

But on the other hand, the Beeb seemed scared by the implications of what it had done. That same year, 1967, the corporation banned two Beatles songs – 'A Day in the Life' and 'I am the Walrus' – because they contained references, however oblique, to drugs. Other songs, including the Beatles' own 'Lucy in the Sky with Diamonds' and Procol Harem's 'Whiter Shade of Pale', with their equally 'mind-expanding' lyrics, slipped through the net. The Beeb wanted to move with the times; it wanted to be a part of the psychedelic sixties, but it was worried by the knock-on effects of keeping up with the Jaggers and the Bests, the reckless rogues who were enjoying both fame and notoriety for their social and sexual misdemeanours.

If the Rolling Stones' pouting front man and Manchester United's goal-scoring genius were having fun, it was due in no small measure to the easy availability of the Pill in the 1960s. It brought new-found liberation for women (and men), but it also generated a certain angst, even among those who were in favour of its transforming role in society. Writing in the *Guardian* in 1967, the author Margaret Drabble was concerned that 'two of the most profound experiences of human nature, sex and child-rearing, which used to be so inseparably connected, are now only marginally so, and by choice. It is hard to see how morality will adapt itself to this alteration.' One assumes this fastidiousness over the nation's morals was not shared backstage after a Stones concert or, if the hype be believed, during the half-time break at a Man U game.

And in what looked like a recognition that in this no-holds-barred Britain things wouldn't always go according to plan, the government passed the 1967 Abortion Act, which made voluntary terminations available on the NHS. For good measure the Family Planning Act meant local authorities could now openly provide contraceptives and contraceptive advice and the Sexual Offences Act meant that homosexual activity between consenting adults was no longer a criminal offence.

It's as if one half of Britain was jumping headlong into a new era while the other half was scared stiff. While one lot were dreaming about tearing down the walls of the establishment – with 'peace and love, man' – the other lot were content to sit back and remember the good old days when everybody knew their place. The nation's favourite TV programme in 1967 was *The Forsyte Saga*, an Edwardian period piece set in London's Eaton Square.

I've often thought that if my parents had had the tiniest inkling of what was going on in Britain they might have changed their mind about sending me to school here. Instead they were enticed by an altogether different vision of the country. Having grown up under imperial tutelage, they were convinced Britain was a place where the Queensberry Rules still applied, where fair play and honour were the qualities prevalent in public life and, above all, where a hard-working Sri Lankan boy could prosper.

*

In one sense they were absolutely right. Whatever was going on in town, within the walls of St John's College I was beginning to develop in a way that would not have been possible in Sri Lanka or Ghana. Boarding school is a closed and unreal society. If there was turbulence outside, inside it was steady as she goes. Under the watchful eyes of brothers from the De la Salle order – now a mere shadow of what used to be a powerhouse of Catholic education – I was becoming an able student and a budding athlete, the sum of which made me more confident than my parents could have hoped.

But the truth is that I was advancing so rapidly despite what was going on in Britain rather than because of it. Had the whole family emigrated to Britain, had we settled down in some inner-city borough, my prospects would have been altogether different. Even in 1967 there were some neighbourhoods where immigrants – usually from the same part of the world – made up 50 per cent of the population. The separation of Britain's communities – and the shutting down of opportunity and aspiration that too often goes with it – was in its nascent stage.

My good fortune wasn't down to wealth or status. For sure, St John's was not an ordinary school, it wasn't your 'bog-standard' comprehensive, but equally, it wasn't a bastion of privilege. The vast majority of the pupils – the 'day boys' – did not have to pay fees. If my parents had been looking for status or privilege, and if they could have afforded the fees, they would have sent me to a school like Ampleforth or Stonyhurst which brought cash, class and Catholicism together in one neat and divisive package.

The key point about growing up at St John's was that I was allowed to develop largely protected from the prejudice that the colour of my skin might have provoked outside. Two things can hold back an immigrant child – poor expectations from those around you and a poor self-image brought on by the drip-drip effect of a society that does not welcome you. Neither of those things applied to me. In that sense, and only that sense, I was indeed privileged.

The parents of other immigrants would sometimes hold their own children back precisely because they lived and worked here and experienced the daily humiliation of petty racism. One of the most revealing passages in James Baldwin's searing indictment of racism in America in the fifties – *The Fire Next Time* – is a description of his father's foreboding when confronted with the young Baldwin's ambitions:

> The fear I heard in my father's voice, for example, when he realised that I really believed I could do anything a white boy could do, and had every intention of proving it, was not at all like the fear I heard when one of us was ill or had fallen down the stairs or strayed too far from the house. It was another fear, a fear that the child, in challenging the white world's assumptions, was putting himself in the path of destruction . . . You were not expected to aspire to excellence, you were expected to make peace with mediocrity.

It was not so different here. Thousands of African-Caribbean and Asian children were expected to opt for safe back-room jobs. Trevor Phillips, the youngest child of Guyanese parents who went on to become chair of the Commission for Racial Equality, spoke about it in a speech he gave in Darlington in 2004:

> . . . every child like me grew up knowing that if we followed the rules we would be doing pretty much what our parents did. I got lucky – the right combination of parents, teachers, and sheer luck gave me options other than putting on the uniforms that my older brothers and sisters and my cousins all wore at some point – nurse, soldier and postal worker.

My father and mother, caught in the blissful ignorance of a time warp, could throw caution to the wind. Because the Britain they saw from afar was the Britain of tolerance and justice, they had no trouble expecting us to exploit the opportunities before us.

In any case, what little experience they had of Britain left them confused about the state of race relations here. My father talks about the occasion, on his first ever visit to this country, when he couldn't work out which train he needed to board at Victoria station in central London. Worried by the reaction he might get from white people, he made a point of searching out a black uniformed official. 'Caan't you read, maan. Go and look on the board,' was all the help he got. The white train guard he went to next was much more sympathetic. It was a not-so-subtle reminder, and a very early one, that race relations could not always be reduced to black and white, though that is the division that is easiest to expose and most corrosive in its impact on the nation. There are plenty of Asians who look down their noses at African-Caribbeans and plenty of African-Caribbeans who can't stand the sight of a Johnny-come-lately Somali immigrant. Today there are plenty of Hindus and Sikhs who think the Muslims are giving all Asians a bad name and prefer not to be called Asian at all for fear of being tainted by association.

The first racially motivated incident I remember occurred in my third year at St John's. It was a dark winter's evening. Dick Allen – who would later be my best man, and later still become a self-made millionaire – and I were walking back towards the college after a trip to the fish and chip shop. We were aware of a group of skinheads behind us and attempted to do what only the genuine hard men pull off – look tough and unruffled even from behind. We failed miserably largely because we were not at all hard and we were scared shitless. First came the taunts.

'Oi! You fucking wog. Come here.' We abandoned the I-couldn't-give-a-toss amble and set rather a quicker pace back to the boarding house. We hadn't quite got to the hip-swivelling, shoulder-pumping motion those speed-walkers have, but it was close. We were more like a couple in those old black-and-white silent movies in which everyone walks in quick, jerky movements.

'Who's your friend? Likes nig-nogs, does he? Come on,

you black cunt!' The quick walk turned into a thinly disguised run.

'Getting scared, are we? Come on, let's have a look at you.'

And then we heard the sound of breaking glass. It had the same sort of effect a starting gun has on eight lanes of finely tuned flesh at the Olympics, except that in our case it was not adrenalin, but pure, undiluted fear that kicked in. We sprinted. We were both on the 100-metre team, and I reckon we broke a record or two that evening.

Back in college we had a story to tell. And the way we told it, it was a close-run thing, a near miss with the forces of evil. That's how I dealt with the incident in public. Alone in bed, later that evening, it was different. I knew I had learned something about this country that I had not really been prepared for. I'm not sure that the word racism entered my head, but I understood from that day on that there was an ugliness in British society and that I might see it more often than most simply because of what I looked like and where I came from.

Those skinhead taunts introduced a splinter of fear that niggled away for years to come. Over time I developed a sixth sense that told me when I could be myself and when I should be as unobtrusive as possible. When I went to London for the holidays, I was more careful about where I sat on the tube train. When I was queuing up for a late-night doner kebab after a night at the pub, I knew instinctively who I could smile at and whose eyes I should avoid. I honed the skills that every black person needs when he navigates a white society.

I'm not going to pretend that I was a victim of racism in the way that countless others were at the time and thousands are today. Back in the sixties and seventies, when I confronted prejudice it was something to talk about, something to rail against, but it never became something that derailed the direction in which I was moving. It simply did not happen often enough. At boarding school I lived in a state of splendid isolation. For every time that I was subjected to racist abuse – there was the occasional abuse on the sports field and even the odd snide remark in the classroom – I can remember many more times when my colour simply did not matter. Or, if it was remarked upon at all, it was in what I think was an endearing way. Occasionally one of my friends would call me 'black magic', a pun on a brand of chocolate popular at the time.

As I write this, I can already hear the barbed comments from those of my immigrant compatriots who will, no doubt, accuse me of being either naïve or stupid – probably both. They will say I was being patronised and was too dim to notice or too brain-washed to care. My response is this: I know what it is to be patronised and it makes me mad. When friends called me 'black magic', I didn't get angry because I could see what their motives were. Far from trying to belittle me, they were, in an admittedly gauche way, trying to show how at ease they were with my colour. I was happy to judge people by what they meant to do rather than what they appeared to do.

In any case, I was getting to the age where I was far more inter-ested in what this black magic might do for me at the annual disco with the Girls' Public Day School Trust across the road. If Britain was experiencing its sexual revolution, I was experiencing a sexual awakening – but it was one shot through with contradictions.

The only Asian girls I knew were my sisters and the daugh-ters of family friends, which, in my eyes, was practically the same thing. For sure, in the background there was always the demure ideal of womanhood my parents encouraged, but in front of my eyes was something quite different. Whether it was on TV, through which I learned so much about Britain, or out walking down Palmerston Road on a weekend exeat, I was con-fronted by a singularly English, and white, representation of femininity. Remember, this was the late sixties and seventies – an era of liberation for everyone, but none more so than English women.

This juxtaposition of what I had been brought up to expect of a woman and what I saw around me created its own private battle-field. While the burgeoning adolescent in me imagined all sorts of possibilities with these emancipated girls, I found it hard to accept that my own sisters, down the road in Littlehampton, might be equally freed of their Asian restraint. I remember one particularly boisterous argument when one of my friends told me what he'd like to do with one of my sisters, whom he'd recently met.

There was always a race from the refectory on Thursday evenings when *Top of the Pops* was on BBC 1. Virtually the whole boarding house – I'd moved on to Woodlands House by this stage – would be crammed into the TV room in an atmosphere as rank with overcrowding as with adolescent expectation. The curtains were drawn and in the dark you could catch the strobing light from the TV glint across the faces of boys mesmerised by what was going on on the screen. Years later when I went to see a striptease show, I realised that the very first time I had experienced anything like that was in Woodlands' TV room. We waited for the cameraman to offer up the low-angle shot where all you'd see was a mass of legs and hips. We weren't interested in the blokes, just the girls, especially the ones in miniskirts. Someone would always shout, 'Come on, let's have a proper look,' before furtively glancing at the TV room door to make sure one of the brothers hadn't popped in to check on us. In truth, you couldn't see anything. It was all in the imagination, and ours were overheating with possibility.

The climax of the show – at least as far as we were concerned – was the appearance of Pan's People, an all-woman dance troupe that accompanied one of the songs on each show. Occasionally they were dressed in virginal white as they performed a fauxballet routine to some ballad, perhaps Simon and Garfunkel's 'Bridge Over Troubled Water'. But more often than not they highkicked and gyrated to the more tempestuous rhythm of a rock-and-roll bass guitar. Their zip-up boots came up to their knees and their hot pants were as brief as you could get. There'd be a hush in the room. Twenty, thirty boys watched with tumescent fervour, transfixed by these sirens. At the end of the show everyone would shuffle out with an air of studied nonchalance. You'd be careful to pass some comment about one of the bands just to show that – unlike all the other dirty buggers – you'd been concentrating on the music. *Moi?* Turned on by Pan's People? Never.

Even in this most formative of adolescent experiences my mental picture of what was attractive looked no different to that imagined by my white classmates. It wasn't that I didn't fancy any Asian or African girls; there were simply none around to fancy. There weren't even any to fantasise about. Naomi Campbell had yet to strut the catwalks, and instead of Halle Berry sashaying out of an emerald sea in her bikini and into the ever-ready arms of Pierce Brosnan's Bond, we had Ursula Andress doing exactly the same, except she ended up in a clinch with Sean Connery.

When I started mixing with girls, as part of a group, they were all white. I can still remember their names: Christian, Jane, Anita, Carol, Sarah, Theresa, Francesca, Sally. There were no Shanthinis, Nalinis or Shermilas.

The very idea of who was beautiful and what that beauty looked like was shaped by what I saw on TV or billboards. I'm not talking just about the women but the men as well. Imagine what it is like when everything that is considered desirable is everything you can never be. Today the Bollywood look is fashionable; then it would have been risible. Today the whitest kids from the wealthiest suburbs affect an inner-city drawl and dress like the boys from the 'hood. In those days it was David Cassidy and Donny Osmond – clean and white, the pair of them – who had the girls screaming for more.

I cannot think of a single Asian man who fired the popular imagination in my teen years. The cricketer Imran Khan, whose confidence and competitiveness was like a shot of Viagra for the wilting Asian male ego, had yet to burst into public consciousness. When he did – in the early seventies – his charms seemed to work best on the Sloaney set in west London or on the ladies of Home Counties England. I suspect his appeal – which so many of us Asian lads coveted – would have been lost on the streets of Pompey.

Many women say they too have to live with the dissonance between who they are and what the world seems to expect of them. They say they are made to feel inadequate next to the impossibly shaped women portrayed in a thousand magazines and advertisements. All of that may be true, but if you want to try to understand what it was like for a fourteen-year-old Asian adolescent at boarding school, you have to understand the difference colour makes and you have to weigh up the cost of isolation. Few girls or women are cut off from the hinterland of their peers in the way in which I was estranged from the people I had grown up with as a child. When I looked out across the playground there was no one there who could come over and say, 'Don't worry, I know exactly how you're feeling'. If you are overweight, you can try to lose some pounds; if you're unhappy with your hair, you can dye it. But skin colour is immutable. Colour attracts comment and derision in a way that virtually no other physical attribute is subjected to. Colour carries its own unique baggage, its stereotypes.

To the anti-racist campaigners there was never any difference between being Asian and being African-Caribbean – we were all supposed to be the same in the extent to which we were subject to discrimination. But on the ground it never felt like that. Subtle distinctions were made in everyday talk. These things were never said that openly, but I picked them up through implication and inference. African-Caribbeans were thick but they were strong. Asians could be clever but they were snide bastards, slippery customers. The Chinese were just chinks and nobody cared much about them as long as they kept the chicken chow mein coming. These stereotypes – unwarranted and abusive – still linger.

But I did have one way out. In the almost exclusively white milieu in which we mixed, I think I had a sort of novelty value. I was a rare thing. There were only a handful of other non-white pupils at St John's. In my eight years at the school I can count just over a dozen others – four Asians (with east African roots), two brothers from the Bahamas, two brothers from Malaysia, a mixed-race boy from Hong Kong, another Sri Lankan and a couple of others – and they were not all there at the same time. If I'd been one of hundreds of Asian youths I would have been just another 'Paki', but in my uniqueness I could be seen as exotic. There was irony in this. While I was trying to become as English as possible, people around me may have found a certain attraction in the fact that I came from somewhere else. It may be that what made me different – the source of some personal anxiety – was also the very quality that gave my embryonic love life a bit of a kick-start.

The first time I was told I was like Omar Sharif, I remember wondering what on earth I could possibly have in common with this – to my teenage mind – ageing Arab actor with a weedy little moustache and a gap between his front teeth. I didn't look like him and I didn't sound like him. But over the years it was a comparison that was made over and over again – and every time it was meant to be a compliment. The David Lean film *Doctor Zhivago* had opened in 1965, and by the early seventies its tale of true love set against the turbulence of the Bolshevik revolution was responsible for setting many an adolescent girl's heart a-flutter. Omar Sharif's tortured and wistful Yuri was the perfect foil for Julie Christie's ravishing and heroic Lara. Sharif's soft, swarthy features against Christie's porcelain-white Englishness gave their illicit love the unspoken dimension of colour. Yuri was exotic.

So where did I fit into this fantasy world? The truth is that there was only one attribute, and one alone, that I shared with the Egyptian actor – we both had brown skin. The fact that the comparison was ever made speaks volumes for the extent to which my colour played a part in people's assessment of me – even if they didn't know it or admit it. No one ever said, 'You're brown like that actor,' but I began to understand that that was precisely what they meant.

Crucially, my 'exotic' charms came in an acceptable and unthreatening parcel. My education, my adopted accent, my religion, even my looks, all combined to make me the right kind of foreigner. Admittedly, even that wasn't always enough to shield me – or indeed the people I was with – from the odd barbed comment. One girlfriend was taken aside by a woman at a bus stop we were queuing at and asked what she thought she was doing with a boy like me. The mother of another used to get 'concerned' enquiries from friends and colleagues about how she coped with her daughter going out with 'a coloured boy'.

And long before either Frances Robathan or I knew we were going to get married, her grandfather had had a *sotto voce* conversation with her father that ran something like this. 'Is Fannie's Ala-what's-it educated?' To which Charles Robathan replied, tartly and promptly: 'My dear chap, that boy is better educated then you and I will ever be.' It was quite a rejoinder coming from a man who had been to Marlborough and Oxford. Charles's comment was a triumph of loyalty and affection over breeding and experience. What I did not know at the time was that he had, at some point in our relationship, taken Frances aside, not to put her off, but to warn her that it wouldn't always be easy. There were also one or two others in the family, apart from her grandfather, who had had their worries.

Today it is commonplace to see mixed-race couples. In fact Britain has the highest rate of inter-racial relationships in Europe. Thirty-five years ago they were still something of a rarity, whereas the 2001 census recorded 238,000 mixed-race children. In the 1967 film *To Sir, with Love*, in which a class of largely white inner-city teenagers is confronted with a black teacher, the director James Clavell allows a trace of sexual frisson to quiver under the more dominant theme of racial tension that the film tries to explore. In reality the flame of cross-racial passion had yet to take hold. If, today, it is approaching a bonfire, then it was barely a flickering ember.

If St John's College shielded me from the anti-immigrant sentiment that was bubbling up to the surface across England, it could not protect me from a far more insidious and self-inflicted contagion. Like many immigrant children I began to shrink from the crippling fear of failure. From very early on I began to believe that I was being judged not as an individual but as an Asian boy, a foreigner. My successes or failures were not for me alone but for all of us, all brown people. It was a sense that if I got things wrong I was letting the side down. Nobody told me to feel like this; it came from inside me.

I remember exactly when I first sensed this burden of expectation and it happened while watching football on TV. I knew very little about the game. Supporting a club is a tribal thing; for the most part you inherit an allegiance from your father. Going to your first match is like a rite of passage. At least that was how it seemed when my friends talked about it. They'd tell me about the ritual. They'd tell me how, like warriors before battle, they'd get dressed for the game in the right colours (the manufacture and marketing of team kits had yet to develop into the multimillion-pound business it is today). Then dads would meet other dads at the pub before going on to the chippie. Fed, watered and pumped up, they'd walk to the stadium.

I, of course, had had none of that. The only football team I had ever heard of was Asante Kotoko in Ghana, and that wasn't something I dared admit to. I wanted to support a team in England's top division but had no particular reason to choose one over another. Then one day I found something – someone – I could latch on to. In 1969 a Bermudan-born player named Clyde Best made his debut for West Ham. I had no idea where West Ham was or how good a record the team had, but I was drawn to this black man, then such a rarity on a football pitch. I didn't know what being offside meant (and was too embarrassed to ask) or the difference between a direct and an indirect free kick. All I knew was that I desperately wanted Clyde Best to get the ball.

But I remember that from the very first time I saw him with the ball at his feet I also feared that he would lose it. Success and failure seemed to lie far too close for comfort. The other boys would shout obscenities at all the players who failed to perform to perfection, but when their screams were directed at Clyde Best, I took it personally. It was as if their derision was a slur on all black people. I felt a kind of shame. In my mind poor old Clyde was not allowed any off days. If he couldn't do something fantastic with the ball then I began to feel that it would be better if he didn't get it in the first place. The very reason that had brought him to my attention – his colour – was also the reason I couldn't allow him to be like any of the other twenty-one players on the pitch.

Actually, what was happening was that I had turned this footballer into a lightning rod for my own anxieties – the worries I had about Clyde Best's performances were really the worries I had about myself. I can't remember ever having that carefree sense of doing something because I simply wanted to do it. There was always a silent calculation to be made. It got to a stage where the possibility of failure loomed larger in any decision than the prospect of success. It wasn't simply the fear of letting myself down, but the fear of letting 'us' down. Whatever challenges I faced on the outside – in the classroom, on the sports field and even at the school disco – were never as great as the challenges I confronted inside my head. At times it felt as if I were caught in the middle of a psychological vice, crushed between the aspiration to do well and scared by the thought that it could all go horribly wrong. How tempting it would be to settle for the middle ground, to bob along the surface without ever taking any risks. I have spent much of my adult life shaking off this dead weight of anxiety, fighting off the allure of mediocrity.

By the time I got to university in Durham, I had learned to accommodate all these anxieties. Or perhaps it would be more honest to say that I had learned how to suppress them. I wouldn't say I was the finished article – aren't we all, to the very end, just a work in progress? – but I had reached a sort of evolutionary plateau. Some eight years after I had arrived in Britain I had matured into a relatively confident young man with much to be thankful for and much to look forward to. England had turned out to be everything my parents had hoped it would be – a place where opportunity was based on merit. At least that was how it felt. I was, you could say, comfortable in my own skin. Indeed, so comfortable that no one seemed to notice my skin colour at all. After showing one friend a family photo I can remember him telling me how, for a moment, he'd been surprised that my parents were Asians. It began to dawn on me that my transformation from Asian boy to English adolescent might have been rather too successful.

I'm not sure how deeply I was aware of it at the time, but I think I had become a sort of honorary white, that most demeaning of racial stereotypes. It wasn't the way I felt inside but it was certainly what I had become in some eyes. The honorary white is like a mannequin in a shop window. People get to dress it up any way they want to – and usually it ends up looking reassuringly like themselves. No fuss, no threat.

The honorary white has a long pedigree in British culture. As early as the seventeenth century, it was fashionable for aristocratic ladies to be seen with a black pageboy, they were just another ornament in the drawing room. A perfect example is Sir Anthony Van Dyck's portrait of *Henrietta of Lorraine* at Kenwood in London. In it the black pageboy, an emasculated version of black manhood, looks up adoringly at his lady. Much later, in the early 1900s, there were the Indian prince-cricketers who went to Oxbridge and showed off their flamboyant talent at Lord's but whose countrymen might have found it rather more difficult to enter the members' enclosure. In the seventies sitcom *Rising Damp*, the black actor Don Warrington played the cool, calm and highly articulate tenant to Leonard Rossiter's hilarious portrayal of the mean-spirited landlord. If Warrington's character had in any way resembled real black tenants, who – more often than not – felt cheated, put upon and abused by their rapacious landlords, it wouldn't have been funny. The comedy was in the reinvention of the black man as honorary white. I'm not saying I didn't laugh with the rest of them, but I always secretly wished that Don Warrington would suddenly morph into a Jamaican Yardie who wouldn't play the game. Who'd be laughing then? I would.

And it was precisely because my colour didn't seem to concern anyone around me, or was overlooked by them, that it suddenly began to matter more to me. For the first time I began to feel that the ready and open acceptance that I had encountered, and which made my life so much easier than for so many immigrant contemporaries, may not really have been proof that race was not an issue. On the contrary, I began to worry that my Englishness had made it possible for people to ignore race altogether.

It was at Durham that the scales fell from my eyes. It was here that I began to see England as she really was rather than the cloistered version I had grown up in at St John's. It wasn't so much that Durham University looked and sounded like the real England but that it looked and sounded precisely the opposite. Up there in the north-east, once the cockpit of the labour movement but already fading into insignificance like the scene of some fabled but ancient battle, the university felt as if it were a privileged outpost. Town and gown rarely came into contact except when the former were serving or clearing up after the latter. Boys with striped scarves lying floppy and lifeless over their shoulders like the dead weight of tradition and girls in quilted green jackets wondered around from college to lecture theatre apparently oblivious to the world around them.

Whereas at school I'd taken it for granted that I was often in a minority of one in the classroom, the scarcity of any other black or Asian faces on Durham's Palace Green or in the Junior Common Room began to strike me as odd. I couldn't vouch for the numbers, but it certainly felt as if there were more overseas students (Durham had links with universities in Africa) than there were undergraduates from Southall, Brixton or Birmingham. The university's admissions culture was inevitably reflected in the preoccupations of the student body. In the student union we noted the iniquities of life in Pinochet's Chile, resolved to do something about supporting the Sandinistas in Nicaragua and closed down our overdrawn accounts with Barclays Bank in the name of fighting apartheid. But rarely, if ever, did we even recognise the home-grown deficiencies in race relations. I don't remember any motions about why so many students came from the leafy suburbs of south-east England and so few from the inner-city boroughs.

I had arrived at Durham naïve enough to believe that the opportunities I had had were there for all those willing to grasp them. I left the university convinced England was socially skewed and riven with racial inequality. It was at Durham that I learned to read the hidden signals that tell you who people are and where they come from. The cut of a man's collar, the way he knots his tie, the gold signet ring placed ever so discreetly on the little finger – the tiny details which constitute a social code to be understood by those who know the rules. I saw how middle-class girls thought nothing of wearing daddy's baggy jumper or big brother's old rugby shirt, while girls from the estates spent more than they should on clothes they often looked uncomfortable in. Later, I noticed how some people would invite me to a party, while the invitations from others simply told me they would be 'at home' – where else would they be. All of it was part of a social semaphore that helped me manoeuvre my way through a landscape in which the obstacles of race and class were often hidden, but no less real for that.

It wasn't Durham's degree that completed my education, but the way the place jolted me out of an uncritical ambivalence about the role race – and class – played in the shaping of English lives.

Hanif Kureishi's debut novel, *The Buddha of Suburbia*, is the first book I remember that tried to chart the fault line between the immigrant experience and English society. I knew straight away that I could never have written a book like that, even if I possessed Kureishi's abundant talent. In turns comic, raunchy and satirical, the novel derives its force from the friction between two cultures. In it, Karim, the child of a Pakistani father and an English mother, is both genetically and metaphorically caught in the middle. I have never really been in that space.

What happened to me was that I went from a total immersion in one culture, my hybrid Asian-African experience from the family's time in Ghana, to a complete submergence in English life. The dissonance between the two went on in my head, not out in the open. For me there was no clash between values at home and values at school, no struggle between language in the house and language in the playground. From the age of eleven there was only transition from the place I had left behind to the place I had arrived in. I have accomplished that journey so successfully that I have been able to exploit to the full everything that Britain has had to offer. I have gained so much – an education, a career, a country – and yet I am sometimes left with a nagging doubt. What have I left behind? Like Eva Hoffman in *Lost in Translation*, her powerful chronicle of a life of exile, I have had to ask myself, 'How does one bend to another culture without falling over, how does one strike an elastic balance between rigidity and self-effacement?'

When people say I am a role model for a new generation of immigrants, I often feel guilty, or a bit of a fraud. I wonder whether someone who has embraced and absorbed so much of English culture has any right to lead the way for people whose experience of living here is so different. It's one of the reasons that I was ambivalent when, in my days as a foreign correspondent, I won awards from organisations trying to promote the fortunes of ethnic minorities. I had never asked to be an example to anyone. I never wanted to be the best black journalist. I simply wanted to be the best reporter that I could be. Later I came to understand that I performed a function regardless of whether I wanted to or not. The accident of birth coupled with the rewards of hard work have given me a fairly unusual foothold in English society – I am Asian and successful. What's more, my achievements, unlike some of the hugely successful Asian businessmen in Britain, have been very public. They are measured in the millions who watch me every night on TV rather than the millions the others have stashed away in their bank accounts.

But what the public sees is only a part of the story. It's like judging a marathon runner by the smile on her face when she is bursting through the finish tape and ignoring all those days of painful preparation. In a sense, I too trained to become English. It started the minute I was left on my own at school. In those first years in Britain I wasn't a part of any community other than the one in which I found myself – an English boarding school. There were a few other foreign students at St John's College, but there were never enough of us to represent a community of foreigners. We didn't compare notes. And even if we'd recognised the challenges we faced, or understood that they stemmed from the dislocation of culture from place (and I don't think we did), we would not have admitted it to each other. We were far too busy and engrossed in our own private struggle to fit in. To have admitted that it was a struggle would have smacked of weakness, and weakness opened the door to failure. That was a door I wanted to keep slammed shut. It took many years, decades even, till we were confident enough of our place in Britain to begin the conversations we should have had in our youth.

It was only in researching this book, for example, that I discovered how Anna Eliathamby, the eldest daughter of the Sri Lankan couple who acted as guardians during my boarding school years, coped with being an immigrant child. She told me how she would dread Mondays at school. The other girls – mostly English – would ask, in all innocence, what Anna had been doing and who she had seen. Invariably her family would have spent the weekend with other Sri Lankan families. But Anna would be too embarrassed to admit that, and so her descriptions of the family's weekend activities were contrived in such a way as to leave open the possibility, in her friends' minds, that she had mixed with white English friends. It was a lie of omission rather than commission.

Another friend, Dori Chetty, also a Tamil but from Mauritius, thought she would be laughed at if she told her friends that her aunt, with whom she lived, only ever cooked curries. So Dori would tell her friends about the toad-in-the-hole she'd never seen or the bangers and mash she'd never eaten.

Anna, Dori and I, and thousands of other immigrant children who grew up in Britain in the sixties, were part of a generation that spent its formative years here without the benefit of multi-culturalism – the credo that has dominated race relations for the last thirty years or so. Not for us the celebration of Diwali and Ramadan. Not for us the role models of black premiership super-stars. Not for us the fascination with Indian fashion and film. Not for us the strident advocacy of a Yasmin Alibhai-Brown or the hectic comedy of a Lenny Henry. Not for us the famous talents of Meera Syal or the fat-wallet confidence of Lakshmi Mittal, one of the richest men in the country. Come to think of it, not for us the dulcet tones of a Trevor McDonald, Britain's first black network newsreader, or the war reporting of a George Alagiah, the BBC's first black TV foreign correspondent.

No, we were the generation that felt we had to hide our light under a bushel. We knew we had much to offer but couldn't be sure that our new-found compatriots were ready to accept our gifts. We used to worry about the smell of garlic on our breath and on our clothes. We wished our parents would learn to speak prop-erly and take us on holiday to southern Spain. It didn't seem to matter that the place was already filling up with the kind of Brits who would detest our presence. It was what everybody talked about when they got back from the long summer and we wanted to have a story to tell as well. Saying you'd gone back for the wedding of a distant cousin in even more distant Gujarat didn't seem to have the same ring to it. Not in those days. Today you'd be asked to address the school assembly about it. Then it served only to prove how different you were.

In that tug of war between heritage on the one side and assim-ilation on the other, I never really had much of a choice. It had to be assimilation. That, to some people, suggests suppression of one's own culture. But I didn't so much suppress it as set it to one side. It is still there, and every now and again I dip into it. It asserts itself every time I travel for work as a reporter. I believe I have an affinity with people in far-flung places – whether it be the earthquake victims of Pakistan in 2005 or the victims of genocide in Rwanda a decade earlier – precisely because my 'other' side comes to the fore. It's evident every time I spend time with my father, or even with distant relatives who breathe new life into it with the oxygen of cultural familiarity.

In my case the alternative to assimilation was to stick out like some exotic cactus in a bed of spring meadow plants. I had found out what that was going to be like in my very first days at boarding school, and I knew I wasn't going to let it happen again. By becoming English, I escaped the square-peg-round-hole fate that befell so many of my fellow immigrants.

My transition from Sri Lankan boy to English man has taken decades. It started out of necessity, then it became a convenience, and finally, in my thirties, it became an attachment. Britain began to feel like home. That sense of belonging was far more momentous than I realised at the time. I know now that it was only when I was secure in what I had become that I could explore what I had been. And so it was that thirty-five years after I had begun my English journey, I set out on a new one to Sri Lanka – the land of my birth. I was to discover a home from home.

2

A Home from Home

'I'll send you a postcard when I get there.' Getting there, the destination, that's all that counts these days. Once, the journey itself was something you could write home about. It took so long and you saw so much on the way. Today, it's just beginnings and endings. You start and then you finish. A few hours separate a northern winter from a southern summer. You can fall asleep in the east and wake up in the west. You can leave Christianity one day and immerse yourself in Buddhism the next. In the morning you can look around you to see only concrete and glass; by the evening nothing will interrupt your gaze till your eyes settle on a distant, purplish horizon.

Take-off and landing. There's hardly a moment to adjust. Departure and arrival. Virtually no time to contemplate. Embark and disembark. A clingfilmed, microwaved meal to distract you. London–Johannesburg; Gatwick–Lagos; Paris–Dakar; Frankfurt–Bangkok; Zurich–Rio de Janeiro. The world has shrunk. Thousands of miles apart on a map, just a dash separates them on an airport departure board. Accents, cultures, languages, and customs – all squeezed into that tiny little space between two cities on a screen.

This is the story about another journey on the departure board – London–Colombo – and how it has changed my life, or the way I think about it.

There are still some journeys where the distance travelled in the sanitised capsule of a plane is nothing compared to the distance travelled in the mind. The trip I want you to join me on now is not about what a person can do when he gets to a place, but about what a place can do to a person once he's there.

Back in December 2002, when I returned to Sri Lanka some forty-odd years after I'd first left it, nothing could have prepared me for the sense of umbilical connection I would feel for the land of my birth. Even as I set off for Heathrow airport, I began to realise that this was a journey not just from one part of the world to another, but from one place in my head to another. The flight would be the bridge from the part of me that felt British to the part of me that wondered if there was any of Sri Lanka still left in me.

It crept up on me – this feeling that I wanted to be Sri Lankan again. Or, at least, allow Sri Lanka to be a part of me again. Imperceptibly, hour by hour, day by day, I found myself wanting to acknowledge something that I had contrived to forget. For forty years or so, I had defined myself by where I was going to rather than by what I had left behind. First it was Ghana and then it was Britain. Now my past was about to reclaim its rightful share in my identity.

This is not about citizenship. I am British. This is not about allegiance. I am loyal to queen and country – whatever that means these days. This is not about where I call home – it's London. This is about a *feeling*. What do you do when you discover a home away from home?

I have always loved airports and aircraft. From the moment I set foot on my first plane – an Air Ceylon DC3 Dakota flight out of Colombo in 1961 – the whole business of flying from one place to another has held a special fascination for me. From that hold-your-breath moment when the nose of the plane tips up, or the thrill of bursting through a canopy of grey cloud to find a sunny blue sky, to the neck-twisting peek you get of a new land as the plane drops down – all of it, every single bit spells discovery and adventure.

As a child, planes were a bit of an obsession. I used to cut out pictures of them from magazines, make drawings of my own intricate designs (I thought of a double-decker long before Airbus got around to it), make Airfix models of them, and tick off the ones I'd seen in a spotters' book.

By the time I was eight or so I was the captain of an airliner. Our front garden, with its turning circle around the most generous of guava trees, was the airport apron and our house was the terminal building. I'd skip down the steps from the veranda and climb on to my made-in-Czechoslovakia bicycle (the country had yet to be split up). I was in the cockpit. I would creep around the guava tree very slowly and then pick up speed as the path straightened out. The tyres would spit out bits of gravel. It was time to check my instruments. Fuel tanks, fasten-seatbelt signs, lights – they all had to be imagined, but I was meticulous, just as the real pilots were. I had no gears and the brakes were applied by pedalling backwards. Testing them meant locking them hard enough to cause a little skid, exposing a gash of red earth beneath the gravel. At the front gate I would wait for the control tower to give me the all-clear. Second Avenue sloped ever so gently uphill – the perfect angle for a take-off. I'd turn into it, stop for the briefest of moments, before opening up the throttle. I'd pedal furiously, my lungs fit to burst, till the road levelled off and I was in the air. Landings were even more exciting. I'd fly down the hill as fast as I could, always aiming to touch down by the third neem tree from the gate. I chose it because it only just gave me enough distance to reduce my speed before having to turn into our corner home at number 10. If I missed and ended up in the main road it would mean a telling-off from my mother and, what was much worse, danger for my passengers, all of whom relied on me to bring them back safe and sound.

Looking back, the fascination with flying appears to have been a family trait. I was not alone. My sisters were willing accomplices. Growing up in Ghana, one of our favourite outings was a trip to the airport. It's as if we were drawn to this symbol of our journey from the stultifying atmosphere of an ethnically divided homeland to a life of opportunity in west Africa and, later, the United Kingdom. All those years earlier Colombo airport had been a gateway – we'd walked through it and into a new life.

Even now, when I sit in a departure lounge, I think I can tell which travellers are embarking on that life-changing journey we call migration. For a start there are always more bags and bits and pieces than anyone would need for a mere holiday. They dress in a style they think will suit the place they are going to, but it is a style they have gleaned from tattered old magazines – it's out of date. There is that look of trepidation in their eyes. It is a singularly brave thing to do, to leave all that you are familiar with for the promise – though never a guarantee – of better things in a place you have never seen before.

My parents would take us to Accra airport at dusk – that was when the long-haul flights would take off. Pan-American and BOAC (British Overseas Airways Corporation); Boeing 707s and VC10s – the airlines and aircraft that first began to shrink the world in the age of jet travel. It was the best time of the day – the heat which at noon would bear down on you simply caressed you now. We'd wander over to the only terminal building to check the departure times. I used to look up at the ceiling fans arranged in a line above us like wheels spinning towards each other without ever actually catching up – what would happen if someone made them go as fast as the propellers on the planes on the tarmac? Perhaps the whole terminal building would start to float upwards – that was one of my fantasies. Outside, the evening breeze would carry the tell-tale smell of meat being grilled on charcoal embers – *chichinga*, the spicy Ghanaian kebab. But my mother's concern for hygiene meant we were only allowed an ice cream or roasted ground nuts wrapped in a paper cone made from a sheet of yesterday's *Ghanaian Times*.

This was an age of innocence, before anyone thought of using a plane as a weapon of mass destruction. All that separated us from the airliners was a flimsy chicken-wire fence. You could smell the kerosene and hear the rattle of the baggage carts as they were trundled over to the plane. The cabin lights were already switched on, like a luminous tickertape ribbon that stretched down the fuselage. I used to pick out a passenger, watch her as she climbed up the gangway and disappeared out of sight. Then I'd try to guess her progress inside the plane; try to see if I could place her wherever she sat down. Slowly the long queue would dwindle until the final passenger made a late dash from the terminal building. One of the ground staff would always go into the plane at the last minute – I used to worry that he wouldn't get out in time. But it always took an age for them to finally shut the door.

There was one man on the ground whose job it was to pull the chocks away from the aircraft wheels, and I used to watch him like a hawk. As soon as he made his move, I knew we were just minutes away from the climax of the whole show. The jet engines would come to life, spewing out a heat haze which made even the last sliver of blood-orange sun look like it might wobble and melt into the Atlantic. Then there was a surging roar as the engines worked up the power to shift the plane. And slowly, almost imperceptibly, it would begin to move. We knew exactly what was coming next. It would have to turn, point its nose towards the runway and away from the terminal. That was when my parents would turn their backs; that's when we would dare each other to stand stock-still to face the heat-wave as it raced over us.

In those days people would dress up for the journey – it was not unusual to see men in ties and women in high heels. Now we look for something comfortable to put on. Flying represented success and elegance. I remember those street-side hoardings advertising Peter Stuyvesant – a masculine but neatly manicured hand holding a filter-tipped cigarette. In the corner of the picture you could just see the navy cuff of a suit with the gold braid of an airline captain's uniform. That was enough, that was all you had to show to get the message across. Smoke this, it said, and you'll be in high-flying company.

I used to watch open-mouthed as the flight crew breezed through the terminal, heading for a side door reserved especially for them. Shiny shoes, dark glasses, their caps tipped to one side, their jackets slung nonchalantly over a shoulder. From my waist-high perspective they looked like gods. What style, what confidence!

And the stewardesses! How fragrant, how cool they looked when all about them people were losing their heads over stray bags and connections missed. I envied the easy intimacy they seemed to share with the men from the flight deck. It was in some teeming terminal – perhaps it was Cairo or Beirut; it could have been Accra or Bombay – that I felt the nascent stirring of sexual frisson, that heady mix of desire and admiration that takes you on the road from like to lust.

It's all changed now. What the package tours started, the no-frills airlines have perfected. Flying has been reduced to a glorified bus service and the staff seem to behave accordingly. As for the passengers, they look as if they might be embarking on something as mundane as popping out to get the newspapers. And, of course, many of them will end up on pretty familiar territory. They might cross a border or two on the way, but the whole purpose of modern, pre-packaged travel is to avoid any surprises. Heaven forbid that you might actually have to speak a foreign language! Those who are loudest when it comes to condemning the immigrants who can't speak English properly are often the least likely to take a phrasebook when travelling abroad. Where once there was a thirst for adventure and discovery, now there is simply the desire for a new backdrop against which to do the same old things. Why hang around in Inverness or Portsmouth when you can get inebriated in Ibiza or have a piss-up in Prague?

Time it right and the cost of your ticket will be less than you'll pay for a round of stale sandwiches at Luton airport.

As for me, airports and planes have been the punctuation marks in the story of my life and career. I've now travelled too often to be surprised by the process, but the prospect of disembarking in a new place, with new faces, new accents, new smells and new customs, still excites me.

What I like best are those moments before landing when the plane is low enough to catch some detail on the ground below. It's like looking down on a model village, except it's all real – people move, the trucks belch out diesel smoke and the children play barefoot soccer in a rust-coloured haze of whipped-up dust. You feel just a bit like a voyeur as you look down into a courtyard that you'd never glimpse from the street. You're not supposed to see that woman as she takes water from a bucket to wash her hair. That man wouldn't like it if he knew you could see him as he sleeps off a night of excess under a palm-thatched awning. But in a few minutes you'll no longer be the detached observer looking down on him from your lofty perch. Soon you'll be down on his level, in his town. That will even things up a bit. You will have to do what travellers through the ages have always done – make friends with the locals.

But what happens if you were once one of the locals? In December 2002, forty-one years after my family's first ever journey on a plane, I was about to embark on a flight that would become – though I didn't fully appreciate it at the time – just as significant, to a family reunion in the country we had left in 1961. Then it was Ceylon, now it was Sri Lanka. While the country had changed its name, I had changed my life. I had traded my birthright, my Sri Lankan passport, for a British one. I had left as a child, I was returning as an adult.

So there we were, working our way towards the check-in desk at Heathrow's Terminal 4. It was 17 December 2002. You only had to look at our party to begin to understand what happens to people who leave their homeland, how they are transformed by the miracle of migration. My wife Frances is English, English as they come. Our sons Adam and Matthew carry a Tamil surname but look like they could be from South America or southern Italy and all stops on the way. There was my eldest sister Mari, and her husband Tony, the child of a wartime romance between an English lass and an African-American GI, who was left first to the care of Dr Barnado and then a loving foster family. Their children: eighteen-year-old Lara, all hips and cascading hair; Nicholas, forever checking that the flight hadn't taken off without us.

But this was only one part of the Alagiah entourage. My father had already been in Sri Lanka for some weeks. Another sister, Rachel – second out of five children – had arrived there a few days before. Her journey had started in Geneva, where she is settled on the shores of Lac Leeman with her Czech émigré husband Joseph, and their daughters Lisa and Maya. The girls spoke French to their parents and English with the rest of us. There were still more to come. Sisters three and four were leaving on a later flight (part convenience, part superstition). The plan was for Christine and her English husband Guy, with their four children, to meet my youngest sister, Jenny, who was en route from her adopted home in Florida with her husband, Mark, and her own brood of four. Charles, Grace, George and Paul would say things like 'awesome' in their endearingly wholesome American way, while Louise, Stephanie, Philip and Joselyn would say 'wicked' in their endearingly English way and, what's more, mean the same thing. 'We'll hear Uncle Mark even before he gets off the plane,' quipped one of the children. Mark's booming American twang was part of family folklore.

There was one person whose absence we all felt so keenly. My mother, Therese, had died in 1996. Our family was her creation; it was her life, and it seemed so unfair that she could not share this journey with us.

There was a rather special atmosphere at the check-in queue for Sri Lankan Airlines Flight UL505 out of London – more than the usual flutter of anticipation as people head off for a couple of weeks in the sun. For many of the passengers, the tickets they clutched represented a passage of rediscovery, a journey back to a place they, or their parents, had left in more uncertain times. In many ways, what they held in their hands was a return ticket, though the initial journey might have been, as it was for us, decades earlier.

For some years the sun, sea and sand of Sri Lanka had made it a popular, exotic addition to the burgeoning list of long-haul destinations favoured by the ever-increasing numbers of Europeans bored with the condominium culture of Spain's Costa del Sol. The Germans, whose wallets could take the strain better than most, were among the earliest to sample the delights of this most favoured of tropical isles. But as Britain's economy began to turn around in the eighties, its people, too, started to look for new playgrounds.

The irony was that while growing numbers of tourists were sampling the delights of Sri Lankan hospitality, an equally steady stream of locals was heading the other way. Beyond the tourist enclaves, with their picture-perfect vistas of emerald seas and arching coconut trees that seemed to bow in thanksgiving for the trade the tourists brought with them, there was a deep disaffection in the countryside.

In 1983 the sporadic bouts of inter-ethnic rivalry and violence that had marred Sri Lankan politics since independence in 1948 coalesced into a full-blown civil war. A rebel attack on a military garrison in the Tamil-dominated northern city of Jaffna led to violent reprisals against Tamils – thousands were killed in the predominantly Sinhalese capital, Colombo, and elsewhere in the country. It marked the beginning of nearly two decades of sustained violence. The Jaffna attack was masterminded by the guerrillas of the Liberation Tigers of Tamil Eelam – or the Tamil Tigers – who had grown out of a frustration with conventional politics. In the eyes of even moderate Tamils – who constitute a little less than a fifth of the country's population – the 'boys', as they came to be known, were making up for lost time.

The conflict gave rise to a second wave of Tamil migrants. My parents' generation had been the first – they fled from institutional discrimination, while this new diaspora was fleeing for its life. Forty years ago the Tamils (and moderate Sinhalese) who left were educated people, fluent in English, with professional skills they could sell abroad. My father was a civil engineer. The Tamils who were leaving in the eighties and nineties were a different, more desperate breed. Their education had been disrupted, and even if they had been in the classroom, they were forced to learn in the vernacular – there's not much use for a top grade in Tamil abroad. These were the people who began to swell the asylum queues in Germany, France and Britain. These were the people who seemed to land the overnight shift at every other petrol station in London.

And it wasn't always the Sinhalese army they were trying to avoid. Tamil propagandists would never admit it, but a sizeable number of these Tamils were also escaping the overzealous, not to say coercive, nature of the Tigers' recruitment and fund-raising drives. There were plenty of stories of Tiger officials commandeering properties and enforcing taxes on those who lived within their territory. The double whammy of government offensives and the Tigers' persuasive tactics was enough to prompt even the most patriotic of Tamils into an expensive, miserable and often dangerous search for somewhere else to call home – at least until things returned to normal.

In December 2002 things did, indeed, look as if they might be returning to normal. A team of Norwegian negotiators had cooled down one of the hottest and most vicious wars with a dose of their Nordic chill. For the first time in nearly twenty years the guns were silent, the roadblocks had been lifted and it was possible to believe in new beginnings. Our planeload of returning migrants was testament to that. That's not to say that anybody was planning to uproot their family for a second time and return to Sri Lanka like prodigal children. Most just wanted to remind themselves of the country they had left behind.

The flight itself was like a halfway house, a no-man's-land between Britain and Sri Lanka. It was somewhere to get acclimatised. Without even knowing they were doing it, people were beginning to shed their Western outer layer, the one they wore for protection in Britain. Like boxers who sense the threat is over, they were letting their guard down. The chatter was free-flowing and the accents were changing. People who, just a few hours earlier, had studiously managed not to confuse their v's with their w's no longer felt it mattered that much.

There was an air of revival and reunion on the plane. The sense that this journey was taking me full circle to where it had all started was reinforced when, on a walk through the cabin, I was stopped by one Upali Jayattileke, a man who, like my father, had left Sri Lanka for Ghana in the sixties. He told me he used to watch me play as a child in Kumasi, a provincial city there. Also on the flight were friends from London: Sri Lankan-born Neil Fernando, his wife Amanda and their children – Luke, Tarin and Mala. Neil is more or less my age and shares the same birthday. Amanda, who is English, has exactly the same birthday as my wife Frances. What are the chances of that happening between any two couples? What are the chances of that happening between any two mixed-race couples? If you understand the lottery that is migration, then we had hit the jackpot.

As a BBC TV journalist I was a familiar face and there were plenty of knowing glances and friendly taps on the back. But it wasn't the Z-list celebrity status they were acknowledging; it was the sense of kinship. Nobody actually said it, but what they meant was: 'You may be a big chap on the world-famous BBC, but still you're one of us.'

Ever since I reached the point in my career where I was recognised on the street, there has been a marked difference in the way people have reacted. From the English there is always a nod of recognition and then a whispered 'It's that newsreader' to a friend as they walk past. From black and Asian people there is always a handshake followed by the words 'We're proud of you' or similar. They have a sense of ownership. What I have achieved, I have achieved for them. It's been a salutary experience.

I have never asked to represent black or Asian people, but for some of them that is precisely what I do. I used to feel rather ambivalent about being described as the BBC's first black foreign correspondent, or being voted the Media Personality of the Year by the judges at the Ethnic Minority Media Awards. Is it so good, I asked myself, to be the best black journalist? I wanted to be the best journalist full stop, period, case closed. Now I accept that among people who still feel their country does not appreciate everything they bring to it, my success represents a counterblast that might topple the hoary stereotype of the indolent outsider. On Flight UL505 I personified that most potent element of the immigrant dream – to go forth and succeed. To make it in the white man's country, now that is what it's all about! There were many people on that plane who, I am sure, had made something of their British sojourn, but mine was a very public success – and it was acknowledged freely and generously.

It was a first gentle reminder that however British I felt, in some eyes I would remain forever Sri Lankan.

As the plane headed eastwards into an ever-fading sky, as the colours turned from blue to pink to purply-black, I began to see that for over thirty years I had been preoccupied with being British – first it had been a conscious effort, later a reflex. Now, perhaps for the first time since I'd arrived in Britain in 1967, I had to start thinking about what it meant to have started my journey in Sri Lanka.

I'd prepared myself to find something smaller than I remembered. The things that are writ large in a child's mind diminish with age. That much I was ready to accept. But was it really so modest, so run-down, so ordinary, so dirty? Number 16 Charles Place – that was where my parents lived when I was born, the third child and only son. Everybody needs a place to start, a point of reference, a place where the memories – conscious or subliminal – start to grow into the mental ballast we all carry around. This was my beginning. In my mind's eye this is what everything else in my life would be compared to. Here was the first place I would call home – an unremarkable, somewhat dilapidated bungalow at the wrong end of an ordinary street in a modest part of town.

Charles Place was no more than a dirt track. The fetid gully into which I had once fallen still ran along the side of the property. Steel-sheet gates now protected the compound. I didn't remember those. There was a grille at eye level. We peered through it and into our history. A dog was barking; I knew it would look mangy. It was that kind of place.

We'd gone to Charles Place on the day after we arrived in Colombo. I'd always felt it would be an important part of our trip. Later there would be the usual tourist destinations, but first came the family history. When planning the holiday, I'd made a mental note to try to be with the kids when we arrived at the house so I could be on hand to explain the remarkable journey their family, their grandparents, had made. But when it came down to it, I found that I had to start explaining it all to myself.

Ever since I came to Britain, people have asked me where I'm from. Some say the question itself is loaded, but I've never minded it. After all, if you're an Indian and you see someone white in the middle of your country, you'd be inclined to ask the same question. And in those days, back in the sixties, it was a fairly good bet to assume I was from somewhere else. They weren't – most of them anyway – trying to deny me my place in Britain; they were just curious. More recently they ask because they want to know more about a man who's been in the public eye for quite a while. 'I was born in Sri Lanka,' I used to say. But that was only ever a sort of conversational holding statement. I realise that now. Because no sooner had I finished that sentence than I would follow it up with the words, 'but I grew up in Africa, in Ghana.' I'd always dealt with Sri Lanka in a clause, a grammatical way-station to Ghana, where the real action began.

In *A Passage to Africa* I wrote about how, as a child, I'd wanted to be a part of something big, not some insignificant little island in the Indian Ocean that had rejected people like us – Tamils. I'd clung to Africa – not just the place, but the idea. A vast land where we could, as the Americans put it, 'start over'. I reinvented myself. It's as if I had manufactured a new beginning. Certainly going to west Africa did open up new opportunities. My father's career and our family's fortunes blossomed. But Ghana was not the start of our journey, it was a milestone in it. As a child I'd ignored that; as an adult I'd chosen not to remember.

I used to say that I felt at home in Africa. But *this* was home. This shabby little corner of the world was where I was from. If Africa had a claim on the person I'd become, Sri Lanka had a claim on the person who started out. Nurture and nature. And where did that leave Britain, the place I've lived in longer than anywhere else – and by a mile?

The whole party trooped down the lane – there were nineteen of us at this stage, six short of the full complement. I looked over at my father to see if his reaction was anything like mine. It wasn't. There was recognition, but no surprise. He hadn't tried to forget anything, so there was nothing to shock him. He was checking his memory; I was checking my conscience.

We knocked on the gate. The dog barked even louder. It was scolded, possibly beaten, judging by the yelp that ended the noise. My father spoke in English. It had always been a predominantly Sinhalese area, but ethnicity had been less important to my parents than its proximity to the Catholic church. Most people in Dehiwale had that in common. There was a tentative reply, a silence, some footsteps, and then the bolt was pulled back. We poured in like water through a narrow hole. And, like water, we seeped into every nook and cranny of the tiny garden.

The slight, elderly woman who'd opened the gate turned

straight back to the security of her porch, retreating from this horde of foreigners. For a moment nobody said anything. We gawped, she looked down. It was my father who broke the silence.

'You are?'

'Abeyaratne.' That was it. Hardly what you'd call a conversation. Her eyes moved across from my father to the rest of us. We began to understand what it must feel like for her. There we were like visitors to a zoo. She was in her home, except we'd made it feel like a cage.

'Is the man of the house here?' my father asked. He spoke in English. Abeyaratne is a Sinhalese name, and English is the language common to both communities. To us the question sounded terribly formal, even patronising. Later my father explained that it would have been considered impolite, too familiar, if he'd tried to address her directly from the beginning.

'He's inside,' she replied, still suspicious.

'These children were born in this house and they have come back to have a look,' he said tentatively. You could see her doing a mental calculation – which children; there were twelve of them.

'No, no – these are my grandchildren. Come, Mari, George. Where are you all?' We shuffled forward. 'Jenny and Christine, come, come. Here, these are the ones that were born here.'

We nodded, not quite sure whether to try to shake hands. We could hear a sound just inside the front door. Tired, sleepy sandals dragged across a cement floor shining with wear. Mr Abeyaratne walked out, blinking into the sunlight. The old woman said something to him in Sinhalese.

'Can I help you?' he asked.

'Max, is it Max?' My father was excited.

'Yes, yes, I'm Max.'

'Alagiah. I'm Alagiah. Donald. You can't remember?' Why should he? It had been more than forty years since they'd last met.

'Donald! Oh my God. Donald.' At last there was some point of real contact. They shook hands.

Max Abeyaratne had been the rent collector. He'd married the daughter of the owner of the house, and the property had been a part of his dowry. Once a month he'd come round. I imagined the scene. It would probably have been my mother in charge of the rent. She'd handled the money side of things. I can remember the ledger she kept for household accounting. Marble-effect covers with a dark blue canvas spine. She would have taken the money from somewhere in her bedroom, hidden away with the rainy-day money – not that there was ever much of that, from what I'm told. She'd unfold the notes, smooth out the creases, count them and then count them again. Forty rupees – about three pounds at the time. At last she'd hand over the money – a transaction that reminded her she had nowhere she could call her own. My parents did move to a property they owned – briefly – in Sri Lanka. But then they upped sticks. It was to be over two decades before my mother would have another place that was hers and hers alone. It would be in East Finchley, suburban London. But all that was in the future, in places she couldn't even begin to dream about as she handed over my father's hard-earned money.

I wondered if Mr Abeyaratne was depressed by the discovery that while we'd moved to another country, he'd merely moved down the road. While we'd laid claim to the world out there, he'd simply claimed his dowry. We'd started out the same, but ended up so far apart. What was the difference between my father and him? Hope. Hope and ambition. My parents had always hoped for something better and had the ambition needed to look for it. As for Max, perhaps he was happy just the way things were. Or maybe he too had tried but had failed.

'Do you remember this fellow?' Dad pulled me forward.

'He's a big chap now.' It was a clever answer. It avoided having to say he couldn't remember a thing about me. We shook hands.

'He's a TV presenter on BBC 1 in England now.' Not that it meant a great deal to people out there. The BBC's World Service, which is beamed into tens of millions of homes around the planet – now that would have been different. It was to become my father's standard introduction on this holiday. It would embarrass me at first. It sounded as if he was boasting, emphasising the gulf that had opened up between us, who'd got away, and them, who'd been left behind. But over the next few weeks I came to see that nobody else was embarrassed or offended. Coming back taller, richer, more confident – that was what people expected. It is what migration is all about. It is confirmation that there is a better life to be had out there.

'Do you mind if they have a look inside?' We left my father to do the talking. It was a tacit acceptance that this was his territory, that he would know what to do and how to do it.

'Oh, why not,' Max said. 'Come, come. Of course, they'll be used to much bigger things now.'

Indeed we were. There was a living area with a rattan-backed divan at one end and a table at the other. My grandmother – amma-amma – used to have a colonial-style lounger with the same rattan webbing. The way the strips of rattan were woven, they'd form pentagonal holes. She'd lie back after lunch with her legs splayed apart on the fold-out leg-rests. The umpteen pleats in her sari would ensure her modesty was spared. For us the best part was the way her weight would force her fleshy body through the holes. We used to poke those little protruding bumps. When we were feeling really brave, we'd get under the lounger and poke her bum.

There were two bedrooms leading off this front room. My parents had slept in one with Christine, the youngest child at the time. The two elder girls and I had had the other room. We didn't ask to see the kitchen or the bathroom. When we lived here, there was no bath, just a cold-water shower. And there was no sewerage. The latrine was cleaned out once a day by a man who pulled his tank from house to house.

'Would you all like something to drink?' We declined. 'Some water, maybe?' My father said he wouldn't mind a glass. We declined again. Once we would have drunk it from the taps; now we were worried about hygiene. We said we weren't thirsty.

My father started telling a story about the occasion my mother had baked a birthday cake for one of the girls and then gone out to the market, leaving the cake on a table to cool. She came back to find a neat little hole in it, just about the size of a child's finger. She'd called three of us to the table (Christine was still in her arms). None of us admitted to being the culprit. Then she'd pointed up at the picture of the Sacred Heart (there's been one in every house my parents ever lived in) on the wall above the table.

'Jesus is watching,' she'd said. 'Jesus sees everything. Now who was it?'

Apparently there was a long silence, and then I'd moved to the other side of an arch that divided the front room.

'Well he can't see me now,' I'd said triumphantly.

I suppose it was in the telling of this story that I first began to take ownership of this place. If I didn't recall the deed, I certainly recognised the tale. It was a part of the family folklore: how stupid George got caught pinching the birthday cake (the girls' version). It placed me here in this little bungalow, bucket-loo and all. If as a child I'd been embarrassed by such humble beginnings, felt that such a modest start diminished me, I began to see then that it actually enriched me. It put my achievements into perspective; it gave context to our family's journey. It allowed us to say: 'Look back, look how far we have come.'

We thanked Max and his family, then headed off back to the other world, the world of high-rise hotels, lunch by the pool and bottles of 'pure' water.

Charles Place – for all its ordinariness – marked a turning point for me. It wrought a subtle but important change in the way I saw myself. This was about kinship. It wasn't that I hadn't thought about any of this before. On the contrary, I had given it a lot of thought. I'd spoken about it, I'd written about it. But I'd done it all in my head, now I did it with my heart. After that morning, every day on the holiday would throw up new experiences that cemented my sense of connection. Finding Charles Place was like finding that crucial piece in a jigsaw puzzle. It wasn't the final piece, but it was the one that opened up a whole new part of the picture I was trying to recreate. On its own, it's as jagged and confusing as all the rest, but when you find its place in the whole, it's a revelation. I had found the missing piece.

One evening later that week we gathered at the house my father had rented. Months before, when we were still looking into which hotel best suited our needs, my father had decided he would find somewhere else. He claimed the hotels were all too expensive, but I suspected another motive. In a hotel you're treated as a tourist, as a foreigner, and I don't think he was ready for that. This was still his country, this was still his city. He'd found a place near one of his oldest friends, Thiru.

We were there for a dinner party. We had invited the extended family. Partly this was because we didn't have the time to visit everyone separately. But there was also another reason. We felt that going to see them at their homes would be too much of an imposition, even if we left our children behind at the hotel. For some it would simply have entailed a lot of work; for others it would have been awkward and embarrassing. While we had made good abroad, the lives of some of our relatives who'd stayed behind had been less than successful.

It was, in effect, a gathering of the Alagiah clan, my father's side of the family. Most of the relatives on my mother's side, the Santiapillais, had left the country. There was only one aunt left, and she was in Australia, on holiday with one of her sisters. Their flight from Sri Lanka, coupled with my parents' own emigration, spoke volumes for the brain drain suffered by the island from the sixties onwards, when institutional discrimination against Tamils took root in the politics of the country.

One uncle, Victor, ended up a UN undersecretary-general. He ran the organisation's International Trade Centre in Geneva, a precursor to the current World Trade Organisation. Another, John, set up an electronics business in New Zealand. Two aunts, Lily and Daisy, both ended up in Australia, where their husbands were respectively in insurance and medicine. Daisy was herself a consultant anaesthetist, while her husband became a highly acclaimed neurological expert based in Sydney. My own father's last posting had been as the World Health Organisation public health engineer in Zimbabwe. Their collective success was unusual but by no means extraordinary. Sri Lankans of that generation – well educated and utterly comfortable in English – left their mark wherever they went. The majority of them were Tamils.

My mother's family had prospered in the colonial era. Though not of the highest caste, my maternal grandfather had been a *mudliyar* – a traditional title of some significance but one that had been appropriated by the British and then bestowed on their favoured subjects. It was a bit like being awarded a minor gong in the annual honours list. For those who cared about such things, it was something to be proud of; those of a more cynical mould might regard it much as schoolchildren feel about teacher's pet. They were not rich but they were certainly comfortably off. The *mudliyar* had a chauffeur-driven car. The colonial virtues of thrift, hard work and church-going seemed to suit them well. The Santiapillais were Catholic. As a family they were noted for being self-contained, perhaps even a bit aloof. Their self-reliance may have been precisely the qualities that would lead most of them into such successful careers.

The Alagiahs were a complete contrast. My father's father was a postmaster. There were three sons, my father and two others, which meant they were much envied by those fathers of daughters, who were weighed down by the prospect of having to find a dowry come wedding day. It was by all accounts a rumbustious household in which members of the traditional extended family would come and go. What it lacked in order it gained in conviviality. My grandfather was a Methodist; his wife converted from Hinduism. It was a house in which Western values constantly fought for space with traditional ones. More often than not, the potential conflict was resolved in a healthy fusion of the two. When she felt like being English, my paternal grandmother would serve 'courses', which meant little more than bringing out a succession of her usual home cooking at different times during the meal rather than placing it before her hungry brood all at once!

But on one thing the Alagiahs were utterly uncompromising: caste. Given what you know of the two families, you might have thought the Alagiah household would have been over the moon about a match between their son, Donald, and the eldest Santiapillai girl, Therese. Not a bit of it. Though their worldly achievements were comparatively modest, the Alagiahs were of a higher caste. When my parents did eventually marry, they did so against the wishes of my father's parents, who refused to attend the wedding. It was what was called a 'love-match' – something that is far from universal today and was positively rare in the late forties when they began courting. The other two brothers had arranged marriages.

I've always thought the experience made my parents all the more tolerant when it came to their own children. With grace they accepted the Western notion that we should marry whoever we chose to, and that in modern Western culture parental approval was more symbolic than real. Not one of our partners was either Sri Lankan or Catholic when we married them (though one has since converted) – the two things my parents might have been expected to hold dear. As it turned out, nationality and religion were the least of their worries – before long they had to contend with that other bane of modern Western life, divorce. Not once, but twice. And both initiated, as it happens, by their daughters.

If family values shape our futures, it is no surprise that five of the six Santiapillai siblings got out, while on my father's side he was the only one. While the Santiapillais always aspired to something better and had the work ethic to make it happen, the Alagiahs were more inclined to see the pleasure in what they already had. While we had met my cousins from my mother's side – we are all now part of the Tamil diaspora – we had become estranged from our cousins on my father's side of the family, most of whom had never managed to get out. That night at my father's rented house was meant to make amends.

One of the prime duties of a migrant is to look after the people back home. That is why, more often than not, families will come together to decide which of their number will go abroad first. It's a question of putting your best foot forward. It's about making sure that the man who gets on that plane – occasionally it is a woman, perhaps a nurse – is the one most likely to make good. It won't always be everyone's favourite nephew, the one with the ready smile and a way with the girls. Send him and he's likely to end up marrying one of them. No, better to send the studious, hard-working kind. He'll work so hard he won't have time to play around.

Migration is rarely about severing one's links with the old country. It's not about burning your bridges once you've got across, it's about building the bridge in the first place. The whole point is that others might follow, or at the very least you'll be able to send something back. Sending out a migrant is like making an investment, it's like putting money away for a pension. Everyone who chips in to help fund the journey can expect to make a return.

Go to any of the world's great migrant cities – New York, Birmingham, Marseilles, Paris, Frankfurt, Dubai and many others – and you will see the money transfer offices. In my corner of London, Western Union is making the running. Have a look at any one of the hundreds of internet booths that have opened up in our big cities. All of them advertise cheap phone calls. Where to? To Accra, to Colombo, to Kabul, to Lagos. If you could listen in on a conversation, this is what you might hear. Imagine a call back to a village outside Batticoloa in the east of Sri Lanka:

'Hello, *amma*. Is life treating you well?'

'Yes, my son. And are you looking after yourself?'

'Oh yes. I'm very well. I've never been better.'

'It's just that we have not heard from you for a while. I was getting worried. *Thambi* (younger brother) heard on the radio that they were arresting Asian boys and everything. He says they are being put in jail for no reason.'

'Oh no, I'm fine. Those are just some troublemakers. You know I don't mix with that sort. No, it's just that I have been very busy. And how is my father?'

'Oh, the same as usual. You know he's still taking those pills the doctor in town told him about. But still he's the same. Lying around most of the day. Only he gets up for meals. And those tablets are not cheap.'

'Yes, *amma*. One of the boys at the petrol station I am working at night-time is coming back. I'll try to send some pills with him. There's a doctor from Batti here, he usually helps us.'

'*Perya-uncle* (mother's elder brother) is already planning Ramani's wedding. They have agreed the dowry but he is asking for help.'

'*Amma*, I'll try to send something extra next time.'

'And you know, last month we couldn't pay Sharmila's school fees. And that man, the head, he is telling us we should have so much money with our son in London.'

'*Amma*, I know, I know. Landlord has put up rent. Not much left afterwards. But next month I promise. Boss at work tell me he give me extra money if I work one more nightshift.'

'All right, son. But don't forget your studies.'

Who'd be a migrant son? Anyone who thinks they are all a bunch of loafers, scroungers out to squeeze what they can out of the system, needs to know there are literally millions of conversations like that going on every day around the world. I know because I have heard one or two of them myself. These men and women work longer hours, for less money than most locals would be prepared to. If the foreign lad enrolled on a computer course at the further education college nods off during a lesson, it is more likely to be because that extra nightshift is taking its toll rather than because he's spent a night on the razzle.

As a system of shifting money from the rich world to the poor world it works. Indeed, it does so far more efficiently than most official aid programmes. According to the World Bank, in 2002, for the first time, remittances sent home by migrants exceeded the amount of cash that went to the poor world in the form of official aid or private bank loans. Petrol station attendants, pizza delivery boys, nurses and doctors – together they transferred some US$80 billion in that year. And this only accounts for the money that statisticians can keep track of; billions of dollars more find their way to every nook and corner of the world through informal distribution networks. In its report for 2005 the bank estimated that if you include unrecorded transfers, the amount of money that went to poor countries was more like $250 billion. When British politicians boast about their plans to increase the country's aid budget, it's worth remembering that they will have some catching up to do if they are to match the amount sent back by immigrants, most of them at the bottom of the social pile.

Unlike the official aid programmes, there are no expatriate staff on tax-free salaries, no local bureaucrats to be paid off. Governments are not deciding who should get the money, people are. And there is a far smaller risk that the money will be end up paying for some grandiose project to feed the vanity of a tinpot politician. The money transfers end up in new roofs for old houses, in school fees and medical bills, and every now and then in an airline ticket so the migrant son or daughter can return in triumph.

Which, in a sense, is what we were doing. But you cannot return empty-handed. You're expected to lavish your new-found wealth on your relatives. Partly it's about helping out, but it's also about proving that you have done well. Have a look at the luggage of a returning migrant. Check all those cardboard boxes. It's like an inventory of modern electronic gadgetry. The Samsung TV, the Panasonic microwave oven, the Sony DVD player and the Philips short-wave radio. The brands might be different, the equipment more varied, but the general impact is the same – they are all icons of the good life.

We didn't take any cardboard boxes. Over the years my father had done his bit with cash handouts. Help with school fees here, money for a dowry there. It was that sort of thing. He never felt he'd done enough, and no doubt there were some in his extended family who would have concurred. We decided it would be money. Actually, my father decided it would be money.

'God! How embarrassing.' One of us said it, all of us felt it.

'Well, I'll tell you right now, I'm not going to be the one handing out the dosh,' I said. '*Acca*, you're the eldest, you should do it.' Much has changed in our lives, but I still call Mari *acca* – it means elder sister.

'Oh, thanks a lot. So I'll play Lady Bountiful handing out money to the plebs!'

'It's not like that, children,' my father intervened. 'Nobody will mind, it's the normal thing to do. It's just a gesture. After all, you're coming after such a long time. George should do it, he's the son, but if he won't, then Mari, you can do it.'

At least that part was settled. But how much? These days ten pounds is practically small change in Britain, but converted into rupees it's quite a tidy sum. Actually, it wasn't the amount that worried us. Between us we could afford to give each family a lot more than ten pounds – and we did. We were uncomfortable with the whole process; we'd been away for so long, had had such little contact with our cousins, that to us it did seem somewhat paternalistic. It was a very British way to feel. More accurately, it was a very middle-class British way to feel. These were the drawing room sensibilities of a certain kind of Britain, the boarding school milieu in which we had grown up. We were uncertain migrants, people who had lost touch with the way things worked back home. In fact, we'd long since stopped thinking of it as home.

Our relatives arrived. We hugged and we kissed. We willed the decades away. There was a smell of newly ironed shirts and recently oiled hair. The most obvious difference between us and them was stature. We seemed to tower over them – perhaps it was all that school milk we'd drunk before 'Thatcher the snatcher' took it away. Our jeans and trainers looked positively tatty next to Rukshini's salwar kameez and Shanthini's Bombay blue silk sari.

Jeya, Rajkumar, Sathian, Shanthini, Rukshini, Sahuntela, Nirmala, 'Baba' and son, Felician, Anita, Chitra, Christopher, Johnny, Sister Joyce-Marie (née Jeyala). Cousins and second cousins. Their husbands and wives. In-laws and more, about forty in all, including us.

Just names on a page now, but on that evening a powerful evocation of what it means to belong. We hadn't written to each other. We hadn't talked to each other. The last time we'd all been together like this had been way back in 1967, when my father's brother had died while we were on a holiday. Thirty-five years with virtually no contact, except vicariously through my parents. We hadn't been like other migrants. It must have seemed as if we were the kind who had pulled up the drawbridge once we were over. If there was disappointment, malice, it didn't show. On the contrary, we were accepted for what we were – family.

As discreetly as she could, Mari handed out our offerings in white envelopes. They were put into purses and wallets and no more was said about it. There. It was done. Nobody thought it was strange, nobody felt awkward. My father had been right. We could get on with what we really wanted – to try to catch up after a lifetime away.

I felt more acutely than I would ever have thought possible a sense of closeness. At least, that's what I thought it was. Now, as I think more about it, I can see it for what it really is. What I actually felt was a sense of responsibility, a sense of guilt even. Individually they were long-lost relatives; collectively they represented my past, the past I had escaped from. It was like looking into a mirror and seeing not the man I am today, but the man I might have become. And truth be told, I preferred what I had achieved abroad to what I might have settled for at 'home'. The difference between the two outcomes was not about ability but about ambition. That evening I understood that Britain's most precious gift to me was not education, health or confidence but aspiration. So in that room I felt I belonged and didn't belong. I was conscious both of how British I was and how Sri Lankan I could feel.

I was trapped outside on the porch. That's where the men were sitting. The women were inside, where the awkward silences slowly gave way to a lively babble. I watched how Frances made friends. She has that gift for crossing cultures. I saw how they accepted this English woman, took her into the fold. After a while we joined them. First we traded pleasantries, then we traded memories. What is kinship if it isn't shared experience? You can't touch or feel or see the bloodline, but you can remember good times – and bad – together.

It was a modern version of an ancient ritual. As oral histories were to clans, tribes and villages, so memories were to us. With each one remembered, we drew each other more closely into the web. There was the time we all went to Pasi Cudah, a beach on the east coast. What about when we used to play 'church'? Jeya always got to be the priest, which meant he was in charge of the sweets-made-into-hosts. Is the old house still standing? The one where the three uncles have their footprints in the foundation stone?

It went on for hours. They sang Tamil songs, classic tales of unrequited love and betrayal. Our children sang pop songs, also about unrequited love and betrayal. Our children shot video; their children just wished they had a video camera.

I can't pretend that in the space of an evening we had clawed back over three decades of lost friendship. But I will say this. As a migrant, you can try to leave it all behind but it doesn't mean it has gone away. The place, the people – it's still all there, waiting. It is like the desert grass, dormant till the rains come. Then it will blossom. You have a choice: nurture it and see it flourish, or turn your back and live without the bloom. After that evening, I knew I wanted to give it a go.

We said our farewells (there'd be one more family gathering

later on in the holiday) and watched them leave. In the morning we were heading out of Colombo. Off to explore their country. Truth be told, it was beginning to feel like our country too.

It was my brother-in-law, Guy Denington, who suggested we take the train, at least for a part of the journey. He is a railway fanatic. Cupboards crammed full of old magazines in their London home attest to a lifelong passion. His kids call him an anorak, my sister would like the cupboard space back and the rest of us think it's rather sweet. The subcontinent is a train-spotter's paradise. You will find ticket offices, rolling stock, signals, even staff uniforms dating back to the great age of imperial railroad building. Travelling by rail is also a great way to learn about a country.

Sadly, our preferred itinerary and the Sri Lankan Railways timetable failed to fit neatly enough. So we settled for a day trip from Weligama, on the south coast, where we had rented a villa, to Galle. We travelled west with the Indian Ocean more or less always in sight to our left. It's a distance of about twenty miles. This was the same line – perhaps it was the same train – that I would report on almost exactly two years later when the great Indian Ocean tsunami engulfed the Matare Express and killed the 1,500 souls who were traveling on her that fateful Boxing Day. Our five second-class tickets cost under a pound. We hopped on board the 09.29 to Anuraderapura via Colombo and all stops along the way. It would take us an hour; those going the distance were looking at another day.

When the kids were growing up and I used to read Thomas the Tank Engine to them I became rather adept at making all those chuff-chuff noises. I could mimic the rhythmic sound of the wheels going over the rails – *diddip-diddip* (slight pause) *diddip-diddip*. And I knew exactly when Thomas would blow his whistle – *toot-toot*! The curious thing, of course, is that our children never actually got to ride on trains that make noises even remotely like that. Had they been brought up in Sri Lanka, it would have been different. They would have known why their dad made all those noises. Our train did the full repertoire.

It was past the rush hour and there were plenty of seats to choose from. The faux-leather upholstery stuck to our skin – it may have been mid-morning, but it was already humid. You could see how those of us who were wearing shorts kept crossing and uncrossing our legs to ease the discomfort. It was only a while after I'd settled down that someone pointed out that my seat was reserved for the clergy – for the type who wear an orange robe rather than a white cassock.

Sri Lanka is a predominantly Buddhist country, but as a child growing up here I had little inkling of its religious pedigree. A sapling of the bo tree Buddha is said to have meditated under was brought to Sri Lanka from the subcontinent and planted in the ancient city of Anuradhapura. Kandy in the central highlands is the focus of an annual pilgrimage in which Buddhists congregate around the temple of the tooth relic. Ours was a family so immersed in the more recent importation of Christianity that all else paled into insignificance. So, from our very first after-hours drive out of Colombo airport on the night we arrived back in Sri Lanka, I had been as surprised as the children to find the road lined with Buddhist temples. There was something surreal about the way in which the statues of a cross-legged Buddha were all lit up, a dazzling and watchful presence in a night-time scene otherwise given over to scavenging dogs and the unsteady footsteps of Colombo's homeless and rootless.

I blame my parents for not telling me about this other part of my heritage. I had grown up knowing that our ethnicity had set us at odds with the rest of our countrymen. But I had failed to grasp, and had never really been told, how our religion, too, meant we were doubly alienated from the majority of Sri Lankans. One or two of my close friends have turned to Buddhism, disillusioned by the tired and institutionally petrified Christianity they have been handed down by their parents. They have found solace in the religion of my homeland, while I was not even properly aware of it.

But on this morning there were no Buddhist monks who wanted to claim their rightful seat on the train. Sri Lanka's south-west coast – along which we were trundling – is the engine of its economy. The tourists have always been there (their precise numbers rising and falling with the country's political fortunes), but recent years have seen the development of export promotion zones. Kogalla, about halfway on our journey, is one of them. It is an implanted pocket of industrial order and efficiency in a countryside of coconut groves and seafarers' villages. It's as surprising as finding a Bedouin tent on a Sussex lane or as incongruous as a steel-and-glass home in the middle of a Victorian terrace. Instead of the sun-blackened fishermen who once perched on stilts in the water, pulling out the silver-backed *hal masu*, you now have men in uniform guarding the gates to this enclave of Western capitalism.

Inside its neatly spaced warehouses garments are stitched together for some of the Western high street's most famous names – Banana Republic, Tommy Hilfiger and many others. When the shifts change, an army of women marches out and another marches in. Compared to the uncertain profits to be made by their husbands and brothers in the fickle ocean a few hundreds yards away, this work – as regular and predictable as the up-and-down jab of a sewing machine – is a blessing to the hundreds of families who depend on the income.

Once, in the fifties and sixties, it was the workers from the poor world who migrated to the jobs, to the great textile mills and garment factories of the Black Country in England. Now it's the jobs that are migrating to where the people are. When the immigrants came to work in the textile industry all those years ago, the cry went up: 'The darkies are taking our jobs – send them back.' Now when the darkies stay where they are, the cry from the unions is almost the same: 'They've taken our jobs and we want them back.'

Export zones like the one we passed at Kogella are part of the new economics of globalisation. Some, like Naomi Klein in *No Logo*, see them as modern versions of the old tenement sweat shops. But to those women we saw waiting for the company bus to take them home, they are a godsend. You can always fight for better conditions, but you have to have the job first.

In any case, the fashion-label garment factories are at the bottom end of what the business-school executives like to call outsourcing. Further up the chain the products become more sophisticated – such as TVs and car parts – and beyond that there are no products at all. The service industries are the latest to move, lock, stock and computer screen. Some of the biggest names in British business – Norwich Union, Lloyds TSB, BT, British Airways, Prudential, Powergen, Standard Chartered, BUPA, Reuters and Abbey National – are closing down their telesales and aftercare operations in Britain and reopening them abroad, mostly in the English-speaking countries of Asia.

The sales assistants you get on the phone may never set foot on British soil, but they are taught to make you think they're just down the motorway. Multinational corporations spend millions of pounds training their call-centre staff in poor countries – giving them new names and teaching them new accents. So in this high-tech version of smoke and mirrors, Ranjit may become Ryan and Sharmini calls herself Sandra. In an eerie throwback to the renaming of slaves on the plantations hundreds of years ago, Sri Lankans and Indians are being repackaged to make their identities more palatable to Western tastes. Ironically, they are being asked to develop the habits they might have acquired had they emigrated to Britain. Globalisation has given us the virtual migrant. And now, in the most wonderful reversal of history and fortune, some children of the first-generation immigrants to Britain are opting to go back to the mother country to work in these very call centres.

The colonies, in a sense, are fighting back, but in ways which the pioneers of independence could never have imagined. The colonial masters taught their imperial subjects to speak English, and now, hundreds of years later, that is precisely the weapon they are using to win these most precious of jobs in the international labour market. So there is, it seems, some advantage to having been conquered by the British and not the Portuguese or Dutch – though Sri Lanka had the dubious distinction of playing host to all three over a period of 500 years under the colonial yoke.

The imperial presence is writ large in the city of Galle – where our train pulled in exactly on schedule. The ramparts of the seventeenth-century Dutch fortress overlook the (usually) gentle swell of the Indian Ocean. If the solid walls, with their redundant gun emplacements, speak of an earlier form of conquest, what's going on in their shadow now, in the old colonial quarter, is a glimpse of a more up-to-date version of the expatriate takeover. Some are calling it a new wave of colonialism. Today within the old Dutch quarter is an ever-expanding enclave of foreigners. These are the chequebook settlers, people with a penchant for the easy life and a gift for property deals. Brits who've made a small fortune in Hong Kong, Americans with a taste for the exotic, Australians with a hotel to run, and artists on the hunt for new inspiration – all of them are making new homes for themselves in Galle. You can tell which ones are owned by new occupants: their whitewashed walls stand out like a new crown in a row of old, smoke-stained teeth. House prices are going through the roof. We walked down a terrace of houses, past a juice bar and an internet café, towards the sounds of a makeover in progress. Inside, old timbers had been restored, floors varnished, and tiles polished. You half expected one of those daytime TV presenters, complete with the white chinos and linen shirt, to pop around a newly knocked-through arch to say, 'So what do you think?'

Let me tell you what I think. This is another face of migration. While the poor are moving for jobs, the rich are moving for leisure. Retirement homes and holiday villas in Spain are so yesterday. These new settlers want something much more exotic. It is the destiny of cities like Galle – and there are a growing number of them around the world – to play host to these new settlers. They will become the outposts of the rich world's new empire. These foreigners bring new ideas, new fashions and new money. But I'll bet they'll also bring new resentment. The locals will see how their streets are changing. They'll notice these white women in skimpy tops and see-through sarongs ambling along pavements where once their own women would have scurried to market. They'll feel exactly the way the curtain-twitchers of the Midlands felt when the first darkies moved into a house on their street.

'Come on, Uncle George, you're going too slow, go faster, go faster, take us over there.'

That was the moment I knew I was in trouble. I'd been trying to ignore the pain for about twenty minutes, but that plea from my six-year-old American nephew, Paul, brought matters to a head. The 'over there' in question was a coral reef no more than a hundred yards from where we were paddling about, but I realised that for me it was a hundred yards too far. I needed to go the other way, I needed to get back to the shore – and I needed to do it in a hurry. That much I knew.

It was supposed to have been the highlight of our stay on the coast. Months before, when I had been planning the trip, I'd dreamed up the idea of an afternoon of snorkelling and scuba-diving. I'd guessed that by that time in the holiday, the children – all fourteen of them, ranging from eighteen to six – would be ready for a little adventure after the rounds of relatives, temples and ancient ruins.

Weligama is an undeveloped town, built at one end of a bay and just beyond the strip of tourist beaches in the south-west of the island. It has a hotel, but, like the last stop on a railway line, most people get off at the previous destinations. We were there because it was the only place I could find that had a villa large enough to house most of our party.

Weligama does have one claim to fame. In the middle of

Weligama Bay sits Taprobane Island. It protrudes from the sea like a compass point around which the shore makes a perfect sweep from palm-fringed end to palm-fringed end. The name Taprobane – recalling Ptolemy's ancient depiction of an island of continental size – is a conceit. The local fishermen, in much more prosaic fashion, call it Galduwa, or Rock Island, which is precisely what it is. The palm fronds and tropical shrubs that cover were put there by the man who made the island his home in the early twentieth century. Count de Mauny of Talvande was also the man who started calling the island Taprobane. In 1927, on this unforgiving granite outcrop, he started building his dream house. It was to be his home from home. Today it is a luxury holiday villa but with a price tag that few in our group could afford.

Weligama's relative seclusion was both a blessing and a curse. On the plus side, we weren't constantly bumping into other tourists. A couple of hundred yards from where we were staying there was a beach-side bungalow where young surfers could get a room for a couple of quid a day. They rode the waves in the afternoon, filled the air with the sweet smell of dope in the evening and slept most of the morning. In short, they were ideal neighbours.

Not so the local fishermen with whom we also shared the beach. The problem was that they didn't really see the beach in the same way we did. For them it was merely the bit of land they had to cross in order to get to where they needed to be – in their boats. Not for them the leisurely stroll of an evening. Try telling them how delicious it feels to let the wet sand ooze through your toes and then have it all washed away by the next froth-fringed wave! For them the beach was a place of work: somewhere to park their boats, somewhere to mend their nets and – worst of all – somewhere to have a shit. Exactly two years later these were the very fisher folk who were swept up in that greatest tide of all – the Boxing Day tsunami.

At one end of Weligama's crescent shore sits the Bay Beach

Hotel, built in the hope of a thousand tourist nights but apparently surviving on just a fraction of that. And it showed. If the hotel was well past its glory days, much the same could be said of the man who was about to guide us through the underwater world of coral reefs and darting fish.

Eddie Rupprecht was not what you'd call a man in his prime. The first time I saw him I thought he was naked. I had the same sense of shock and embarrassment you get when you walk in on someone on the loo. I might even have said sorry. He was hunched over a computer screen, apparently bare-bodied. He had the kind of physique on which you can't really tell where one bit ended and the other started. Just one great mass of flesh folding and falling away from smooth, rounded shoulders. From where I stood at the door it seemed as if his ample gut was cradled in his lap, masking his manhood.

'Don't get up,' I said, fearful of the consequences. By the time I'd got round to his side to shake hands, I could see the brown briefs that would save us both from the awkwardness I dreaded. They were the kind of swimming trunks that are worn out of habit, but not for support or modesty, if you get my drift. And there was, it seemed, quite a lot that needed supporting.

It was Eddie's idea for some of the younger children to be paddled around on surfboards while he accompanied the older ones to the reef. Though born an islander I have always been squeamish about any depth of water in which I cannot feel the bottom, and happily volunteered to be a surfboard pusher. I had a couple of kids on my board, and my brother-in-law Guy had two more. While we splish-sploshed and scared anything interesting away, I could see the others fanning out as they followed their curiosity and nature's trail of beauty.

The shallow tropical water around Sri Lanka's coast is the ideal habitat for coral growth. But here, as elsewhere in the world, the coral reefs are under threat, battered by a host of ills ranging from overexploitation to changes in the water temperature. The first signs of coral degradation were spotted in the 1980s. The tell-tale bleaching is obvious even to the inexperienced eye, a testament to how quickly and comprehensively we can undo the patient work of nature. Weligama is fortunate. Here there are, apparently, signs of recovery of some types of coral formation, which was good news for us, and indeed for Eddie and his business.

It was turning into a lovely afternoon – just the kind I had hoped for. Or so it seemed.

'Damn! I've stubbed my toe.' We were nudging up close to some rocky outcrops in the sand, and it was the only explanation I could think of for the stab of pain that shot through my big toe.

'Yes, there'll be a few nicks and grazes to deal with tonight,' said Guy. 'There's going to be a run on the Elastoplasts.'

'Funny thing is, the pain's getting worse, not better,' I said, looking for a bit of reassurance.

'Hmm. That is most odd,' he said in that quizzical English way of his.

It was about this time that I was being urged on to greater effort to catch up with the main party further out to sea.

'I could swim there,' shouted Phil as he lifted his goggle-shrouded face from the warm water.

'Yeah, let's have a race,' said Paul.

'I'm going to stay with you, Uncle George,' said Jos.

'Nobody is swimming anywhere.' I was in firm mode.

'But we could get there quicker than you're pushing.' Phil again.

'Yeah!' came the rejoinder from Paul.

In fact, I wasn't pushing at all. I was beginning to feel quite limp. By now the whole of my right foot was throbbing. I convinced myself that I had probably broken the toe.

'Listen, I think I'm going to head back in,' I said to Guy.

'Oh dear! You feeling all right?'

'I'm sure it's just a sprain or something, but I'd better go and check it out.' It was said more in hope than conviction.

By now Eddie was also back on shore, having left the teenagers with one of his assistants, a local lad not much older than the children he was meant to be looking after. Eddie saw me limping out of the water.

'So we have our first casualty,' he shouted. 'What we need is a beer,' he added, pulling a bottle out of the cooler box. It was for him, not me.

'Actually, I could do with some of that ice,' I said.

He came over with a bundle of ice cubes.

'Yah! You have to be careful. Some of those rocks can be pretty sharp,' he said.

'Too frigging late to tell me now, Eddie' was what I wanted to say. Instead, years of acquired British understatement came to the fore.

'Thank you,' I said. 'I'm sure it'll be fine once I get this ice pack to work.'

But it wasn't working, and it wasn't going to work. It was Eddie who first noticed a row of pinprick dots on my big toe. Ominously he started speaking a mixture of German and pidgin to his crew of beach boys and diving assistants. They, in turn, would reply in a mixture of Sinhalese and German. All of which left me distinctly out of the loop, since the one language I could understand – English – was the one they seemed to be avoiding. But I didn't need to be a linguist to understand that look on their faces or the tone of their voices. Nobody was panicking, but you had the sense that it was just around the corner. Eddie was doing his best to appear nonchalant but the local lads were talking too loudly and throwing knowing glances at each other. In the middle of it all I heard someone say 'scorpion'.

'Scorpion! Have I been stung by a scorpion?' It was my turn to start thinking about panicking.

'No, man, there are no scorpions in the water,' said Eddie. 'They're talking about a scorpion fish.' If Eddie thought he was being reassuring, he'd missed the mark by a million miles.

'Eddie, that doesn't make me feel any better. What is a scorpion fish and what does it do?'

'It's a group of fish—' I didn't let him finish.

'Forget the marine biology lesson, Eddie, what should we do?'

'We should get you checked out.'

By now the rest of the party were heading back to shore. I struggled to look calm. Inside, I was burning. The pain in my foot was so excruciating I began to fantasise about having it cut off. The big toe – with its tell-tale punctures – was now taut, red and swollen. I moved in and out of dizziness. I felt hot. Then I felt cold. And then hot again. I became conscious of my own pulse; every heartbeat was marked by a throb of pain.

There was no hospital in Weligama – but there was a public clinic, and we decided that would be our first stop. Our driver had been sent off on an errand and he wasn't back. We didn't have any transport.

It is at times like this that you depend on the generosity of complete strangers. Throughout my reporting life there have been people whose names I have now forgotten but whose deeds I can remember only too well. There were countless translators who became peacemakers when the mob got angry with me and my work. There was the rebel soldier who carried my rucksack for miles as I wilted under southern Sudan's noon sun. There were the locals who always held back on the food and water because they felt we, their guests, needed it more.

So it was that on this day Janaka Vimal came into his own. Till that point he had been one of many people at the dive school who seemed to have nothing better to do than watch my creeping agony. If I'd had the energy I would have told him and the others to stop gawping or get lost. Now I needed him; now he took charge.

Vimal shouted across the yard. He was speaking in Sinhalese. I felt a stranger twice over. First I was a Brit, and second I was Tamil. What little I might have dredged up of my mother tongue was going to be useless in these parts – this was a Sinhalese region. The only transport on offer was a trishaw – a scooter pulling an open cabin behind it. They are designed to carry two passengers behind the driver. Three of us squeezed in – Vimal, me and my second-eldest sister, Rachel.

Vimal barked out the instructions. *'Igmatte, igmatte!* I'm telling the driver to be quick,' he explained. The driver pulled his sarong up and tucked the folds of multicoloured cotton between his legs – literally girding his loins for the challenge ahead. Then he opened up the throttle. As we swerved out of the hotel compound I felt as if I was going to just topple over on to my sister's lap. I gripped the grease-shiny hand rail in front of me all the harder.

Neither Rachel nor I was in the mood for talking, but it didn't look as if Vimal was going to give us a choice.

'Fish he also bite me one time,' he began.

'At least you're alive to tell the tale,' I said, logging his survival as a portent of what I hoped would be my own recovery.

'But I very lucky,' he added. 'I go find doctor quick, quick. No time for poison to work full treatment on me.'

'How long did it take you to find doctor?' Rachel, chipped in, no doubt calculating the hour or so that had passed since I thought I'd stubbed my toe on coral.

'Maybe one hour or two hours – can't remember everything. Such a long time ago when I was young boy,' Vimal said in the matter-of-fact way you might adopt if you'd been asked to remember a trivial little detail like when you had had your first appointment at the dentist. In my pain-addled mind the time sitting around at the dive school was now beginning to feel like a matter of life and death.

'Pain moving up and up my leg,' he said, running a hand up his skinny little calf. I had visions of mercury rising up a thermometer and bursting through the top.

'It go past my knee, past everything.' He wafted his hand over his lap at this point; there was, after all, a lady present. 'Then pain reaching my stomach. Oh my God, so much hurt I crying, shouting to my friend. It pain so much I pick up sand and put in my mouth to bite.'

I knew exactly what he meant. Anything, even grinding sand

between my teeth, seemed preferable to what I was going through. Rachel was silent; just the odd glance to read my face. If she was worried by what she saw, she didn't let on. That was par for the course. Rachel was good in a crisis. That was why it was her sitting next to me and not one of the others. In a family each child plays a role. What might begin with circumstance is reinforced by expectation. My wife, Frances, is also the kind of person you'd want next to you in the proverbial trenches but she was back at the villa – laid low by a back strain. A fine holiday couple we were turning out to be!

In our family, for as long as I can remember and whether she liked it or not, Rachel was regarded as cool under pressure. If you wanted to party, if you wanted to stay up late to put up Christmas decorations, Mari was your woman. If you wanted true grit, if you were looking for someone to stand up for your rights, you'd call on Christine. If you wanted poise, a certain polish, then Jenny was the one to call on. She combined that particular talent with another one, seemingly at odds with the first – teller of dirty jokes and cruel mimicker of any unfortunate souls who came our family's way. In short, if you had been stung by a scorpion fish and you weren't quite sure what was coming next but you thought it was almost certainly horrible, Rachel was the one to have at your side.

'So which doctor did you see?' Rachel asked. 'Are we going to see the same one?'

'No, no, I go to see village doctor. He very good, he know all about scorpion fish. He put oil on my leg, take candle and burn away all pain.'

Oil, candle, burn. No question, even that sounded like blessed relief compared to what I was going through. I was feeling sick. Sick with fear or sick with poison, I couldn't tell.

'You want I take you to the village doctor? We find same, same doctor?'

Decision time. You're sitting next to a man you've never met before. For all you know, your life is in his hands. He's offering you traditional healing which he says worked for him. The alternative is to press on with Plan A, find the clinic and see the doctor. You know nothing about the doctor except that he has been trained in Western medicine – which, of course, doesn't tell you how good his training was or even whether he is a decent or careless practitioner. East versus West, unknown versus known. Tradition versus convention. Ancient versus modern.

We were being asked to choose between one form of medicine which local people have depended on for centuries, and another which was imported into the country with colonialism. In Sri Lanka, those who could afford to moved between the two systems, the rest did what their forebears had always done – they visited the *veda-mathaya* (literally medicine-master). I had often heard my parents talk about the traditional pastes and ointments that had been administered to them as they grew up.

Ayurvedic medicine is one of the most ancient forms of healing known to man. Its roots go back 4,000 years, arriving in Sri Lanka as early as the sixth century BC. By the time of the great Sinhalese kingdom of Anuradhapura – from around 350 BC – ayurvedic physician was already an established profession. King Buddhadasa (365–337 BC), an ayurvedic practitioner himself, is said to have insisted on appointing a healer for every ten villages. Today, it remains the point of first call for millions of Sri Lankans, a tried and tested solution for the vast majority of ailments – including, it seemed, the sting of the scorpion fish.

So there we were, screeching around Weligama's back roads and alleyways, with a decision to make. Vimal was waiting for an answer to his question, whether to find his *veda-mathaya* in the countryside.

'No,' I said, 'let's keep going to the clinic.'

I've often thought about that response and what it meant. Sure, Vimal couldn't tell us exactly where we'd find his village doctor, or exactly how long it would take to get there but they weren't really the reasons I rejected the option of traditional medicine. The truth is that I didn't really have any faith in it. Over thirty years in Britain had meant that I had lost what my parents had had – trust in a form of medicine that was as old as the country itself. All that stuff about oils and candles and burning: what I really wanted to see was someone wearing a white coat; I wanted a jab or a smooth white pill with a Western manufacturer's name etched into it. I had returned to Sri Lanka to rediscover my roots, but when it came to the crunch, there were limits to just how far down that particular road I wanted to go.

'People's Clinic' – it's both a name and a description. It sits on one end of Temple Road – first you see the doctor, then you go down the road to pray. If one doesn't save you, perhaps the other will. The red board with white writing told us this was clinic number 7515. Dr Ranjith Samerage MBBS was the resident doctor. Initials after a name, that's more like it, I thought.

Vimal jumped out before our trishaw had come to a stop. He shouted at the driver and came round to help me out, then dragged me up the four or five steps and pushed open the door.

The waiting area was no bigger than a modest sitting room. The floor was painted a glossy red – a tell-tale sign of the British legacy in public buildings around the globe. It was still shiny in the middle, but had been rubbed bare along the walls. There were wooden benches along three sides; the fourth was given over to a pharmacy counter. The walls were white – well, let's say tired white. At regular intervals above the benches there was a smudge, the impression left by a thousand coconut-oiled heads leaning against it.

The room was full, but nobody said a word. An old man, his chin flecked with hair he could no longer be bothered to shave, held his head between his hands and looked down at his feet. A mother, bookended by a couple of listless children, pulled her sari over her head as we entered. Vimal went straight to another door – the doctor's surgery. He was giving a running commentary. All we could understand was the word 'tourist'. It clearly gave us licence to jump the queue. Still, nobody protested. We were foreigners, it was what they expected. Imagine if the roles were reversed. Imagine a surgery somewhere in rural England, a local lad brings in a foreigner and says he's got to go to the front because he's a tourist. 'I couldn't care if he's the king of Bongo-Bongo land, he can still wait in line like the rest of us.' Rings true, doesn't it?

I was embarrassed, but I was more worried than embarrassed so I went along with it. Vimal opened this other door. Finally, a look of shock, protest even. It was the doctor, in the middle of a consultation. Vimal spoke to him as he manhandled the patient out of the room. Once again that magic password, tourist.

'Dr Samerage?' Rachel asked.

'No, I am Dr Terence Senanayake, I'm the locum from Galle. Dr Samerage is away at the moment. What seems to be the problem? Your friend tells me you've been bitten in the water.' His English was adequate; it's been improved in the telling.

I looked around the room, at the man first and then his equipment. My earlier faith in the superiority of modern medicine began to ebb away. I noticed a spaghetti tangle of wires behind him from which emerged two metal clips, smaller versions of what you'd find on the end of a car jump-start lead. They were attached to two batteries. He followed my eyes.

'They are for the fans and lights,' he said. 'We get a lot of power cuts. Sometimes they can last for up to four hours. One is a car battery, the other one is a truck battery.' I wasn't sure what I was to make of the distinction. Either way, I can't say I was impressed. I did notice, however, that the sterilising unit was not connected up to the batteries – clearly keeping cool trumped keeping clean.

'My brother has been bitten while swimming off Bay Beach Hotel.' Rachel was speaking slowly and deliberately. 'They said it was probably a scorpion fish.'

'There are many types of scorpion fish,' the doctor replied. I could feel the start of another marine biology lesson coming on. 'We really need to know what kind of fish exactly it was that has bitten your brother. Did he see the fish?' He was talking to Rachel, ignoring me. Did I really look as if I couldn't be relied upon to come up with a decent answer? I knew I was sweating, I knew I probably looked rather pale, but did I look that bad?

'No, it was under water.' As soon as I said it, I realised just how stupid it sounded. Of course it was bloody well under water, it's a bloody fish and that's where they live! I thought I saw the faintest of smiles pass over his face. Maybe he had been right to address Rachel. 'It was over in a flash,' I added. 'And anyway, I thought I had stubbed my toe.'

'What did you do to your toe?'

'I didn't do anything to my toe, I was just saying that I *thought* I'd banged my toe against a rock and that's why I didn't even think of looking for the fish.'

'Okay. But I must say, banging your toe and being bitten by a fish is a very different thing. Anyway, let's have a look.'

I lifted up my right leg. I hadn't looked at my foot since we'd left the dive school. By now it was slightly purplish. And there was another puncture point in the skin that was stretched taut as a balloon, one that threatened to go *pop* at any moment.

'Oh yes, yes, yes. I see the marks. Definitely you have been bitten. This is probably a stonefish. '

'Is it dangerous?' Rachel and I spoke in stereo.

'Not really. It all depends on how you treat it. You see, we don't see much of these in the clinics. Usually it's the fishermen who are getting bitten and they have their own medicine. They go to the *veda-mathaya*.'

Vimal was nodding furiously. If he thought of saying 'I told you so', he resisted the temptation. So it wasn't dangerous, but it depended on how it was treated.

'What is the treatment? Is there an antidote?'

'Sorry, can you say again.'

'Is there something I should take for the poison?'

'No, it is not like snakebite, it is not attacking your nervous system.'

It looked as if I was in the clear. The whole consultation cost a little over fifty pence.

It won't surprise you to know that I've since developed a morbid fascination with the stonefish, a member of the scorpion fish family. Whenever I'm surfing the Web I have to resist the temptation to punch in 'stonefish' just to see if anything new has been posted on the web. Let me tell you, there is an awful lot about this foot-long creature. My favourite – staying with morbid fascination – is an article by one Virginia Wells titled 'The Stonefish – The Deadliest Fish in the World'. She begins her essay with a description of an ancient dance ritual performed by Australian Aborigines, who clearly knew a thing or two about stonefish:

> A man wades into the tide pools in search of fish. Suddenly he steps on something – a clay model of a stonefish with 13 wooden dorsal fins – and screams in pain. The dancer writhes on the ground in agony, and the ritual ends sadly with a death song.

The article goes on to describe in graphic detail how well the stonefish is camouflaged, the number and length of the poisonous dorsal spines and the effect they have on those unfortunate enough to come into intimate contact with them. Victims experience excruciating pain that lasts for hours, and a tremendous swelling develops with the death of the tissues. Temporary paralysis, shock and even death may result. The severity of symptoms depends on the depth of penetration and the number of spines involved.

Happily, I didn't know any of this as we set off back to the villa. I clutched my little white pill – a painkiller – with all the fervour of a pilgrim with a miracle cure. But if I was beginning to feel more confident than at any time in the previous couple of hours, the opposite was the case at the villa. There, they had begun to find out just a little bit more about the scorpion fish.

The news of my encounter in the shallows had preceded me. Everybody had returned to the villa from their separate outings. The place was in a state of controlled tension. Frances, who had been lying on a bed, unable even to turn over on to her side, had leapt into action on being given the news. There is no cure, no drug like adrenalin. She'd started phoning around and had gone to a different clinic, where she had spoken to another doctor. His was an ominous warning. The doctor at the clinic Rachel and I had been to had been right, the sting itself is not necessarily dangerous, but he'd not explained just how deadly the body's reaction to it can be. Frances had been told not to ignore the possibility of anaphylactic shock. The advice was clear: it was life-threatening, and if it happened I needed to be in a hospital.

I limped in and managed to climb the stairs to our first-floor bedroom. I remembered a piece of advice given to me by an ex-military instructor on one of the survival courses BBC foreign correspondents were sent on. 'When you're hurt, when you're wounded, there is nothing more you can do. You'll only make matters worse – for you and everyone else – if you try to charge around. Find somewhere quiet, somewhere dark and lie down. Stay awake but stay calm. Get your pulse rate right down. It's for your buddies to do the worrying.'

One by one the girls – that's how I still think of my sisters – trooped into the bedroom. They were perched on the bed, leaning against the wall, they were around me. I felt safe, I felt secure.

'Do you remember Mum used to do a bread-poultice thing when we had an infection?'

I can't remember who said it, but I do remember the treatment. My mother would take a hot cotton or muslin cloth with a soaked wedge of bread inside it and tie it around the affected part. 'It will draw out the pain,' she used to say. I can see her still. One hand holding the poultice, the other pushing back my hair, a few beads of perspiration on her upper lip the only outward sign of her concern and effort. We decided to give it a go. Perhaps it was being back in Sri Lanka that prompted this revival of an old family treatment. My mother had been dead for over six years; she would have had a wry smile as the girls went off in search of cloth and bread.

It turned out this was exactly what we should have done in the first place. We have since found out that the stonefish venom is a protein, and the way to combat protein is to apply heat. The ice cubes that I had held to my foot all those hours earlier were almost certainly making matters worse. I should have been doing exactly the opposite. Oil, candle, burn. That's what the *veda-mathaya* would have done, and he would have been dead right.

Outside, I could hear quite a debate. Brothers-in-law, Neil Fernando who had flown out with us, Frances – all of them seemed to be talking on their mobile phones. It turned out we were more or less halfway between two hospitals. One was slightly further but more reputable. The other was closer to us but more provincial. Time versus expertise – that was the dilemma. We opted for time.

We explained the situation to one of our drivers, Haridasan, and asked him if he knew the hospital in Matare, further east along the coast road. No, but we could ask when we got there. Frances came with me, as did my youngest sister, Jenny. I sat in the back of the van. I'd put on a quilted jacket. It was sundowner-warm outside, but I had the shivers. Nobody talked much. All eyes were on the road as Haridasan negotiated everything from an oncoming bus on our side of the road to a stationary bullock cart with the nerve and agility of a racing driver.

This was the time of day when people came out of their houses. The road became an extension of their front porches. Conversations begun inside the house would be continued as they walked across the road. Even with our windows shut you could smell the paraffin in the air as stall-holders lit up their lanterns, the flames flicking this way and that in a liquid dance. Under their wavy light you could see little piles of sweets or cig-arettes for sale.

Inside the van it was dark. Every now and again I'd catch Frances' face in the lights of a passing car. I could tell just how worried she was. It wasn't her eyes, or the set of her jaw, or the way she sat on the edge of the seat. It wasn't anything you could point to. When you've been around someone for nearly thirty years, it isn't what you can see, it's what you can feel.

Matare was about twenty-five miles away. I'd never been there, but it sounded familiar. These were roads and places my father had seen as a young water engineer. I'd certainly heard him speak about Matare to friends. My parents had started married life on this coast, an hour or so along the road from where we were headed. I found the thought comforting. I don't think I really believed anything bad was going to happen to me but, equally, I knew there was little I could do to change the course of events. In a way I'd never experienced before, or since I found not knowing exactly what was coming next curiously liberating. I was no longer frightened. If Frances and Jenny were concentrating hard on trying to see any early signposts to Matare General Hospital, I was wondering whether my parents could ever have imagined that their still-to-be-conceived family would one day be back in these parts as tourists – on this occasion tourists in trouble.

Haridasan turned off the main road. We drove into a dimly lit courtyard. If this was the A&E department, it had a peculiarly understated way of advertising itself. Frances went in. We could see her talking to someone through the window. She came out. We'd pulled into a state-run old people's home!

'They can't do anything about your toe,' she said. 'But if you ever make it to retirement, it's not a bad place to be.'

Finally we found it. Matare Hospital was being renovated. The walls in the main reception were bare plaster and you could feel the grit and dust underfoot. As I limped across the reception hall it felt as if I had sandpaper on the soles of my sandals. But no attempt to tart up the building could disguise the accumulation of misfortune that it represented. The benches, the people, the naked light-bulbs, the orderlies, the coughs, the relatives, the groans – all of it told a story. If you want to know how well a country is doing, go to a playground; if you want to know about its losers, go to a hospital. The vast majority of ailments that end up being treated in a hospital are preventable; only a fraction are the kind of emergency that had taken me to Matare. The more poverty there is, the more ill-health there is. It's always struck me as curious the way politicians the world over take such pride in opening up a new hospital. A hospital is a monument to failure; it's needed because everything else has not worked. It is a last resort. Now a standpipe that delivers clean water, that's a victory. Electric power that can keep vaccines refrigerated, that's another advance. A school lesson on nutrition and safe sex, that's progress. Every cigarette that is stubbed out for good, that's an illness averted. Every home that has an income, that is a promise of safety and security.

Dr Kumudu was in the middle of the evening ward round. He abandoned it to attend to us. He led us into an examination room. It was a tiny space, just right for someone like Dr Kumudu – he couldn't have been much over five and a half feet tall. But we crowded it out. We towered over him, a difference in scale made all the more stark as he sat down while Frances and Jenny carried on standing. I took a seat opposite him. Frances explained our predicament, ending with the warning she'd been given about the sometimes fatal risk of an anaphylactic shock.

'No, people can die of it, but I think if you were going to die, it would have happened by now.'

We didn't know whether to laugh or cry, whether to be relieved that the worst was over or shocked that death was ever a genuine possibility.

'But we need to keep you under observation,' he said, taking a good look at my toe. Now we could see five blood-dots. So it wasn't clear-cut after all. It was Jenny who spoke next. She talks with a slight transatlantic twang, the result of twenty-odd years living in America. It can be quite attractive, but allied to her line of questioning it sounded intimidating.

'Listen, we need to know exactly what it is you are worried about. We've been given so many different messages today.'

'No, just in case,' Dr Kumudu said with a sideways rotation of the head that could mean yes, no or something in between.

'In case of what?' That was Frances.

'Well, the effects can last for up to twenty-four hours and different people react in different ways.'

'Look, is there anyone else we could see?' I think that was me. 'Is there a phone we could use to call a doctor in Colombo.' A phone call to the capital. It was a loaded question; its full meaning was implied rather than stated. Perhaps in the big city there would be someone more competent. I hate to admit it, but in my mind I think I may even have wanted to hear a British accent.

'I wonder if we ought to put in a call to the British High Commission. They may have some advice or some medical emergency numbers,' I said to no one in particular.

'That really will not be necessary,' said Dr Kumudu. Leave aside the insult to Dr Kumudu, I was sounding precisely like the thing I despise most – the caricature Brit, banging on about how it wouldn't be like this back home. But of course it *is* like this back home, and sometimes worse. And the notion that the after-hours number at the High Commission was likely to offer any sort of salvation was touching, if a little deluded.

'Actually, along this coast, with so many people getting a living from the sea, we probably see more of this sort of thing than they do in Colombo.' I noticed the beads of sweat on Dr Kumudu's forehead. We'd made him timid, and it must have taken a huge effort for him to try to reassert his authority.

I can see now what I didn't see then. I know how this scene was unfolding, how it was following a very old script in a new setting. I can see how, imperceptibly, we were shifting the balance between him and us. Question by question we were playing the overbearing expatriates and he was retreating into his assigned role of native. When did this role play first start? Five hundred years ago, when the Portuguese arrived on these shores? Later, when the merchants of the Dutch East India company decided that Ceylon could make them and their country rich? Or later still, when British imperialism found Ceylon, a teardrop-shaped bonus that dangled from the jewel in the crown – India? Here we were, at it all over again. We'd already dismissed the traditional healer and now we were denigrating the skills of this doctor, who probably wanted nothing more than to get back to his ward full of patients.

Dr Kumudu could have got up, walked away and told us to come back when we were ready to take his advice. That's probably what I would have done; that's almost certainly what a Sri Lankan tourist in Penzance or Southwold would have been told to do. To his credit, Dr Kumudu was a kinder, gentler, more patient man.

'Anyway, first things first,' he said. 'I should certainly give you a tetanus shot.'

Still we were on the offensive. 'Do you have disposable needles?'

I'd always carried them when travelling for work, but had not thought to bring any on this trip.

'Yes, of course we do,' he said, and added, with just a hint of tetchiness, 'It is standard practice.'

We went into an adjoining room. There was a bin next to the table. It was overflowing with bloodied cotton swabs and discarded needles. I stared at it. Dr Kumudu knew what I was thinking. He pulled out a syringe and tried to click it into place. He must have done this a thousand times, but that night he made a hash of it. The needle snapped. He was nervous and he knew I could sense it. He tried again. This time it worked and he administered the jab I had longed for all those hours ago. He gave me some tablets and told us we were welcome to wait at the hospital. He reassured us that the worst was almost certainly over. We shook hands, apologised for our pushiness, explained what a scary experience it had been and departed on good terms.

The story of that day is worth telling for what it reveals about me. I had always thought of myself as a cross-cultural figure. Someone comfortable in many different places – indeed, I had built a career on my ability to get on wherever I found myself. Yet when my back was against the wall, I discovered that my Britishness ran deeper than I had ever suspected. That's because immigration has worked for me. A few snide remarks aside, the experience has been a good one. As a schoolboy I was protected and as an adult I have been privileged. But for tens of thousands of other immigrants it's been a very different story. From the moment they stepped off the ship or plane they have felt a chill in their hearts – not from Britain's execrable weather but from the attitude of some of its people. It's an ambivalence that has permeated the laws that govern immigration into Britain.

3

They Come Over Here . . .

'They come over here . . .' and what? There are many ways in which that phrase could be completed, but I'll wager the advance on this book that the one you are least likely to hear is: 'and make our country so much better'. Quite often Britain's attitude to immigrants has been at best ambivalent, and sometimes down-right hostile. For every well-argued article in *The Economist* on the virtues of migration, you'll find many more people on the street who will tell you that the country is being overrun by foreigners. It is a view that reared its head in the fifties and sixties, the opening years of postwar immigration, and has coloured the public mood ever since. No wonder Alf Garnett, the cloth-capped West Ham supporting character in the late sixties TV sitcom *Till Death Us Do Part*, became such a cult figure. Johnny Speight, who created the foul-mouthed Alf and wrote the diatribes for which the character became famous, always maintained that the audience was meant to find the man ridiculous, but pretty soon it became obvious that Alf was saying in public what many were thinking in private. People were not laughing at Alf Garnett, they were laughing with him. So in Garnett-speak the most commonly held views about immigrants are probably that they come over here 'and take our jobs', or they come over here and 'live on benefits'. Those views have as much resonance in the early twenty-first century as they did when Alf Garnett first gave them an airing .

In fact little of the available evidence supports either of those sentiments, common though they are. Immigrants do take jobs – that's the whole point of immigration – but usually these are in the sectors where there is a labour shortage, or those jobs that no one else will do. Just have a look at who does the most menial jobs in care homes for the elderly – to take but one example. Sometimes they do take jobs that locals are doing, but they tend to do them for less money. You will not find many of the people who complain about immigration turning away the Polish plumber (who has joined the Kosovan builder and the Somali cleaner in the growing list of foreign stereotypes) ready to sort out their waterworks at a fraction of the cost charged by the locals. And as for benefits, the amount forked out by the taxpayer to support immigrants is outweighed by their contribution to the national coffers. According to a study carried out by the London-based think-tank the Institute for Public Policy Research, the contribution made by immigrants to the public purse grew between 1999 and 2004. On average they accounted for 8.8 per cent of government tax receipts and 8.4 per cent of government expenditure. In the last year for which the institute published figures, 2003–4, the contribution in taxes was 10 per cent, while immigrants' share of public expenditure was 9.1 per cent.

The figures are persuasive but they will not convince everyone. Migrationwatch, an organisation which campaigns for what it calls 'balanced migration', has done its own sums, and finds that the net contribution each immigrant makes is just 14p a week (and it believes even that figure is probably an exaggeration). Small change given the size of the British economy and, if the calculation is credible, hardly an irresistible argument in favour of immigration. The discrepancy between the positions is almost certainly because they are not comparing like with like. Migrationwatch's critics, especially at the IPPR, say the average migrant earns more and therefore makes a larger contribution in tax than the non-migrant. The argument cannot be settled here but one thing is clear – it is not as black and white (pardon the pun) as either side would have us believe. Even on Migrationwatch's estimates the idea that all immigrants are spongers (an allegation it does not make) can't be sustained. Some are, most are not – just like the English, really.

The idea that immigrants must always be a drain on the economy, though it sticks like lichen to a rock in most people's minds, is simply not borne out by the facts. The periods of greatest immigration tend to be the times when Britain's economy has been growing and, conversely, the flow has slowed down when our economy has gone into recession. People looking for a new and better life are hardly going to risk all to come here at a time when their friends are telling them workers are getting laid off and jobs are hard to find! The logic, self-evident though it is, sometimes escapes even the most careful commentators on social policy.

Some time after London won the right to stage the Olympic Games in 2012, the *Guardian* columnist Polly Toynbee noted, with apparent regret, that nearly half the workers needed to build the sporting facilities were likely to be from eastern Europe. What she wanted was a greater emphasis on recruiting people from London's own unemployed. Laudable though that aim is, it is not entirely clear that those without work in London, many of whom are women, could be trained quickly enough or in sufficient numbers to build the Olympic infrastructure on time. In a Europe of free movement, which is what many progressive people want, employing foreigners makes a lot of sense. The outburst of patriotism that accompanied London seeing off the old enemy, France, in the final run-off for Olympic status, did not and will not automatically produce people with the skill or, indeed, the inclination to turn the Olympic blueprint into steel and concrete reality.

In its 2005 report on migration, *A Welcome Opportunity*, the Royal Society of Arts found that as Britain moved further into the 'knowledge' economy, so it would need people who, like worker-bees in a hive, do all the more mundane tasks. London's Olympic bid fits nicely into the society's analysis: Lord Coe and his team had the ingenuity, flair and imagination to compile a winning bid, while it will be left to others – whatever their nationality – to put up the stadiums, build the athletes' accommodation and construct the transport infrastructure. Organising the whole process? That too will be the kind of task British companies should be competing to do. It's really just the old adage about brain and brawn in a new guise.

In any case, the debate about immigration has never really been about number-crunching. That's the pretence. It's the fiction we all collude in because it makes the debate sound scientific. In truth, concern about immigration flows from a more visceral instinct. Indeed, many of those most worried about immigrants live in the countryside, where they are least likely to come across one. If it were about facts and figures, how could the former Conservative prime minister, Margaret Thatcher, have got away with saying people were afraid of being 'swamped' by foreigners? It's hardly plausible to suggest that immigrants, who make up less than 5 per cent of the population, are threatening everybody else. No, Mrs Thatcher was appealing to something much more important than facts, to something in the national psyche that has always found the people of this country ready to feel beleaguered – an odd way to feel for a nation that once ruled the biggest empire the planet has ever known. Perhaps Britain's uneasy relationship with its past is a large part of the problem.

And there is one other self-delusion we might as well get out of the way. When people talk about immigration having become a problem, they don't really mean there are too many Australians or New Zealanders coming over here. What they do mean is that there are too many black and brown people making it into Britain. But because we Brits are awfully polite and not at all racist, we'd never dream of saying these things in public. No, what we really mean is left to the small print in the plethora of laws and regulations we have passed to keep people out (more of that later).

In recent years, things have got a lot more complicated for the poor souls worried about how one of the top five economies in the world is going to cope with all these extra people wanting to work and save in Britain. The trouble is that the newest immigrants – those who started coming over in the nineties – were a sort of hybrid. Mostly they were white, but not white like those tanned South Africans and Zimbabweans. Truth be told, they were more olive complexion than white, and here's the really confusing thing – quite a few of them were Muslim. If any of the Kosovans and Albanians thought that being from Europe gave them a bit of a head start, they soon learned that in this 'sceptred isle' the cultural rules were a little more complicated.

There is a kind of collective schizophrenia about attitudes to immigrants. Curry is a national dish and yet there are some who resent the people who have introduced it into our lives. Trevor McDonald (before he retired in December 2005) was the most respected newsreader in the country, but all too many still think that his fellow African-Caribbeans are indolent and criminal. Virtually all Albanians are caricatured as bogus asylum seekers who ought to be sent packing, but they are employed on building sites up and down the country. It's what I call the 'oh but you're different' syndrome. I can't think of an argument I've had about immigration – going back to my days at Durham University – when someone hasn't piped up with those words.

Again, there is a sort of code at work here. What they mean is that I don't talk funny or eat all that smelly food. No one stops to think that immigration is a process. The me they find so different, so acceptable is the finished article. It's not the me that arrived here in 1967, every inch a foreigner. All that is different about me is that I got the chance to stay and prove, as millions before have done through the ages, that immigration changes people.

The truth is that the people trying to emigrate to Britain now are really very similar to the ones who have already made their homes here. They come with the same dreams, the same determination to improve themselves as did previous waves of immigrants. The

Ugandan girl being deported or the Kosovan boy locked up in a detention centre are just as likely to make good. But to acknowledge that would be to change our collective attitude to immigration. By pretending that people like me are somehow different, we convince ourselves that today's migrants are a new, less appealing breed. By setting our minds against them, we turn this most human of stories into a faceless, abstract process. We throw a veil over a thousand epic stories which, if we heard them in the intimacy of our homes rather than through the screaming headlines of our newspapers, would move us to the generosity and sense of fair play that this country is rightly famous for.

This attitude towards immigration is not something peculiar to the late twentieth and early twenty-first centuries. When he was doing the research for his exhaustive and quite brilliant book on immigration to Britain, *Bloody Foreigners*, Robert Winder says he was surprised at how comprehensively the role of migrants had been written out of the national pageant: 'Time and again I came across delineations of the national character which failed to view it as the product of a cosmopolitan ancestry.' The rest of the book is a telling account of the role foreigners have played in the history of this country. Each new wave has helped to recast and reinvent it, almost always for the better. But the contributions of these foreigners – be they the French Jews who lived in York in the twelfth century, or the Italian musicians and even Africans who gave the Elizabethan era its particular verve, or the West Indians whose labour was so crucial in post-war reconstruction – were hardly ever recorded, far less appreciated. Instead, as Winder points out, even in medieval times they were given the cold shoulder. When things went wrong, it was always those 'cursed forrainers' who were blamed. *Plus ça change, plus c'est la même chose!*

None of this means that I think Britain's doors should be left wide open. Every country has a right, even a duty, to choose who should come in and who should be asked to leave. But there is a world of difference between exercising some discretion and having a default position which is inimical to the whole process.

If you invite someone into your house but do it in a begrudging way, they are never going to feel truly comfortable.

There is a link between immigration policy and race relations. If immigrants have sometimes seemed too inclined to retreat into the enclave, if they have seemed to lack the imagination and courage to take advantage of all that this country has to offer, we might ask whether something we have done or not done is partly to blame.

To accept immigration for what it is, a dynamic process which has brought huge benefits as well as challenges, should be a first step in any attempt to build social cohesion. If we want people to play a more active part as citizens, we need to convince them that we think their arrival here was a good thing. Across the Atlantic, in America, through either history or design, they have approached immigration differently.

What must wee Mary Greig have made of it all? After weeks of being cooped up on board the Anchor Line's *Columbia*, here she was clinging on to her mother's skirt as their family waited in a line that seemed to go on for ever. In comparison to the claustrophobic dinginess of the ship, the room they were standing in must have felt as big as the whole wide world. High above them, sixty feet from the floor with its heptagonal tiles, the vaulted ceiling must have felt like the sky itself. The four towers they had seen as they came off the ship, in red brick and limestone trim, made it look like a palace. There were great big windows high up in the sky through which the spring sun shafted in like a miracle. It was 17 April 1906.

Mary's father, a twenty-nine-year-old from Penicuik in faraway Scotland, looked stern. He was shuffling bits of paper around (passports would not be needed for another 15 years), checking that he still had his meagre savings and nervously looking to see if they were moving up the queue or not. Mary wanted to run about, but her mother Annie, at thirty a year older than her husband, kept telling her to keep still or she'd be in real trouble. 'Grab a hold of your sister,' she might have said to six-year-old Alex. 'Just make sure she doesn't go wandering anywhere. We'll never find her in this lot.'

Never mind, how about a game of peek-a-boo instead? Twenty yards behind them was four-year-old Jessie. The two girls had become best friends on the voyage from Glasgow. Jessie was one of six children, aged from nineteen to an infant of only a few months, travelling with their mother, Mrs Sproul. The Greigs had felt sorry for her on the trip, what with trying to cope with all the children and no husband to help her. But now there was an air of each man for himself, and all Andrew Greig was concerned about was getting his family through. Never mind the other 1,300 passengers.

The Greigs passed the first test. The doctors, in their blue United States Health Service uniforms, eyed each one of them but did nothing. It was awful when one of the other passengers – was it that man named Telford? – was taken away after one of the doctors scribbled a chalk mark on his back. It meant they thought there was something wrong with him. For him, all this might have been in vain. For the umpteenth time Annie checked that they all still had their passenger manifest numbers – 0013 to 0016 – pinned on. Nothing must go wrong. This was the Great Hall of Ellis Island in New York, gateway to America and – please God – the start of a new life.

Ellis Island was often called America's front door, and between 1890 and 1915, the years when it was at its busiest – some 17 million immigrants passed through it and into the vastness of America. In fact 1906, the year the Greig family from Penicuik arrived, was something of a boom year. The economy was growing at full throttle and record numbers of immigrants came to try to grab a slice of the action. As they finally made the short ferry ride towards Manhattan, the Greig family would have passed under Liberty's outstretched arm, her sculpted torch held out like a beacon to all who approached America's shores.

The Statue of Liberty is, of course, not American at all but a gift from the French. Conceived by a group of French liberals to mark the centenary of America's independence in 1886, it was designed by Frédéric Auguste Bartholdi. The man responsible for making sure the mighty statue stayed up (it weighs 225 tons) was none other than Alexandre Gustave Eiffel, better known for the eponymous tower that would come to symbolise Paris as much as the Statue of Liberty now represents America.

If the original intention of the statue was to celebrate the links between the two nations (remember, the French had helped the nascent country in its war of independence), it very soon acquired a different purpose. The statue's special resonance for immigrants comes from the lines of a poem written by one Emma Lazarus. The lines now immortalised at the base of the monument are like a nineteenth-century mission statement for America. Its last lines are as emotive today as they were on the day a New York philanthropist discovered them amongst a number of other poems commissioned as part of the original fund-raising drive to erect the statue:

> Give me your tired, your poor,
> Your huddled masses yearning to breathe free,
> The wretched refuse of your teeming shore,
> Send these, the homeless, tempest-tossed, to me:
> I lift my lamp beside the golden door.

The plaque with Emma Lazarus's poem was fixed to the statue's pedestal in 1903, three years before the Greig family were ferried towards Manhattan. From where they were, they would not have been able to read the words, but as they turned their gaze from Liberty towards the approaching shoreline, they would have been dumbstruck by the skyline that seemed to rise from the very waters of the Hudson. It truly must have felt like a New World. The majesty of the buildings must have spoken more eloquently than words of the city's unabashed dedication to wealth creation. They may have seen the Singer Building going up. When it was finished the following year, it would reach forty-seven storeys high! London's Canary Wharf, built nearly a century later in 1991, only has three more floors.

How do I know so much about the Greig family and their fellow passengers? Well, I may have made up the bit about poor old Telford being dragged away (though he was on the *Columbia*), but the rest of it is true. Names, dates, manifest numbers – it's all available at the click of a mouse. Today Ellis Island is a spectacularly conceived museum, with an online database into which thousands of ships' manifests and other immigration papers have been transferred. This is not a museum full of preserved exhibits in glass boxes, but a living tribute to immigration. In his hugely accessible book on Ellis Island, *Immigration's Shining Centre*, John Cunningham says that 'immigration is America's basic story, the source of the nation's strength and its uniqueness'. It's thought that 100 million Americans – that's roughly one in three of them – can trace their forebears back to this island. This is a place where Americans are encouraged to delve into their past.

Mary Greig's granddaughter is one of them. Her name is Susan Hess and she had just confirmed the Ellis Island connection when I met her. 'It's just so exciting,' she said, palpably moved by her discovery. 'We must have got about two hundred hits on the website.' Susan and her husband now live in Irvine, California, modern-day versions of the westward drift that started at Ellis Island in another age. The fact that they had travelled all the way from their home near the Pacific coastline – a continent away – to see Ellis Island tells you a great deal about Americans' attitude to immigration. It is something to be celebrated, not something to tolerate.

Outside, in the grounds of Ellis Island, is a 'wall of honour'. In return for a donation, people can have the names of their Ellis Island ancestors inscribed on shining steel panels that radiate out towards the Hudson River. From Leigh Ann Aaberg on panel 7 through Ramnath Lakshmiratam and Kee-Lim Li Chai to Wladislaw P. Zyzyk on panel 578, there are thousands of names. They came as individuals and families, but on this memorial they are brought together. They arrived as Austrians, Lithuanians, Indians, Chinese and Polish, but by the time they passed on the baton to the next generation, they were Americans. The message behind this wall of honour is clear: to have had a relation, however distant, come through this place is a privilege. Immigration is a privilege, it is a good thing.

About a third of the many millions who came through Ellis Island settled in New York itself. At the turn of the last century the little corner of Manhattan south of about Rivington Street and east of Bowery was reckoned to be the most crowded place on earth. Wave after wave of migrants headed into the district. Irish, Polish, Germans, Ukrainians and Russians, many of them Jews fleeing the European pogroms, jostled for accommodation and jobs in what is now known as the Lower East Side. Most ended up in the garment business. Whole families would sit around the kitchen table sewing a batch of 'knee pants', otherwise known as knickerbockers. After a while the father of the household might move up the chain, becoming a 'sweater' who contracted out small orders to other, newer immigrants. The Far East sweatshops of today are just bigger and more efficient versions of the teeming tenements of nineteenth-century New York.

Number 97 Orchard Street is one such tenement building. Between 1863 and 1935, when the last tenants were evicted, some 7,000 immigrants from twenty countries had passed through its door. Like those rock exhibits that show the different strata that make up a geological formation, 97 Orchard Street is a cutaway of America's immigrant past. It, too, is now a museum.

Among the earliest residents were Julius and Natalie Gumpertz, who had settled into one of the apartments by 1870. Both were Prussian immigrants who had arrived in New York separately. Julius was a shoemaker. In their three-roomed flat (only one was designated as a bedroom; the other two were parlour and kitchen respectively) they brought up their four children – Rosa, Nannie, Olga and Isaac. On 7 October 1874, at seven o'clock in the morning, Julius set off for work as usual. He never returned and the family never found out what happened to him. Nathalie became the sole breadwinner. Like 35,000 other people in the city at the time she became a dressmaker. Her front room, the only one with natural light, was a workshop during the day, a sitting room when it needed to be one and a bedroom at night.

Among the last tenants at 97 Orchard Street were the Baldizzi family. Adolfo Baldizzi, a cabinet-maker from Palermo in Sicily, made his passage to the New World as a stowaway on a ship in 1923. A year later his wife Rosaria joined him. They lived at number 97 from 1928 to 1935. Adolfo and Rosaria had two children. One of them, Josephine, lived to see the opening of the museum in 1989. In the book published by the museum, *A Tenement Story*, she gives her reaction to how much the area had changed in the fifty years since the Baldizzis had moved on: 'When I came in contact with the immigrants coming here now I said 'Oh my God what country am I in. These are all foreign people. What are they all doing here.' Then I realised that these poor immigrants now are doing the same things my parents did.'

Indeed the area has changed, subject to the constant metamorphosis that is both the muddle and the marvel of migration. When I rented an apartment on Rivington with my wife, Frances, and our sons so I could do a bit of research for this book, the area seemed more Hispanic than anything else. From our overheated flat we looked out on the Havana newsagent where, of all things, you could pick up a plate of sushi to go. Across the street was PS 140 (in a triumph of order over imagination, all the public schools run by the education department are given a number). To be fair, the sign also said *Nathan Straus School*. The Straus family had emigrated from Rhenish Bavaria, today's Germany, in the early 1850s. Nathan, a shrewd businessman, would go on to open Macy's at Herald Square, which was dubbed the 'world's largest department store'. In 2005, the head teacher at the school was Esteban Barrientos. What will his pupils leave to posterity?

All immigrants help to shape the countries they land in, but in

America their influence seems to have been felt more quickly and deeply (and in the case of the native Indians, more savagely) than in Britain. That most quintessential of American songs, the hand-on-heart 'God Bless America', was penned by a Russian immigrant whose family had arrived in the country in 1888. Born Israel Baline, legend has it that a printer's error gave him the name that will forever be associated with popular entertainment in America – Irving Berlin. If ever you want an outpouring of patriotism, this is it:

> God bless America, land that I love.
> Stand beside her and guide her
> Through the night with a light from above.
> From the mountains, to the prairies,
> To the oceans white with foam
> God bless America,
> My home sweet home.

Written in cold black and white the words seem tacky and the tune mundane. Hear it sung, as I have standing in a large crowd outside St Patrick's Cathedral on Madison Avenue in New York, after the attacks on that city and Washington in 2001, and you understand the emotive hold this song has on Americans.

It was another turn-of-the-century immigrant who first came up with the phrase that for decades encapsulated America's apparent ability to absorb millions of immigrants with such differing traditions and turn them into the kind of people who would all sing 'God Bless America' and, what's more, mean every word of it! In 1908 a play by one Israel Zangwill, a Jewish immigrant from England, was first performed in Washington. Apart from the aficionados, nobody remembers the plot but everybody knows the title. It was called *The Melting Pot*. I've often wondered what words Zangwill might have found to describe the immigrant experience in Britain, where he lived and worked before moving to America. Clearly he found some inspiration there that was lacking in Hackney, east London.

Whether the 'melting pot' is any longer a credible metaphor for America's race relations is a hotly debated subject. There, too, people are beginning to question the model, seeing it replaced by what some call the 'hyphenated' identity. There are fears that instead of the one America of apple-pie fame, the country is splitting into factions based on ethnicity. So you have African-Americans, Italian-Americans, Asian-Americans and the like. The counter argument is that in all these descriptions being American remains the baseline. In fact some of this was prefigured in another theatrical production, this time a Broadway musical of the late fifties. *West Side Story* came closest to illuminating the modern immigrant experience in America. It was huge on stage and an even bigger sensation when it was made into a film in 1961. It went on to win ten Oscars.

Based in the New York of the fifties, it was a contemporary rendition of a much older love story, Shakespeare's *Romeo and Juliet*. In this version, though, the rivalry between the Montagus and Capulets is rendered into an Upper West Side feud between two gangs – one drawn from established European immigrants, the other from the more recent arrivals, the Puerto Ricans. One of its signature tunes is 'America' in which the entire Puerto Rican half of the cast is assembled on a rooftop. It is a biting and deeply ironic take on the American dream. If one character presents the best of America, another shoots back with its darker side. Listen to this:

> ANITA: Skyscrapers bloom in America
> ROSALIA: Cadillacs zoom in America
> GIRLS: Industry boom in America
> BOYS: Twelve in a room in America
> ANITA: Life can be bright in America
> BOYS: If you can fight in America
> GIRLS: Life is all right in America
> BOYS: If you're all white in America

The song is remarkable for its honesty, particularly given

Hollywood's predilection for sanitising everything it touches – especially in the late fifties and sixties.

Now, whether you are of the *Melting Pot* school of thought or more partial to the *West Side Story* interpretation of the immigrant experience in America, you have to be impressed by the extent to which the subject has provided such a strong and enduring narrative to the country's popular culture.

The same cannot really be said of Britain. True, the nineties saw the emergence of a genre of film that explored what it was like to be Asian and living in England. Gurinder Chadha's *Bhaji on the Beach*, Damien O'Donnell's *East is East* (based on a play by Ayub Khan-Din) and others use Asian immigration as their subject matter. In an echo of the *West Side Story* formula, *The Big Life* turned Shakespeare's *Love's Labour's Lost* into an energetic take on the lives of four Jamaicans who've just got off the good ship *Windrush* in the late forties. Kwame Kwei-Armah's *Elmina's Kitchen* is a rather more unnerving portrayal of what happens when a second-generation African boy is pulled between the modest accomplishments of a father who runs a café and the bling-bling returns of a life in Hackney's gangland. These and others have certainly opened a new window on British life, but it would be difficult to call them a part of our popular culture. More BBC Four than BBC One, perhaps? And if they are only the first artistic salvos in a new tradition of entertainment, how come it's such a recent phenomenon?

And we don't have an Ellis Island in Britain. Nor do we have an Orchard Street Museum. I'm not really talking about a building (though that is partly true). What I really mean is that we don't have the sentiment. Immigration barely makes a footnote in the national story. We have the history but appear not to have the inclination to exploit it. Like 97 Orchard Street in Lower East Side, we too have an address in London, but in our case its parlous structural state tells you a lot about how we view immigration.

If you click on to the website for 19 Princelet Street, two words emerge from a line drawing of the building in question – 'under threat', it says in a stark red font. It is no exaggeration. Though it is Britain's only museum dedicated to immigration – indeed, it may be the only one in Europe – it is not generally open to the public. It was set up as a charity in 1983. The unstinting efforts of the group of volunteer trustees, led by the indefatigable Susie Symes, a one-time treasury economist, has yet to yield the funding necessary to renovate the property so it is safe enough for people to walk around in. Where are all the self-made millionaires whose families came here penniless? In America they would be fighting each other to contribute to a project like 19 Princelet Street. Instead this architectural gem, this historic jewel sits largely unseen.

The property was erected in 1719 by one Samuel Worrall, a master-builder and a sometime associate of Sir Christopher Wren, who built St Paul's Cathedral. Much of this area of London, northeast of the cathedral, was completely rebuilt after the Great Fire of 1666. Later the Princelet Street house became home to the Ogier family, Protestant Huguenot exiles from France. When the Edict of Nantes (under which France's Protestants were tolerated, if not exactly encouraged) was revoked in 1685, Huguenots knew what to expect. Their churches were destroyed, their trades were limited and their children were forced to be baptised as Catholics. Tens of thousands of Huguenots sought refuge in England, where many became successful traders and artisans. They virtually reinvented the silk industry. Standing outside 19 Princelet Street, you can see the silk-weavers' garrets protruding from the roofline. The large windows, which were added in the 1760s, meant the workers could make full use of what daylight there was.

In time-honoured fashion, the Huguenots became more prosperous and eventually moved out of the area. Number 19 Princelet Street became home to successive waves of immigrants, just as the area around it did. Up the road, on Brick Lane, the original Huguenot church, L'Eglise Neuve, has gone through several incarnations. It was a Methodist chapel, then a synagogue, and in 1976 it became the Jamme Masjid Mosque, which it still is today.

Number 19 Princelet Street was eventually divided up into lodgings and workshops. After the Huguenots, it was the turn of the Irish, and then Jews from eastern Europe. It has variously been used as an 'industrial school' by a Mrs Ellen Hawkins, who prepared women for service or work in local factories, a workshop for the gilder and carver Isaiah Woodcock; and even the headquarters for the Loyal United Friends Friendly society, set up by immigrant Poles. In 1869 Jewish occupants built a synagogue in the garden that had once been the playground for the Ogier children.

Below the synagogue, in the basement, is a meeting area. It was here, in the 1930s, that Jewish groups met to organise their defence against the anti-Semitism that was sweeping through this part of London. Imagine what it must have been like in the weeks before the Cable Street riots of 1936, when Oswald Mosley's Blackshirts led the violence. Groups of Jewish men in dark suits, black felt hats and grey beards speaking to each other in *sotto voce* Yiddish. Their people had fled the pogroms in eastern Europe; now they were faced with this. 'Will it ever stop?' they must have asked each other.

A hundred years later, in 1969, one of the last tenants in the building was one David Rodinsky. He was a mysterious figure about whom little is known, since he simply disappeared. In their book *Rodinsky's Room*, Rachel Lichtenstein and Iain Sinclair write about how the room was discovered in 1980 virtually in its original state. There was a pan of porridge on the stove and an imprint of a head on the pillow. Some said Rodinsky was a scholar, others that he was mad.

After first hearing Rodinsky's story, I couldn't help feeling that his unheralded life, his disappearance without trace and the knowledge he took with him was an apposite metaphor for the fate of 19 Princelet Street. We know what it represents, we can guess at the secrets and stories that still lie dormant within its walls, and yet we cannot unlock them. When I talked about this and the contrast with America to Susie Symes, she said it was not, in the end, about money, but about an attitude to where we all come from: 'It's the difference between the two countries,' she said. 'In America they make out as if they've all just got off the boat. Here we like to think we have always been here and it's other people who are the immigrants. They are both myths, but in America they have acted on their myth.'

Just imagine you want to start the process of applying for British citizenship today. You'd make the trip to Lunar House in Croydon, one of those outer suburbs that seem to stretch London halfway down the road to the south coast. A stamp in your passport at a port or airport gives you permission to enter the country, but a stamp from Lunar House is the one that allows you to become a part of Britain.

You could do it all by post but let's pretend you've decided on a face-to-face application. You'd probably take an early morning tube to Victoria Station for the final leg of the journey by overland train. You've already filled in the appropriate form – SET (O) for 'indefinite leave to remain'. Getting the form was easy enough. A friend downloaded it at an internet café on the Kingsland Road in Dalston, east London. You've got the banker's draft for the hundreds of pounds application fee you have to pay in advance. It's a lot of money and you will not get it back if the application fails. The other things in your plastic folding file are a letter from a relative saying he is ready to support you, and a copy of *Life in the United Kingdom: a Journey to Citizenship*, a handbook from the Home Office.

The handbook is a bit like a teenager's revision notes. Since November 2005, all applicants for UK citizenship have had to pass a test designed to assess whether the would-be Brit has a rudimentary knowledge of British culture, tradition, history and the way the country is governed. One of the twenty-four questions might be 'What is the Church of England and who is its head?' It would be interesting to know how many of a random sample of born-and-bred citizens would put the Archbishop of

Canterbury, and not the Queen, as the answer. The pass mark is 75 per cent but, like the driving test, you can take it any number of times, though whether the applicant can afford to pay the fee is another matter. If you make the grade you will join the 140,795 immigrants who became British citizens in 2004, a record year at the time. On average it takes six years for the majority of people born abroad to acquire British citizenship. But all that seems a long way away as you sit nervously in the underground carriage.

You take comfort from the fact that hundreds of thousands have done the same thing before you. Around you there's plenty of evidence to prove the point. Quite a few of the other passengers look like they're from somewhere else. They're not all tourists either. That's obvious. They aren't constantly looking at a route map, or wearing one of those ridiculous safety wallets hanging round their neck – just where it's easy to snatch and run. No, the immigrants are the ones who are nodding off; they've just come off the night shift somewhere. You remember someone telling you that one in three Londoners is from an ethnic minority. You didn't believe it when you came here, but it's obviously true. In fact, when you hang around the Ridley Road market in Dalston, it's easier to count the white people.

You start to look at the advertisements above the seats. The first one that catches your eye is a poster for 'alpha telecom' (written in the kind of fashionable lower case that would have driven your very proper English teacher back home mad). It shows four phones, each one depicting the national flag of an African country. There's a green and white Nigerian one, the Ghanaian one is red, yellow and green, the other two are harder to make out but the ad helpfully gives the countries underneath. Right next to it is another advert for a phone company. This one is for 'just-dial'. Unlike the other company, this one helps you to make cheap calls from mobile phones, not just landlines. No flags this time, but the countries are listed: Ghana, India, Jamaica, Nigeria, Pakistan and South Africa. There's yet another cheap call advert. This one is for a company called 'liquidphone', but you can't be bothered with the detail, you've got the idea. With a few stops still to go, you just pray you are one of those lucky ones who gets the chance to stay and make the call to your wife back home. A thousand times in your head you've fantasised about the call: 'I've made it! Now we'll see about getting you in.'

Lunar House, all twenty floors of it, is part of a huge Home Office complex. On the day I made my visit, happily as an observer and not as a 'customer', which is what they call applicants these days, the queue outside was modest. The legendary procession of people that used to snake round the building like supplicants at this cathedral to nationality is largely a thing of the past. The greater use of computers and an appointment system means that everybody gets their chance as long as they stick to their allotted time slot. Yolande from Colombia was on her second visit; she was looking for another extension to her visa. She was checking her make-up in a little vanity mirror. Behind her was John from Sierra Leone. He was neatly dressed in the kind of checked sports jacket that people made fun of when I was at university. Or has the fashion come round again? He wouldn't say what he was after. Robert from Uganda looked more nervous than the other two – he was a student and it was his first visit.

There are three stages. At reception, after you pass through an airport-style security check (a sign on the wall says 'Special Notice: the state of alert is currently Black Special'), they make a quick check just to make sure the applicants have all the relevant paperwork. There are about fifteen booths. It's a bit like walking into a bank except there's a lot more at stake than your overdraft.

Next comes the payment area. Unlike at your bank, there's no credit here. The buy-now-pay-later culture does not extend to immigration. It's cash up front or it's goodbye.

On the second floor there's row upon row of benches fixed to the floor. They are made of red plastic and are not designed for comfort, but the Home Office mission statement says this part of the procedure is only meant to take about forty-five minutes. In fact the whole process should take about two hours, with a return visit later in the day to find out the result. If you're successful, there's another hour and a half or so to get the resident's permit inserted in your passport and to collect your other documents. Think of it, same-day service. Just like the dry cleaner's.

I noticed that many of the people on the other side of the glass-fronted booths looked as if they themselves were immigrants. According to the Home Office, a 'fair proportion' of the staff at the Immigration and Nationality Directorate, including the ones who do these on-the-day assessments, have what's called 'indefinite leave to remain' status. They're not full-blooded Brits yet. It occurred to me that if you are one of those immigrants accused by the people back home of wanting to pull up the drawbridge once you're over it, this would be the place to work! In all it's a rather sterile, efficient business. You get more drama at the average supermarket checkout. That's because the people here have taken the legal immigration route.

Upstairs is where the asylum seekers are handled. A third of all the claims for refuge come through this Croydon office. It looks much the same, except the benches are green not red. But I sensed the real difference in the air. The signs are there in the tired, hunched bodies, in the smell of clothes that have been worn for too long, and above all in the eyes that are wide open but appear to see nothing. Some of these people have reached this point after journeys that are in themselves proof of desperation or determination, probably both.

Come over with me and listen to what I heard at booth 15, where a female officer is talking to a claimant through an interpreter. He's from Sudan and says he's fifteen (it's harder to turn a minor away), though to me he looks older. That's just another of the judgements the official is going to have to make. I'm glad it's her and not me.

'When did you arrive in Britain?'

'Five days ago.'

'How did you arrive?'

'By lorry.'

'Where did you start your journey?'

'From Sudan, from Darfur.'

'And when did the journey start?'

'July this year, 2005.'

It was 21 September when I made my visit, two months later.

'Where in Darfur did you leave?'

'From my house.'

'So do you know when you actually left the country, when you went outside the border of Sudan?'

'It was August. I do not know the date.'

'Then where did you go?'

'I don't know. It was on a ship.'

I didn't stay any longer. But just think of the questions that little interchange threw up. Was he really a minor? Was he really from Darfur (from where there was every reason to flee if you were an African at the wrong end of the programme of ethnic cleansing that began in about 2003)? Who helped him to get out of Sudan, and were they human traffickers? Why didn't he claim asylum as soon as he arrived here? Or had he been in Britain much longer and was now hoping to regularise his stay? Did he pass through another European country, and if he did, why didn't he apply for asylum there? But beyond all those questions is the big one, the moral one – what is the right thing to do?

As I thought through the implications of what I had just heard, my mind wandered back to my old university city, Durham, and in particular to the great Norman edifice that is the cathedral. The North Door of the cathedral dates back to 1140. Fixed to it is a huge bronze knocker moulded into the shape of a lion-like beast; at least that was what it seemed like to me. The story of that knocker is an eloquent reminder that the notion of refuge, of giving someone a safe place to stay, is much, much older than the modern argument about asylum.

Throughout the Middle Ages Durham Cathedral was a place of sanctuary. Any fugitive from the law could claim protection by knocking on that door. There were always two watchmen in a chamber above the entrance. They were under instructions to open the door and take the person to the monastery. There he would be fed and watered and given thirty seven days' grace. It was a time when the law-breaker, if that was what he was – for there must have been many who were falsely accused – could decide between facing trial, and admitting his guilt and being sent into voluntary exile. If he chose the latter, he was escorted to a port – usually the Bishop's port at Hartlepool – wearing a badge in the shape of the cross of St Cuthbert (the cathedral is the last resting place of this early English saint) stitched to his shoulder and carrying a rough wooden cross tied together with rope. Some accounts say the runaway had to wear a black cloak as well. Once at the port, he was required to embark on the next ship that was due to set sail. It didn't matter where the ship was going – he had to be on it. It was part of the deal. Durham was not unique. Other churches offered sanctuary too. It was an early attempt to protect the innocent from the summary justice so often meted out.

I'm not sure that I want to see churches offering protection to criminals, but to me, the lesson of this Durham story is that there was such a powerful notion of sanctuary at all in this country. It is as old as modern England if, as some do, you mark the birth of the modern state with the Norman Conquest. It is a precious ideal and we sully it at our peril. Those who misuse the idea of refuge, bogus asylum seekers in the language of the red-top dailies, are as guilty as those who believe that the notion of sanctuary is simply no longer relevant. Durham's Benedictine monks may have protected criminals, while we are only being asked to support the desperate. It may be breaking the rules to claim you are a refugee when, strictly speaking, you are not, but is it a crime to want something better for yourself and your family?

But such ethical dilemmas are a world away from the reality of administering Britain's immigration laws, a process in which Lunar House is the front line. When the politicians have had their say, when Parliament has passed the laws, it is here that they have to be put into practice. In the same way as the Ministry of Defence is really about preparing for war, so too the immigration rules are not really about letting people in but about keeping them out.

That was certainly the purpose of the Aliens Act of 1905, and it has remained the preoccupation of virtually every law since, with the odd notable exception. The 1905 act was the first to place a formal restriction on entry into Britain. There had, of course, been many previous occasions on which foreigners had been maligned or thrown out of the country (Jews were famously expelled from England in 1290), but the Aliens Act was the first piece of legislation preventing people from coming here in the first place. It achieved its goal by stating that any ship carrying more than twenty foreigners could be barred entry without the express approval of an immigration officer and medical inspector. You could be deemed an undesirable immigrant if you were a 'lunatic or an idiot' or in any other way likely to become 'a charge on the rates'.

That was the fundamental breach with the principle of free entry to Britain. After that it was really a case of refinement, or so the proponents of ever tougher conditions would claim. The invention of the passport in 1915 made the business of tracking people much easier. But very soon a pattern began to emerge with every adjustment to the law; those who found that their movements were most restricted were people who were not white. The 1925 Alien Registration Act (Coloured Alien Seamen) left very little to the imagination. Don't you love the way the real purpose of the act is placed in brackets, as if it were an afterthought and not at all the real intention behind the law? By 1935 it was out in the open – shipping companies were offered subsidies to employ white British seamen.

But necessity often breeds change, and the huge demands in men and materiel brought about by fighting the Second World War wrought a toning down, if not an end, to the antipathy towards foreigners. As in the Great War, men from the colonies and dominions played a huge and vital part. They fought with what now seems like touching good faith for king and empire.

The numbers involved are staggering. The Indian Army provided over two and a half million men and women. It amounted to the largest volunteer army in history. From the Caribbean colonies some 16,000 men and about 100 women fought for the 'mother' country. Six thousand of them ended up in the RAF, the only service seriously to lift the colour bar that had been in operation hitherto.

The end of the Second World War saw Britain in a state of limbo. It had, with its allies, won the war, but the effort had been ruinous on the economy. On the other hand it still had an empire. Like a nobleman who has fallen on hard times, it had the airs and graces of the past but faced a future without the hard cash to sustain the old lifestyle. What to do? The imperial instinct, ingrained over hundreds of years, won through. In an act of imperial largesse, Clement Attlee's government passed the 1948 Nationality Act, which gave all Britain's colonial subjects scattered across the planet the right of entry into Britain. It was a symbolic gesture, in keeping with the mood of the day, rather than a formal invitation, but that is precisely how some saw it. From the Caribbean to the Indian subcontinent, people who had been taught to believe that an Englishman's word was his bond began to wonder whether they could make it in Britain. They were encouraged by memories of their experiences during the war, when they had been treated civilly and sometimes with affection. In Andrea Levy's award-winning novel *Small Island*, the contrast between the Britain of West Indian imagination and its reality for those who came over here is a constant backdrop to the trials and tribulations of Gilbert and Hortense.

If the new legislation offered a pull factor, there was plenty to push the would-be immigrants away from their homes as well. In the Caribbean, the economy of Jamaica, the most populous island in the West Indies, had collapsed. A violent hurricane in 1947, the worst for a generation, made matters worse. As for the subcontinent, independence in 1947 and the violence and ethnic strife that went with partition into a largely Hindu state in India and a

Muslim one in Pakistan prompted many to look for refuge abroad.

Over the years and in much of the writing about post-war immigration to Britain, the SS *Empire Windrush* has acquired near mythical status as the ship which began the whole process of mass migration. Whether it did or not is a moot point. In fact, a number of the passengers would have preferred to head for America, where many of their friends and relatives had already gone, but new immigration laws there meant Liberty no longer offered the same open-armed welcome to West Indians. The voyage of the *Windrush* was certainly not a part of the planned migration that came later, when the British government actively recruited in the Caribbean, but its place in history should be assured if only because the views of its passengers and the reaction to their impending arrival in Britain is a most telling vignette of the larger story.

In their painstakingly researched book on West Indian immigration, *Windrush*, Mike and Trevor Phillips publish the recollections of several passengers on that fateful voyage. One of them was Aldwyn 'Lord Kitchener' Roberts, a Trinidadian famous throughout the region for his calypso songs, who recalled that 'When the boat had about four days to land in England, I get this kind of wonderful feeling that I'm going to land on the mother country, the soil of the mother country.' What 'Lord Kitchener' did not know was that in the mother country the impending arrival of over 400 West Indian men had given rise to considerable consternation. There was a quiet horror in the corridors of Whitehall, with cables, memos and files being passed from one department to another. They all had one sentiment in common: 'There's not a lot we can do about this lot, but for heaven's sake, we can't have the whole of the bloody Caribbean following them.' The words are mine, but their meaning is authentic enough. Here's an extract from just one message from the Lord President of the Privy Council, in which he asks the Secretary of State at the Colonial Office to explain 'what he is doing to ensure that further similar movements either from Jamaica or elsewhere in the Colonial Empire are detected and checked before they can reach such an embarrassing stage'.

So there you have it. The juxtaposition of hope on the part of the Jamaicans and fear on the part of the British establishment, as it began to understand the true implications of the 1948 Act. It was a poor footing on which to build any sort of relationship, as subsequent decades would prove. If some of the *Windrush* passengers had imagined that the Nationality Act was like being invited to a party – and in truth, few of them were quite that naïve – they soon discovered that they would be treated more like gatecrashers.

One bald fact is enough to show what the real problem was. All this anxiety was generated over fewer than 500 Jamaicans when, in the decade after the war, Irish workers were pouring into Britain at the rate of 60,000 a year! Around the same time, about 160,000 Poles had been naturalised, given permission to work and, sometimes, offered homes in Britain. It simply wasn't, and isn't, about numbers.

In fact the governments at the time didn't really know which way to turn. They were caught between a rock and a hard place. The ever-sensitive antennae of the political class could sense the social ructions that 'coloured' immigration might bring about, but at the same time, they knew that Britain was suffering an acute labour shortage. Some said agriculture and industry needed an extra million workers if the economy was going to break free of the ration-book era. There was an open conflict in Clement Attlee's government between the interests of the Home Office and those of the Board of Trade.

And despite all the private concerns, economics is what drove policy in the fifties, at least until public pressure towards the end of the decade saw those immigration laws refined once again. So you had the irony of Enoch Powell – the politician who would warn of racial strife in his notorious 'Rivers of Blood' speech in 1968 – talking to audiences in the West Indies about job prospects in Britain. Not to be outdone, London Transport advanced the cost of the fare to those who would come and work on the buses and trains.

In any case, immigrants are a hardy breed. People who have been brave enough to leave behind the security of kith and kin are not the kind who will be put off easily – even by the incipient racism of Britain in the fifties. Whatever they were hoping to come up with in Downing Street, the Privy Council or the Colonial Office, the die was already cast. Britain's monochrome image of itself was about to change irrevocably. In 1949 there were just 100 Indians in Birmingham; by the 2001 census, 55,000 people living in the city were of Indian origin. Nearly a third of the city's one million population was from an ethnic minority.

Among the first Indians to arrive were the Sikhs in the mid fifties. Being a minority on the subcontinent, they had more to fear than most in the ethnic convulsions that followed Britain's 'divide and quit' recipe for independence in Pakistan and India. Pretty soon they were joined by Hindus from Gujarat, and Muslims from what was then West and East Pakistan. None of them found it easy, but for all of them immigration was a chance to earn and save money.

The fifties saw the arrival of 300,000 immigrants from the New Commonwealth countries. In the following three years, 1960 to 1962, more immigrants arrived than in the whole of the twentieth century up to that point. In fact the rate of immigration, already brisk, reached unprecedented levels as it became clear that the government was going to act. Families raced to get relatives into the country before the door was shut, as many feared it would be.

When the legislation came, the 1962 Commonwealth Immigration Act, it didn't quite shut the door, but it severely restricted entry to Britain. It was aimed squarely at what was called 'coloured' immigration. The act divided immigrants into those with job offers, those with credible skills and those without either – strict quotas were set for this last category. Nine hundred work vouchers were granted every week, and no country was allowed more than a fifth of the available vouchers.

That was a Tory law, criticised by Labour in opposition, but it soon became obvious that as far as immigration was concerned, there was little to choose between the two main parties. In 1967, the newly elected government of Harold Wilson fell in with the public mood and tightened up the legislation even further. The number of work vouchers was cut back, and in a regulation that would cast a shadow over family life, children over the age of sixteen were no longer allowed to join their immigrant parents in Britain.

There was more to come from Labour. This time new legislation was prompted by upheaval abroad. In 1968, Jomo Kenyatta, Kenya's first freely elected leader, began what he called the 'africanisation' of the country. Indians, who had something of a stranglehold on business, were threatened with the loss of permanent residence if they chose not to adopt full-on Kenyan nationality. The 1968 Second Commonwealth Immigration Act in effect narrowed down the options open to the Kenyan Indians even further. Jim Callaghan, who was Home Secretary at the time, and his lawyers came up with the idea that henceforth only British subjects with a 'close connection' to Britain would have the right of residence here. What this meant was that you had to have had a parent or grandparent who was British. Now guess who was most likely to fulfil that condition? No, not the Kenyan Asians who were about to be made stateless. At a stroke the rights of some 150,000 Asians were discarded while the white settlers of Kenya could carry on as if nothing had happened.

Three years later it was Edward Heath's turn, as the new Tory prime minister, to add his refinement to the immigration laws. His 1971 Immigration Act was a consolidation of all the previous laws, with one or two new twists. Citizens of the UK and its colonies who were patrial (conforming to the 'one grandparent rule') were clearly demarcated from citizens of independent Commonwealth countries. In order to live in the UK, the latter group needed special work permits, which would be renewed on an annual basis.

If the 1948 Act represented what Britain, in another age, wanted to be, then the 1981 Immigration Act illustrated what it had become. Where once to have been born in the empire over which the sun never set was enough to be accorded membership of the British club, it was now clear that the club itself had ceased to exist. It represented the final nail in the coffin for the expansive, albeit imperialist concept of *ius soli* (literally 'the right of the soil', where citizenship results from being born within the British Empire).

Margaret Thatcher's act created three types of nationality. In the kind of sophistry that found a home in Orwell's *Animal Farm*, everybody was British but some were more British than others. There was full British citizenship, dependent territories citizenship and British overseas citizenship. Only one of those categories, the first, had full rights of entry and abode. The British passport the others ended up with was absolutely useless for the one purpose they might have had for it – to come to Britain. At least Willie Whitelaw, Maggie's old-school and patrician deputy, had the decency to admit the true motivation behind the new legislation: 'It is high time,' he said '[that] we ditched the notion that Britain is somehow a haven for all those countries we used to rule.'

Looking back at immigration law in the twentieth century, it is clear that the 1948 Act was an aberration. All the others, from the Aliens Act of 1905, held up a version of the no entry sign to the majority of people wanting to come here. All the laws were justified by those who passed them on the grounds that they were about regulation not race. In practice, race was a key determinant and anybody born with a black or brown skin knew it.

At university I wrote a dissertation on immigration law. I called it *Racism Made Respectable*. I cringe when I look back at many of the things I wrote and said in those carefree days, but the title of that dissertation is not one of them.

The steady, incremental shift from open borders to the highly selective and restricted access that we now have is not a peculiarly British phenomenon. The changes have seemed starker here because they were always bound to be compared with our stated

intention of having a special relationship with the countries that
we once ruled. But that aside, Britain's changing attitude to immigration reflects a Europe-wide concern. Even some of the
countries that have had the most liberal of approaches – such as
Denmark and Holland – have retreated behind a wall of new
regulations.

In Holland, two men, both murdered – the outspoken and
flamboyant politician Pim Fortuyn in 2002 and the controversial
film-maker Theo van Gogh two years later – catapulted immigration into a key issue, perhaps *the* key political issue of the early
twenty-first century. Fortuyn was a rising star who made his
name by running on an anti-immigration ticket. His popularity,
which within weeks had extended well beyond his political base
in Rotterdam, showed the extent to which the once laissez-faire
Dutch had begun to change their minds about immigration. In
Rotterdam, along with Amsterdam and the Hague, immigrants
outnumber native Dutch among twenty-year-olds and are
expected to become the absolute majority towards 2020. Fortuyn
openly challenged the notion that multiculturalism was working,
citing the number of Moroccan immigrants in the country who
had said they supported the terrorist attacks on New York and
Washington in 2001. His murder in May 2002, the first political
assassination in the country since the seventeenth century, was a
defining moment. Even though the man who killed him was an
animal rights activist (and not an immigrant), his death had a
profound effect on a country that had for so long prided itself on
its liberal race relations policies.

If Fortuyn's death had prompted a hardening of people's attitudes towards immigrants, the ghastly murder in November 2004
of the director Theo van Gogh cemented them once and for all.
Van Gogh was shot dead, his throat cut and the knife used to pin
a letter from the killer on to the corpse. The murder followed an
extremely provocative film, *Submission*, which van Gogh made
with the help of a Somali-born politician, Ayaan Hirsi Ali, on how
Islam condoned the abuse of women. That Hirsi Ali had once

been a Muslim herself gave the film a credibility it might not otherwise have enjoyed. The man arrested for the murder was a Muslim extremist.

Together the murders created an atmosphere in which Holland now has some of the toughest immigration and race relations policies. Fortuyn's calls for a greater emphasis on assimilation and tighter controls at the borders – which were regarded as controversial when he first made them – are now enshrined in law and will, no doubt, be superseded by more stringent measures.

It's hard to condemn the Dutch for their response. They had been the most welcoming of nations for generations of immigrants – mostly from Turkey, north Africa and their old colony, Suriname. Recoiling from their ambivalent role during the persecution of Jews under the Nazis (a higher proportion of Jews were killed in Holland than anywhere else in Europe), post-war Holland was founded on a notion of openness to other cultures. The parliament even passed special legislation allowing Moroccans to have dual nationality, because under Moroccan law, Moroccan citizenship is inalienable.

As in Britain, multiculturalism became a guiding principle for race relations, and in Holland there is growing evidence that it has not led to greater integration. (See the next chapter for the effect of multicultural policies on British race relations.) Between 70 and 80 per cent of Dutch-born immigrant families import their spouses from their own country, mostly Turkey or Morocco. According to a parliamentary report in 2004, policies which encouraged children to speak Turkish, Arabic or Berber rather than Dutch in primary schools have been disastrous for integration. In Holland immigrants have been eligible for generous social benefits. In 2005 ethnic minorities accounted for about 40 per cent of social security benefits, a rate six times higher than for the native Dutch population. Ethnic minorities account for just over 10 per cent of a total population, in 2005, of 16.3 million.

Yet many Dutch people, regardless of their political affiliation, now ask what they have got in return. Many have come to suspect that their own studied tolerance has only earned them contempt from a portion of the immigrant population. There is a sense that the freedom the extremist immigrant groups have enjoyed in Holland, and which they would almost certainly have been denied in their mother country, has been abused.

In Denmark, 8 per cent of the population are non-native and 5 per cent are non-white or refugees. Despite the fact that it gives more of its wealth in aid to the developing world than almost any other country, and has one of the most generous welfare systems in the world, Denmark now has the most stringent immigration policy in Europe. Permanent resident permits are now granted after seven years rather than three, and full welfare benefits are denied for that period. Non-Danes no longer enjoy the automatic right to be reunited with their spouse and no immigrant under the age of twenty-four is allowed to bring their wife or husband into the country. Denmark may have been the first to sign the 1951 UN refugee convention, but from 2005 its interpretation of its duties under it are more narrowly defined than ever.

Of course neither the experience of Denmark nor that of Holland is proof that an assimilationist approach – as opposed to a multicultural one – would have been better. The riots that started in Paris and then fanned out across France in the autumn of 2005 were shocking precisely because most French people believed that they had found the right way to deal with immigration. Every vehicle set alight, every brick hurled at the police told them otherwise.

In France the concept of nationality is an absolute one – you are either French or you are a foreigner. The hyphenated identities that are tolerated in Britain and America would be anathema in France. The us-or-them definition of nationality goes back to the 1789 revolution, when the country was re-forged not as a class-ridden, divided society, but as a nation of equals before the law. Hence the national motto: *liberté, egalité, fraternité*. It's been axiomatic that the state should reject anything that divides one Frenchman from another. So since 1905 even religion has been treated as a political issue rather than a cultural one, as it has been in Britain. It is something you have the freedom to indulge in at home but not something you have a right to bring into the public realm. It is what the French call *laïcité*, or secularism. So from across the Channel they look quizzically at the extent to which we in Britain have tried to accommodate different religions. They can't understand why we have prayer rooms for Muslims in many public buildings or why we allow Sikh policemen to wear their turbans while on duty.

But what France has learned, and the rest of Europe should take heed of, is that there is very little chance of *liberté, egalité and fraternité* if immigrants don't have access to the most basic pre-requisite for integration – a job. The unemployment rate in the *banlieue* where the violence kicked off is two to three times higher than it is for the rest of the population.

Seven years earlier, when France won the World Cup with a multicoloured team under the captaincy of a black man, all of France had been seduced by the idea that their country had found the magic formula to race relations. Their prime minister at the time, Lionel Jospin, posed this rhetorical question: 'What better image could there be of our unity and diversity?' On that steamy summer night when France beat the favourites, Brazil, it would have been difficult to argue with him. After all, the star of the show, Zinedine Zidane, had started out as the son of an Algerian warehouseman. As it turns out, all that game proved was that sport – whether it is football, boxing or athletics – has been the route out of poverty for generations of immigrants.

The emergence of 'Fortress Europe' has to be seen in the context of the ever-widening gap between the rich world and the poor world. The Africans clambering over razor-wire fences to get into the Spanish enclaves of Melilla and Ceuta in Morocco in 2005 were a sign of things to come. Even shooting the would-be migrants – as Moroccan border police did in October that year – will not stop the flow of people heading towards the bright lights and even brighter prospects of the rich world. There is a law of human migration that every Year 11 chemistry student will understand.

It's like osmosis really. When two solutions of liquid are divided by an artificial barrier, there will always tend to be a movement from the more dilute to the more concentrated.

In the case of migration, it is the lack of money on one side and the concentration of it on the other which makes movement virtually inevitable. The average per capita income in Britain is, for example, about sixty times higher than in Somalia. That fact alone (let alone the civil war) explains why in the 1990s Somalis were the single biggest national group applying for asylum in Britain. Many of them may have been genuine refugees, but you don't have to be a rabid Little Englander to accept that looking for a better life may be just as much a driving force for the thousands of Somalis who arrive here.

It's not so much that Britain and the rest of Europe need better immigration policies; they need better foreign policies. If rich countries fail to address the ever-growing gap between them and the poor world, they had better get used to the idea of a never-ending queue of people trying to get in.

The proliferation of internet facilities, even in the most remote corners of the world, means that some of the poorest, least educated people now have a window on life in the rich world. In October 2005, to mark his fiftieth birthday, Microsoft's Bill Gates spoke about how his company was spending hundreds of millions of dollars creating a virtual planet. He described how it would be possible to log on anywhere in the world and literally navigate your way through the streets of London. In this virtual walkabout you'd be able to enter even the smartest store in Bond Street and have a look at what's on offer. If that isn't a 'come on', I'm not sure what is. It's like waving a loaf of bread in front of a hungry man and being surprised when he makes a grab for it. The age-old admonition 'look, but don't touch' is simply not going to do the business. There is no barrier high enough or wide enough that will withstand this force of history, for that is what migration is. By simply trying to slam the door in people's faces all we achieve is to humiliate and degrade them.

It makes you wonder why anyone wanted to come here and why those who were already here didn't think about heading back home. After all, most of them never really meant to settle here, not for good. At least that's what they told themselves. They thought that they might be like the colonisers. Hang around till they had squeezed everything they could from the place and then retire to the home country with enough money to see them through old age. If it was good enough for the whites to do it in our country, why shouldn't we go and do it in theirs? They were just going to do it in reverse. That's what they told their friends as they prepared to leave for Britain. I'll be back, they said, and what's more, they meant it. But little by little, imperceptibly, Britain got under their skin. Year by year, despite the rain and the racism, they started putting down roots, or their children did. They started to look around at some of their neighbours, the ones who stayed separate, the ones who wouldn't change, and they said, 'That's not right.' They told their wives, the women who had once been taunted by 'ruffians' on the high street, that with all its faults this place was still better than the country they had left. That is the moment the migrant becomes British. It's not the day the immigration department put the 'leave to remain' stamp in the passport. That was nothing compared to the very private moment when he realised he wants to be of this place, not just in it. It is the tragedy of race relations in Britain that more immigrants haven't talked about this moment of transition. It is even more of a tragedy that they believe no one would want to listen.

We made very slow progress up the stairs. I couldn't help noticing the way the slippers had become lopsided, furry moulds of the gait and tread of the woman who now had to take a couple of deep breaths as she approached the first landing. A uniform twelve inches above each floral-carpeted step the wallpaper was all scuffed up, as if someone with a tiny scraper had given up on the tedious job of stripping it away. 'It's the cat,' she said. 'She's so naughty, but I don't know what I would do without her,' said Betty Allen, her accent still rich with its Caribbean lilt. 'She's my company now.' Betty was taking me to her bedroom to show me the dresses she used to wear in the old days when they used to go dancing. That was when they were new here.

There they were, still wrapped up in cellophane, as if she'd just brought them back from the dry cleaner's. Betty *had* brought them back from the dry cleaner's but it wasn't yesterday, it wasn't last week or last month or even last year. It was in the early sixties. That's the time she was now thinking of as she pulled the creamy ankle-length dress down from the wardrobe and held it against her body. 'It's a long time since I got into this.' She fingered the label. 'John Charles. I can't remember where I got this one.' She put it back on the rail and pulled off another one. 'This was always my favourite.' It was a long, light green waisted jacket under which she wore a dress with a patterned bodice in pastel pinks and blues. 'I got this one at D. H. Evans.'

Betty had an eye for clothes. She used to work in just the right place to do some window shopping. For a while she was a ticket collector at Knightsbridge Underground station.

'I even went into Harrods. I used to try on the hats and jackets. You know, spin around in the mirror. Used to get some pretty funny looks from the staff there, mind. I used to do it in the lunch break. Sometimes, if I had a bit of money, I'd even have coffee and a cake.'

These were the early days, when Betty and people like her still thought everything was possible and when the views of the English people she knew hadn't hardened into indifference.

'We used to go to the West End, even Park Lane. There was no problem as long as you were dressed nicely and didn't make noise. We wouldn't go into town till about midnight and then we'd dance till the morning. We used to look like penguins shuffling out of the dance halls in our high heels.'

Betty Allen was our neighbour for twelve years. She still lives in Stoke Newington in east London, less than half a mile away from where she had her first lodgings in 1956. Back in Jamaica she was a 'lady's maid'. She worked for the English wife of a German who ran a brewing business. One of their products was Captain Morgan rum. 'I used to have to lay out her clothes and things.' She left without telling her employers. 'I didn't like the work. I wanted to do things for myself.'

It wasn't just the job she was fed up with; it was Jamaica, or her life in Jamaica. Her mother had died when she was thirteen and Betty lost her father seven years later. 'My second brother did his best to look after me. But you know he had two stepchildren, his own children, his wife and there was me. I remember going to his wedding and I was barefoot.' She knew someone who knew someone who had gone to Britain and they seemed to be doing all right. So Britain it was.

And that is how she ended up standing outside 77 Stoke Newington Church Street on a damp and foggy sort of day. Those were the days before gentrification. It was the sort of place the taxi drivers would avoid if they could. The son of another friend lived at the address. There were four flats in the building. The basement, two floors and the attic. She was in one of the middle ones.

'There was a kitchen, a dining room and living room all in one. There was a bedroom and a bathroom. In the evening we had to decide how we were going to sleep. Well there was this West Indian man who already had the sofa in the front room. And my friend's friend and his wife had their bedroom. You know where they said I should sleep that night? Right there in that bed! I was so embarrassed. But it was cold so that's what we did – all three of us in the one bed.'

Within days of her arrival Betty had a job as a seamstress in a Jewish clothes factory up the road in Dalston. Pretty soon she had enough money to move into the attic with a friend when it became vacant. Later still, after she got the London Transport job, she took the basement on her own. It was the start of a typical immigrant journey. There was marriage, there were children, and in her case, there was a divorce.

And there was the race business. Like many West Indians Betty belonged to a credit union club. Everybody put money into it and every week it was someone's turn to get what was in the pot. It was a way of getting credit, because the banks were not too keen on lending to them in those days. Once, when it was Betty's turn, she got about £40. She put it in what she thought was going to be a safe place but it was stolen.

'I knew it had to be someone in the building,' she said, still angry at the thought.

'Did you tell the police?'

'Of course I did. But you know the first thing they said to me? "So where did you get so much money?" Can you imagine the cheek of those men. I had a good mind to throw them out there and then.'

It was her first brush with the petty racism that blighted so many lives. It wasn't her last either. That kind of attitude was never enough to derail a person but it was enough to breed a kind of apathy and cynicism.

'So has it been worth it, Betty?'

'What you talking about?'

'I mean coming over here. Do you sometimes wish you had gone back to Jamaica?'

'You must be joking. Jamaica is not so special, you know. There's plenty of problems there too. I escaped all that.'

Betty looked around the room. At the faux-leather sofa, the piano, at the framed certificates from St Michael's church up the road, and at Cindy her beloved cat.

'You know, George, I made a good life for myself here. This is my home now. I see lots of people pack up and go, and soon as they get there they want to come back. No, I'm not leaving old England.'

My guess is that Betty's attachment to Britain is mirrored in hundreds of thousands of homes across the country. Betty, like so many other older immigrants, looks back at a golden age, even if all the evidence suggests it was far from idyllic. If they remember the good times, it is because dwelling on the bad times would make a nonsense of that decision in a faraway place in a long-gone era when coming to Britain seemed the right thing to do. And by and large, it has worked for them. They have made a life for themselves even if it's not exactly the one they dreamed about when they first set foot on these shores.

In her own gentle way Betty has overcome the prejudice she found. Through her worship, through her work, and above all through her language, she has forged relationships across the racial divide. But there are many other immigrants who have not been so well equipped to deal with Britain's ambivalence to their arrival. Like so many minorities throughout history, they have preferred the security of the enclave to the risks involved in branching out. In choosing to settle for a microcosm of the place they left behind, they have been aided and abetted by a social policy that has put a premium on diversity. Under multicultural-ism, parts of Britain are beginning to look like another country.

4

Another Country

Joshua Theobald knows all about being different. When he walks from his home in Bow, down Upper North Street and through his school gate, there is hardly anyone who looks or sounds like he does. His pallid skin, his red hair, his language, his accent – all of it marks him out as an outsider. Joshua's experience is the mirror image of what I went through all those years ago. For me, arriving at boarding school in 1967 meant an abrupt and unnatural dislocation from the culture of my home. So it is for Joshua, except for one crucial difference. He is a stranger in his own land. It's as if he has walked into another country. You see, he's English; English as they come, but at Mayflower Primary School in the London Borough of Tower Hamlets that is an unusual thing to be.

In the borough that was once home to the quintessential cockney, there are areas where the English are an ethnic minority. When I phoned the head teacher at Mayflower to find out how many English families had children at the school, she had no problem finding the answer. They are conspicuous by their rarity. There are only three. When I asked where all the other children came from, Lisa Zychowicz, herself the product of a previous wave of immigration, rattled off a list that tells its own story about what is happening in the world around Britain. The latest entrants to the school are from eastern Europe. There are children from Poland, Lithuania, Albania and Bulgaria. As for the rest, there are two Somali families, one West Indian family, one Thai family, one Chinese family and two Vietnamese families. But they are all dwarfed by the number of children whose families came to Britain from Bangladesh. They make up 92 per cent of the school roll.

Joshua says he knew he was different as soon as he started at the school. He was six at the time.

'I knew only one other white boy,' he told me. We were sitting in the head teacher's office about half an hour before lessons got underway. The autumn sun shone through the window, catching Josh's face and hair, highlighting just how fair he is. He sat there, hands tucked under his thighs, with Lisa and his mother, Michelle, for company.

'What, even when you were that small you knew about things like that?'

'I knew he was my only white friend.' The other boy's name is Jack. They are best mates. They live on the same estate. They've known each other since they were two going on three.

'So who are your other friends?' Joshua reeled off a list of names. Suffice it to say that there was no Bill, David, Shane or Christopher.

'And at break time what language do you all speak?'

'When they speak to me they speak English, but the rest of the time it's mainly their own language.'

'What's that?'

'Bengali.'

'Do you know any Bengali?'

'I know a few words. Some of the bad ones,' he said with an impish smile. 'And I know some numbers.'

'And do you like it when they speak Bengali to each other?'

'I don't mind. It's just that I don't know what they are saying. You know, if they are saying bad things.'

'And do they say bad things?'

'No. It's just that they are all together. I'd like to know more of their language. Sometimes I feel different.' If Josh did try to learn their language, as he put it, he would be trying to pick up a dialect spoken in just one part of Bangladesh. The vast majority of the Bangladeshis in the borough of Tower Hamlets originally came from Sylhet.

'Do your school friends come to your home? Or do you go to their homes?'

'I've played outside their houses. I don't think they are allowed to bring people in.'

'What about having them over to your place, then? Maybe for a birthday party or something?'

'I did invite them at the beginning but none of them came. They said they would but the next day at school they said their mum wouldn't let them.'

Till then Michelle had let her son do the talking.

'I think it's because we have dogs. The Bengali children are all frightened of dogs.' It felt to me as if she was searching for an explanation. For Michelle to accept that the reason the Bangladeshi boys haven't been to her house might be because they simply don't want to or because they are not familiar with the social etiquette of playground friendship or even because they are discouraged from doing so would be like a kick in the teeth. It would be a blow to everything she's trying to be. Michelle could have been like the friends who told her that she was mad to send Josh to Mayflower because the place was 'full of Pakis'. She could so easily have given way to the racist reflex. But she didn't. She wanted to make it work. She has that rare quality – a mother willing to live by her principles in a situation where many others would have cut and run.

'So, Josh, you've never had them for a sleepover or something?'

'No. But Jack comes.'

So after all that, after all these years, it's still Josh and Jack. Best friends. Just like they were when their mums got to know each other on the estate. Michelle has given it her best shot, but when it comes to secondary school for Josh she'll do things differently. She'll be looking for somewhere more mixed. Somewhere more white.

'It's not about being racist,' she says. 'I'd be more worried about what would happen to Josh. I'd worry about it being racist the other way. He's a sensitive boy and you could get bullying. I've got to think about the social side of things.' And who can blame her?

It was early in the autumn term when I visited Mayflower Primary school. Lisa, the head teacher, had organised an induction for support staff. It was in one of the top-floor rooms. Next to the speaker, on a flip chart, I noticed the title of the morning session: 'Welcome to the diversity and equality workshop'. There they were, the buzzwords of multiculturalism. It's as if no one had actually looked into any of the classrooms. There was nothing multicultural about Mayflower Primary School. One community, one culture dominates this school.

That, of course, is not how Lisa Zychowicz sees it. As she says, when she takes school assembly all she sees is a hall full of eager pupils, not an experiment in multiculturalism, far less evidence that it has failed. 'I think things are changing here. We have a waiting list for our English class for mothers. Four Bangladeshi parents have joined the governing body, three of them are women.' She feels the Sylheti community can be encouraged to open up. On a visit to Bangladesh to familiarise herself with the country with which so many of her pupils are still connected she noticed that people were more open than the community here in England. 'There are valuable lessons to be learned from what's happening in Bangladesh,' she says.

Lisa's enthusiasm is reflected in the school's performance. The previous occasion on which it was checked by government inspectors – back in 2001 – it was deemed to be an 'improving' school. And in 2004 Mayflower came eighth out of sixty-five primary schools in the borough when measured for the progress made by pupils – the so-called value-added score. But progress up the league table is of little comfort to parents who want something more than test results for their children.

The irony is that there are some parents on the other side of this segregated community who also want to see more mixing but feel let down by officialdom. Mohammed Shahid Ali lives with his wife, Fatima, and three sons in a two-bedroomed flat on the Robin Hood Gardens Estate. Their frustrations range from living in a flat that has been waterlogged with leaks ten times in the twelve years they've lived there to an inability to find white friends for their children. 'If he don't meet others how can he handle job where he have to mix with people,' asks Shahid.

Shahid's one aim in life is to ensure that his sons do not end up following him in the taxi trade (a job he first did on the streets of New York) or waiting on tables in a curry house. He understands only too well that to break out of the cycle of low-skill, low-paid jobs that so many of his fellow immigrants are caught in his boys will need to develop the social skills that come from being around the children of white families. But there's little prospect of that. He told me that at Woolmore Primary School where his two younger children studied less than 10 per cent of the children were from non-Bangladeshi families. And at Stepney Green Secondary School where his eldest boy was a pupil the only non-Bangladeshi child in his class was from a Chinese family. In his eyes the answer is obvious: 'There are some schools with lots of white childrens, so Borough should mix them up.'

If school is an incubator for life, Mayflower's children start with a handicap. The Bangladeshi children can spend six years there without ever seeing British life first-hand, only through the limited window of the national curriculum. And children like Josh go through school life in a no-man's-land, cut off from the culture of their parents but estranged from the heritage and traditions of those he spends most of his waking hours with.

For decades now what's happening at Mayflower and so many other schools has been passed off as multiculturalism, but by any honest measure of what's occurring on the ground it is a form of segregation. The result of racist housing policies in the seventies and eighties? Almost certainly. The consequence of a self-imposed ghetto where parents prefer the security of their own kind? Without doubt. In many other parts of Britain, too, we have separate development, a state of affairs that apartheid's social engineers once dreamed of and for which they were roundly condemned in the court of international opinion.

Unlike South Africa, though, this form of separate development is the exception rather than the rule and it has occurred largely by accident rather than design. But it is no less alarming for that. The places where communities have become segregated – such as Tower Hamlets – also happen to be the places of greatest deprivation. It is a combustible combination which bodes ill for wider community relations. I'm convinced the answer lies not in getting rid of multiculturalism altogether, still less in trying to end the diverse flow of people to Britain, but in trying to resurrect its original goal – the mixing of people of different races on an equal footing. Like a garden that has been allowed to run wild, multiculturalism has given rise to a plethora of policies and practices that have little to do with its founding principles. It's time to get the secateurs out, time to cut back the extraneous growth.

One could start with the language teaching policy at Tower Hamlets, itself a hand-me-down from central government, which illustrates what a muddle multiculturalism has got us into. In schools across the borough head teachers have recognised that trying to improve their pupils' English is a lost cause so long as they go home to families where English is rarely, if ever, spoken. Their enlightened response has been to arrange after-school classes for parents – especially the mothers. Lisa Zychowicz's success at Mayflower is not necessarily mirrored across the borough. At another primary school (where the only non-Bangladeshi children in the final year were an English girl, a Chinese pupil and two Somalis) only about ten to fifteen parents attend evening classes, and that after a lot of 'prodding and pushing'.

But in a multicultural world English classes for parents would be far too simple a solution. In a classic case of conflicting policies, Tower Hamlets Council also pays for after-hours Bengali classes for the children. In a policy that began in the seventies, local government has taken on the responsibility of nurturing the 'mother tongue'. And since that made it sound as if the language was foreign – heaven forbid – nowadays these extra sessions are called 'community language classes'. And while we are on the subject of the language to use when talking about language, the multicultural experts would never dream of simply saying that too many children have a poor grasp of English. No, officially they are classified as having EAL – English as an Additional Language. Out of a total school population of about 37,000 children in the borough, 25,000 fall into this category. When I inquired about 5,000 children – mostly Bangladeshi – were taking these classes. According to one official, it costs the local tax-payer about a million pounds a year. With some ninety languages spoken in the borough, you might wonder what the full financial implications of the policy might be.

So when Joshua Theobald longs for more of his Mayflower schoolmates to speak English in the playground, he might, with some justification, blame an official policy that has put a premium on diversity at the expense of encouraging a degree of uniformity. Though it almost certainly was not intentional, this aspect of multiculturalism has exacerbated a situation in which an English child can feel as if he is living in another country.

Mayflower is not unique. According to a report by the Young Foundation, in the borough of Tower Hamlets alone there are another sixteen primary schools in which pupils of Bangladeshi origin account for more than 90 per cent of the names on the classroom registers. The concentration of Bangladeshi children is as stark in secondary schools. In three schools they make up more than 80 per cent of the pupils, while in another two they account for over 95 per cent of the school roll. So in five of the fifteen secondary schools in the borough, children of Bangladeshi origin dominate the classrooms.

And what is true for Tower Hamlets is true for areas right across England. In 2004 two academics at Bristol University – Simon Burgess and Deborah Wilson – published some findings that should send a chill down the spine of anyone who cares about race relations in Britain. What they found was that far from breaking down barriers between communities, schools may actually be bolstering them. The research suggests that schools may be even more segregated than the communities they serve. Burgess and Wilson based their study on the Annual Schools Census for 2001. It is a meticulously argued piece of work, full of references to previous studies, caveats about the limits of their observations, comparisons with similar studies in the United States, charts, maps and diagrams. It even has a formula:

$$D = \frac{1}{2} \sum_{i=1}^{N} \frac{BAC_i}{BAC_{total}} - \frac{(ACC-BAC)_1}{(ACC-BAC)_{total}}$$

It's called the index of dissimilarity. Happily, their conclusions appear in language you and I can understand:

Our main findings are that ethnic segregation in England's schools is high . . . We identify areas of particularly high segregation, especially for pupils of Asian origin.

And here's the sting in the tail:

These areas coincide almost exactly with the locations of urban unrest in the summer of 2001.

It may be on the last page of their research paper, but Burgess and Wilson appear to be saying that there could be a link between segregated schools and the unprecedented violent disaffection that disfigured the cities of Bradford, Oldham and Burnley in 2001. It may be stretching their research, but could it be that the radicalisation of the young men who bombed London's transport system on 7 July 2005, and the ones who tried to do the same two weeks later was a by-product of the segregation these researchers found?

Forty-odd years ago the playground at St John's College in Portsmouth was the place where I learned how to become British, but today, for tens of thousands of immigrant children, school may be the place that prevents them from becoming British. It's just possible that their very isolation breeds an indifference, even contempt, for the nation outside their enclave. If you want to understand the mentality of the enclave, there is no better place to go than Bradford.

It was the kind of conversation I'd had in a hundred taxis in a hundred cities:

'Park Grove Hotel, please.'

'Park Hotel?'

'No, no – Park GROVE Hotel.'

'Grope Hotel?'

'NO – GroVVVVVe Hotel! With a V!'

'Don't know V. Where is V?'

Life as a foreign correspondent had been punctuated by these sometimes comical, always infuriating encounters with drivers who could barely find their way out of an airport car park, let alone to the destination I had in mind. In this case, though, I wasn't on assignment in a strange land, and it wasn't an airport. It was Bradford railway station in the north-west of England, though it very quickly began to feel like another country.

I had taken the last train out of London's King's Cross. It was after 11.00 on a Friday night in May. In fact it was 6 May, the day Tony Blair was confirmed as the first Labour leader to have taken his party to three successive victories at the polls. A little earlier that evening I had presented the *Six O'Clock News*, as I had done every day during the seemingly endless campaign. After weeks of listening to politicians and their view of Britain, it felt good to be immersed in life as it is actually played out. And frankly, there is no better place to eavesdrop on the things that preoccupy a nation than a standard-class seat on a train heading away from cosmopolitan London.

A day that I had described as 'historic' to an audience of millions just hours before now felt as mundane as any other. Anyone who looked thirty-five or over was trying to read a newspaper and was either in the process of falling asleep with the effort or had already done so. Flaccid faces bobbed about on droopy shoulders as pages of newsprint gradually fell through the gap between knee and tabletop. Anyone younger seemed to be on a mobile phone, apparently happy for those of us who were still awake to listen in on one side of a conversation that invariably involved the night before or the one to come. I did what I always do – try to guess what the person on the other end of the line might be saying. I always come to the conclusion that my imagined conversations are far juicier than the reality.

Next to me a Nigerian man watched a DVD on his laptop. I knew he was Nigerian because the actors in the film – which I monitored with what I hoped was an ever-so-subtle sideways glance – were wearing the national costume. It appeared to be a comedy. Every now and then he would giggle away to himself. At least that was what it must have seemed like to him, though, as is the way with anyone lost in the acoustic world of earphones, his reaction could be heard at the other end of the carriage. I found myself wondering if he was one of those immigrants who was supposed to be misusing our collective hospitality. During the election campaign immigration had become an issue and there was much discussion about controlling numbers and kicking out anybody who shouldn't be here. You knew, instinctively, that the politicians, of whatever persuasion, were not talking about Australians or Italians, but people like my travelling companion that night.

It was all change at Leeds. I boarded the two-coach Metro line for the short journey to Bradford Interchange. There were a few commuter types who got on first, neatly arranging their briefcases, their umbrellas and their ready-to-heat meals-for-one around their feet. It looked as if the train was going to be virtually empty, but with just a couple of minutes to spare it filled up with the Friday-night generation. It was cold and wet outside (I had a coat on top of my blazer) but they streamed in dressed as if they'd been out for a summer stroll. The boys, at least they looked young enough to be boys, wore shirts and the girls were wearing implausibly skimpy vests with vestigial straps that left their shoulders bare. They clambered on in unisex groups, sat apart – males on one side of the aisle, females on the other – and filled the air in between with banter. With every stop the group dwindled. Through the rain-splattered window I watched them head off into the night, the boys all balls and bravado while the girls, now that the night was over, tottered on their high heels and hunched their round, white, pimply shoulders against the weather they'd barely noticed just fifteen minutes earlier. Bradford was the last stop.

And so it was that I came to be sitting in the back seat of a Toyota trying to help the driver find my hotel. I'd printed a map off the internet and now pulled it out of my rucksack. He switched on the overhead light and turned round. If I'd been worried about getting to my hotel before, now I was alarmed. Of all the taxi drivers I could have ended up with, I appeared to have picked a man with one eye! He had a lazy left eyelid which seemed to decide for itself when and for how long it would stay open. He turned the map round 360 degrees and then rotated it the other way. His forehead creased as he concentrated on the piece of paper. It didn't inspire confidence.

'Ask the controller,' I said. A blank Cyclops stare. I pointed to the two-way radio set through which a voice was blaring out instructions in a language I couldn't understand. Every now and then I'd catch the odd word or two in English. 'Drop off', 'anybody else' were a couple I jotted down.

'What about your controller, maybe he'll know.'

'Okay, okay, I ask.'

I couldn't be sure if the driver was asking the right question until he got to the name of the hotel. This time he had it bang on, but the controller's reply made me feel like I was heading into my own version of *Groundhog Day*.

'Park Hotel?'

'Give me that thing,' I shouted. It was late at night, I'd just finished four of the most gruelling weeks as a newsreader, the following day was going to be tight with interviews and I wanted my bed, a bed, any bed.

'Look, I've already explained it to your driver and shouldn't have to explain it to you. The place is called Park Grove Hotel and I've showed him on the map that it's somewhere off Keighley Road.'

'Is it near the Mitsubishi garage?'

'How the bloody hell should I know? I'm here for the first time and if I knew where the hell the Mitsubishi garage was I wouldn't be sitting here talking to you over a microphone, would I?'

'Please don't be using dirty language.'

'You're a fine one to talk about language. Some plain and simple English would be nice.' Well, that was what I wanted to say but I didn't. Instead I apologised. It occurred to me that I should treat this a bit more like one of my reporting assignments abroad. Over the years I had come to realise that in most countries – especially Muslim ones – the casual swearing that we take in our stride is considered deeply offensive.

'Look, all I know is that it's off the Keighley Road and opposite the Bradford School of Management.'

'Oh, you should have told the driver. Everybody is knowing the management school.'

So it was my fault. At least we were on our way. Now I could do what I had always done on assignment. Taxi drivers are often the reporter's first source of information. For me it was a way of acclimatising. The taxi driver is the first friend you have in a foreign land, and survival in a strange and often dangerous place is about making friends. This wasn't a war zone, but it was beginning to feel quite strange. In any case, old habits die hard.

'So how long have you been a taxi driver?'

'Twenty-seven days,' he said with a brevity and accuracy at odds with everything else that had happened that evening. I could see why finding the hotel had turned out to be such a palaver.

'Have you just come to England?'

'England very nice.'

'No, I was asking whether you have just come to England. Where were you before you started driving this taxi?'

'I work in textile.'

'In a factory?'

'Yes.'

'What was the factory called?'

'John Haggis,' he said. At least that was what it sounded like. In fact the company, now closed down, was called John Haggas.

'How long were you working in the factory?'

'Fifteen years.'

'Fifteen years! You mean fifteen months.'

'I no understand.'

'Have you been in Bradford for fifteen years? You came here in 1990?'

'Yes.'

'Fifteen years very long time. If you came here fifteen years ago, why you don't speak English very good?' By now I had slipped into the broken English that had become like a second language on the road.

'English no good. All mans in textile is Asia. Speak Pakistan language.'

This was why I had come to Bradford. It was the first inkling that what many said about the place was true. Countless newspaper articles, academic theses and government reports had alluded to the way in which Bradford's Asian community had evolved into a world of its own. Now I had some first-hand evidence.

I sat back and peered ahead. The windscreen wipers left a streak across the glass, blurring everything, making the signs and landmarks indistinct. It added to the sense that I was somewhere different. Inside, all I could see was the driver's skullcap and his prayer beads swinging from the rearview mirror. On the radio, the controller's voice barked out orders to drivers, who replied in the Mirpuri dialect of Punjabi. It felt familiar – not because it was in England, but because it could have been anywhere in the world. In fact, as I would discover on my visits, I was, indeed, somewhere else. I was entering a version of Kashmir, here in Bradford.

If you stand at the bottom of Oak Lane and look up the hill, your eye is drawn to Lister's Mill. It stands there, still solid and majestic, a brick-and-mortar tribute to Bradford's heyday as the centre of Britain's textile industry. Today the urban developers have moved in. The show flat is open – offering not just a home, but a lifestyle. The sales staff are hoping to sell the apartments – in the jargon of regeneration, no one talks about flats any more – to thirty-something couples with their penchant for mounting debts, Alessi corkscrews and Kitchenaid food processors. It's a far cry from the days when you could hardly see from one end of the courtyard to the other – so thick was the smoke and soot that billowed out of Lister's Mill's chimney and many more dotted around the city. If William Blake had a place in mind when he wrote of England's 'dark satanic mills', this was surely it. Lister's Mill is as good a place as any in the city to begin to understand the evolution of Bradford's inner wards into an Asian enclave. The migration of Kashmiris to Bradford is inextricably linked to the needs of the textile industry. It doesn't entirely explain how the city has ended up with a kind of separate development, but it does illustrate how the process began.

The business of spinning yarn and weaving cloth in and around what is now Bradford goes back to the sixteenth century, when it was an extra source of income for farmers. What started out as a cottage industry, with work contracted out to neighbours and friends, had, by the Victorian era, become a massive and lucrative business that made Bradford a focal point in the global trade in textiles. The Wool Exhange, on Market Street, is testament to the enormous wealth generated by the manufacture of textiles, especially fine worsted fabrics. In a photograph of the exchange at the turn of the last century, there are hundreds of traders posing for the camera in suits and hats, but they are dwarfed by the sheer scale of the building. Today its cavernous interior has been remodelled into a Waterstone's bookshop.

The disruption in world trade after the Great War and the economic slump of the 1920s saw contraction in the industry. Tens of thousands of workers lost their jobs in what today's managers would call 'right-sizing'. Some 400 textile firms shut down in this period. The decade before the Second World War saw a marked improvement in business, helped along by the imposition of 50 per cent import duties on foreign textiles and the emergence of new chain stores like Marks and Spencer, which began to change the clothing habits of the average man and woman.

Bradford's manufacturing industries, none more so than textiles, had always relied on inward migration for labour. At first, in the late eighteenth century, the prospect of work attracted families from the surrounding rural areas and from as far afield as Cornwall and East Anglia. In the early nineteenth century there was large-scale migration from Ireland. As the century wore on, their numbers were replenished by an influx of Italians. In the 1930s east European Jews fleeing the Nazis found their way to Bradford. And after the end of the Second World War, Ukrainians, Poles and Yugoslavs got work in the textile mills.

By the 1950s, Bradford's textile factories faced competition at home and abroad. The emergence of new and faster-growing industries in the region meant the mill owners no longer had a captive workforce. If they wanted to hang on to workers they had to offer higher wages. That in turn meant they lost any competitive advantage they might have had over other textile manufacturers in Europe and newer entrants to the industry like Japan. Bradford had to produce more for less if it was to survive in this new dog-eat-dog world.

Enter the Asians. In the early fifties the mills switched to twenty-four-hour production with the introduction of a night shift. In time-honoured fashion it was the most recent immigrants who ended up with the worst jobs. Just as everybody else was trooping home, they were waking up in inner-city 'flophouses' (some men even shared their beds on a rotation basis) and getting ready to walk through the factory gates. This twilight world was the beginning of a form of social exclusion that divides Bradford even now.

The first Asian immigrants came here in the mid-1950s. At first they were drawn from both India and Pakistan (East Bengal had yet to become the independent state of Bangladesh). The Pakistanis, largely uneducated, ended up in the textile mills while the Indians found jobs in the rapidly expanding public transport system. Within this embryonic immigrant world the Indians were an elite of sorts – many sent home studio portraits of themselves dressed in their driver's or conductor's uniform, showing off their new watch and fountain pen. But numerically, at least, they were soon dwarfed by the sheer numbers of Pakistanis who came to keep the spinning wheels turning.

'In those days, I'm talking about the fifties and sixties, you could arrive here one night and land yourself a job the very next day,' says Abdul Bary Malik, who, in a rare exception to the general rule, started in the mills but escaped into his own food preparation business. From their earliest days in Britain, back in the mid seventies, Abdul and his wife Amina have made a conscious decision to avoid the clannishness that was already developing within the Asian community. Today they live in Low Moor, a predominantly white area. 'I have always held the view that living in Britain means living with white people, being their neighbours. If I want to live with Pakistanis I would rather do it in Pakistan itself,' he says. He is a devout Muslim and his family is originally from Pakistan, but a childhood in Kenya, where his father worked for the East African Railways, has given him a semi-detached view of his fellow immigrants. 'In the early days, in the seventies, the ones that came here were honest, hard-working people. Nowadays they screw the system, there is a culture of depending on benefit. But it wasn't like that in the beginning.'

The men came over on their own; if they were married they left their families behind. Contracts were restricted to two years, but in an attempt to ensure an uninterrupted flow of workers, the mill owners allowed those who had worked through their contracts to be replaced by a relative – usually a brother. This revolving-door policy was ideal for the Pakistani families. One man could earn money and, by living in shared accommodation in the most run-down and therefore cheapest areas, send a sizeable proportion of his wages back home. Meanwhile, a male relative could stay behind to keep the family on the straight and narrow, knowing that his turn would come in due course.

For the factory owners the economic logic of this system was impeccable – a self-perpetuating stream of men who would work for the kind of wages that gave the mills the competitive edge they needed. But it had two unintended consequences. First, by restricting the labour pool to relatives of the first wave, it concentrated the workforce ethnically. They all came from a single rural district of Pakistan around the town of Mirpur in Kashmir province. Second, because one brother could always be followed by another, families became totally dependent on remittances. There was little incentive for the brother back home to earn money locally, or if he did, the business was almost entirely reliant on cash sent from Bradford.

On top of this, a decision made far away in the then Pakistani capital of Karachi was to help change the face of this west Yorkshire city. In the late 1950s the government of Ayub Khan decided to build a dam on the Mangla River. Mirpur district, tucked into the outer foothills of the Himalayas, was an ideal location. The project received the enthusiastic backing of the

Washington-based World Bank, which at the time was a champion of these large-scale infrastructural developments around the world. The dam was duly completed in 1966, but while it brought irrigation and hydro-electric power downstream, it left a trail of desolation upstream. In all, eighteen villages were inundated by the reservoir which rose behind the dam wall. Many of the displaced headed for British towns and cities such as Birmingham, Bradford, Manchester and Oldham.

In 1953, there were 350 Asians in Bradford; by 1961 there were 3,457 Pakistanis and 1,512 Indians. In 1959 there were just two Asian butchery-grocery businesses and three cafés; by 1971 there were 260 Asian businesses, and thirty years later there were 250 Asian restaurants alone.

The Mangla dam helped to change the character of immigration from Mirpur to Bradford. What had started off as a conventional flow of migrant labour was transformed into a wholesale resettlement of hundreds of families. The arrival of women and children meant a relatively sudden demand for large houses, and the only place these were available at anything like affordable prices was in the rundown city centre. Black and Asian immigrants across Britain found landlords unwilling to let them decent accommodation, so many families clubbed together and bought houses, sharing the kitchen and bathroom, and sometimes letting rooms out to newer immigrants. Social housing wasn't an option either. During the mid-sixties white families were twenty-six times more likely than their black or Asian counterparts to secure a council home. It set a pattern that still survives. Today, 90 per cent of Asians in Bradford own their own homes. Black and other ethnic minority groups occupy only 3 per cent of council housing in Bradford.

The Pakistani immigrants were rural peasants, deeply conservative in their religious and social views. They brought with them many traditional practices that were, even then, being whittled away in Pakistan, especially in the towns. But here, cut off from their kith and kin back home, and fearful of what they found in Bradford, the immigrant community went into a form of suspended animation. 'I've been going back to Pakistan every other year,' says Abdul Bary Malik. 'I've noticed how people there have been moving on. It's always a shock when I come back to Bradford. Here we have got stuck.'

By 1971 there were already 30,000 immigrants in Bradford. The census of that year records them as New Commonwealth citizens. In practice they were mostly from Pakistan. The vast majority were already crammed into the four wards of the city centre. Early attempts to control the flow of newcomers – such as the 1962 Immigration Act – served only to hasten the rush, as families tried to get as many relatives as possible into Britain before the door was finally shut tight. So as early as thirty years ago, both the geography and the nature of Bradford's Asian ghetto had been shaped. The city's people – both Asian and white – live with the consequences even now.

Today, the ring road around the city is like a boundary – the inner wards are almost entirely peopled by Asians. In three of them Asians outnumber white people by at least two to one, and in another two the numbers are more evenly matched, though white families make up the majority. But even where the statistics appear to show a more mixed population, you would not necessarily see it on the ground because the wards themselves tend to be divided between Asian and white areas. It's not a hard-and-fast rule, but it's a credible enough description of what is actually happening.

In fact the divisions are far more intricate than bald census figures can illustrate. Over and over again during my research, locals corrected my description of two broad categories – Asians and whites. Asif Nasir, who I bumped into on one trip, put it like this: 'Bradford has lots of separate communities. The Patels are in Bradford 7, around Great Horton Road, here in Manningham it is mainly Kashmiris, and the Lahoris are scattered all over the place.' The comment is revealing. The Indian community is referred to not by nationality but by their most common name – Patel. And the Pakistanis are distinguished by the region from which they originally came – Lahore, and Azad (Free) Kashmir.

Victoria Terrace lies in the shadow of Lister's Mill. At one end it runs into Oak Lane, the epicentre of the violence that erupted here back in 2001. The torching of the BMW garage on the street was a defining act. Today the site is empty, awaiting the developers. Businesses owned by Muslims were left largely untouched. They're still there: Café Pakistan, Ifty's Pizzas, and Shiraz Restaurant and Sweet House. At the other end of the terrace is Victoria Road, where the old Anglican church has been leased to the Church of God of Prophecy. The genteel traditions of High Anglican liturgy are out of place and out of time here – it's as if only the more robust worship of the evangelical movement has any chance of survival in this Islamic enclave.

The back-to-back houses in Victoria Terrace are of the style first built for mill workers way back in the first half of the nineteenth century. They are exactly what they sound like – two dwellings share a common wall, one a mirror image of the other. The entrance to the front house is off the street, while access to the other is from a small backyard which you reach through a covered alley running alongside the pair of houses. Today there is sewerage and piped water but little else has changed – except, of course, for the people. Where once the washing lines at the front of the houses might have carried dull Victorian tunics, today they flutter with an assortment of *shalwar kameez* in deep purples and rich greens. A hundred years ago and more the children might have traipsed off in their Sunday best to church, now they head for the mosque and lessons in the Koran.

The wards outside the ring road are where the whites live, though given the way the Asian population is rising, the neat division between inner and outer Bradford is already changing. In the Parekh Report on the future of 'multi-ethnic Britain', the Pakistani population (which is the dominant immigrant community in Bradford) is expected to double by 2020 while the country's white population is likely to stay the same, perhaps even shrink slightly. What is true for the country as a whole is almost certainly true for Bradford.

You know when you have entered the white zone because you start to see evidence of middle England's love affair with gardening. There are window boxes bursting over with the most gaudy petunias, pansies and primulas. This is Ford Focus country, where the men do the DIY and the women choose the colours. As a tribe they stick resolutely to the proverbial 2.2 children per household and tut-tut at the way they're breeding like rabbits down in the city. Mostly they want to be open and tolerant, but they will insist on reading the kind of newspapers which fill them with dread about being swamped by foreigners who sponge off the state – which is the worst sin you can commit in the eyes of these people, who on the whole, pay their way through life.

The division between largely white areas and largely Asian areas is accentuated by the relative prosperity (or not) of the two groups. The Office of the Deputy Prime Minister produced an Index of Deprivation for the whole of England in 2004. What it shows about the distribution of wealth in and around Bradford lends weight to the argument that being Asian means you are also more likely to be poor. Some of the outlying villages of Bradford, such as Rombald, Ilkley and Craven, are amongst the wealthiest 50 per cent in the country. And yet nine of Bradford's twenty-four wards are in the poorest 10 per cent. Most of them are in the Pakistani-dominated inner city. In wards such as Heaton, Keighley South, Undercliffe, Tong, Toller, Bowling, University, Bradford Moor and Little Horton, you can see how poor health, unsatisfactory education, unemployment and disability (just some of the thirty-three measures that make up the index) combine with the refusal or inability of the largely Pakistani population to integrate, creating a ghetto.

Welcome to Bradford – one city, two communities. The division is not new, but its endurance raises questions about race relations in Britain. That there should be such a distinct division of a city along ethnic and racial lines a generation after Britain began a legislative programme to bring about exactly the opposite outcome is staggering. Has Bradford grown apart despite multiculturalism – the principle behind every race-related law

since the Race Relations Act in 1967 – or because of it? Has institutionalised tolerance for diversity led to institutional indifference
to separation? These questions are important because Bradford in
the north-west and Tower Hamlets in the south are merely two
examples in a pattern of urban settlement that is as prevalent as it
is alarming. In Halifax, in Luton, in Southall, in Leicester and so
many other cities where immigrants have settled there is a version
of separate development.

Some research presented in September 2005 by Mike Poulsen,
an Australian academic who looked at changes in Britain's census
data between 1991 and 2001, seem to bear out the growing tendency of certain immigrant groups to live among their own. He
found that the number of people of Pakistani origin who lived in
segregated communities in Bradford and Oldham had trebled
in the decade up to 2001. The number of people of Indian origin in
Leicester – mostly Gujaratis – who live in separate communities
had risen by a third. In these areas they make up over two-thirds
of the local population. Though the degree of separation is not yet
on the scale seen in America – where the average African-
American in Chicago lives in an area that is 75 per cent black – the
trend alone is alarming.

Poulsen would be the first to admit that his findings were a
work in progress, but they appear to be supported by a separate
study. The *Minority Ethnic Groups in Britain* study, published in
November 2004, was also based on a comparison of the 1991 and
2001 census figures. It found, for example, that the proportion of
the population that came from an ethnic minority in the London
Borough of Newham increased from 42 per cent to 61 per cent
over that decade. The study also found that an increase in the
ethnic minority population was often associated with a corres-
ponding decrease in the white population, changing the balance
overall. In some of those inner-city wards in Bradford, for example, the white population decreased by as much as a third. In one
ward the minority population increased from 55 to 69 per cent in
a decade; in another from 54 to 73 per cent.

There is an argument raging among academics about what all this means. Some prefer to describe what's going on as isolation rather than segregation. What they would make of the term I have used – separate development – I don't know. The disagreement over what to call the phenomenon spills over into how to explain its existence. There are those who say the crucial factor is wealth, or the lack of it, while others say race is the defining issue.

The champions of multiculturalism point to other studies which show an apparently opposite trend. In November 2005 Dr Ludi Simpson of Manchester University cited evidence that the number of mixed neighbourhoods in England and Wales was increasing. Also comparing changes in the census data between 1991 and 2001 he found that the number of mixed electoral wards had risen from 964 to 1,070. There was a total of 8,850 wards in England and Wales. Dr Simpson predicted that by 2010 the number of such mixed wards will have risen to 1,300.

But the threshold for what constitutes a mixed neighbourhood is quite low. Any ward in which at least 10 per cent of the population is from an ethnic minority qualifies. By that standard even some of the predominantly white wards in a city like Bradford could be described as mixed. There's no doubt that a combination of overcrowding in the inner-city wards and rising incomes has meant that some Pakistani-origin families have breached the ring road and settled beyond the enclave. To my mind that's hardly a test of integration. The migration of people from one area into another – which has been going on for decades – says nothing about whether people are actually mixing.

Trevor Phillips, the head of the Commission for Racial Equality, now appears to favour the word segregation, with the implication that immigrants are isolated by race as well as economics. In a speech he gave in September 2005 Phillips warned that we in Britain 'are sleepwalking our way to segregation. We are becoming strangers to each other, and we are leaving communities to be marooned outside the mainstream.'

The speech generated a huge amount of attention in the press, but in a sense Phillips was only catching up with what others (including myself in an article in the *Guardian*) had been saying for some time.

But to blame the emergence of isolated communities solely on the way multiculturalism has developed is a bit like attributing benefit fraud to the existence of a benefit system. It wasn't inevitable that multiculturalism would lead to separation. At its best, multiculturalism helped to protect immigrants from racism and so helped them to reap the rewards of hard work. Multiculturalism created the social space in which so many of us have prospered. If some have been left behind, it is partly to do with their own preference for hanging on to an identity which has more to do with the home they have left than the home they are supposed to be making here in Britain. Multiculturalism was the perfect excuse for those who wanted to ring-fence their communities. In continuing to exert control over their communities, these most conservative elements within the immigrant communities could exploit the ample opportunities afforded under multiculturalism – most notably the public funding of difference in the name of diversity.

However you define it – whether you call it segregation or isolation, whether you think people live in ghettos or enclaves, whether you think it all comes down to race or poverty – one thing is clear: it is happening. You only need to take a walk in any one of the places I have mentioned (and that list is by no means complete) to know that for hundreds of thousands of people the great dream of multiculturalism is not working. Under the banner of diversity we have consigned too many people to an also-ran status. They are trapped on the outside track while the rest of us make progress on the inside one. Of course, class is a factor and economics plays a part, but that is all the more reason to get the race relations policy right.

Rizwana Mahmood knows all about separate development. As a child she crossed the divide on a daily basis. She is the product of a brief experiment in bussing Asian children from Bradford's city centre to schools on the outskirts where there were plenty of white children. The word bussing brings to mind images of frightened black children running the gauntlet of an angry white mob – supposedly something that happened only in America's Deep South. But it happened in west Yorkshire too and – incredible as it seems – for one little girl it was a lot of fun. What's more, to meet her today is to question the hoary old convention that bussing is always bad, that it flows from a racist philosophy, and that anyone who endured it must be damaged for life.

There are many ways to describe Rizwana, but damaged is certainly not one of them.

'Where are you?' Rizwana called me on my mobile. She was late and it occurred to me that it was a question I should be asking her.

'I'm standing on the pavement outside the hotel. Where are you?'

'Well, like you said, I'm on the corner of Park Grove and Keighley Road and I can't see you.' I'd forgotten to mention that Park Grove was a crescent and my hotel was at the other end.

'Stay where you are. I'm walking up to Keighley Road and you should see me any second now.' I'm not sure what I was expecting, but even at a hundred yards I could see that this woman broke the mould. Something about the way she waved at me – the sheer abandon with which her arms semaphored above her head – told me Rizwana Mahmood had something I hadn't yet encountered on the streets of Bradford. The Jewish might call it chutzpah, I'd call it confidence. She stepped round her bright blue (brash would be another description) SUV and shook hands. She was dressed in jeans and a short jacket, and her eyes sparkled.

'Do you want to come home? The rest of the family are still getting up so it should be pretty quiet.'

Home is a large terraced house in Great Horton, an area that has remained racially mixed, largely due to the presence of university students in rented accommodation. I've been to enough

Asian families' homes (including my parents' house) to expect the slightly pungent smell of yesterday's curry cooking as you walk through the door; it seeps into the thick pile carpets and heavy curtains that are their habitual preference. The two – curry and carpets – simply don't go together. Here, we walked into a hallway of stripped wooden floors and white skirting boards, a theme carried through into the sitting room. There were two leather sofas; we took one each. In the bay stood a wooden sculpture of flowers and on the opposite wall a photo of Mecca. Muslim and modern; I made a mental note.

Rizwana's father came to Britain in the early sixties to join an elder brother who worked at the Pirelli factory in Burton-on-Trent. He went back to Pakistan to marry and the couple returned to Britain when Rizwana was a year old. The family moved to Bradford, where Mr Mahmood worked successively in textiles and then at the BBA factory, which made landing gear for Boeing aircraft.

She was a bright child. That much was obvious by the time she was six going on seven, ready for school. Her parents knew it; her neighbours knew it; and most important of all the teachers at the West Bowling language centre knew it. The language centres were a kind of educational limbo – a halfway house where immigrant children could be coached in English before being sent on to primary school, or first school as they called it locally (in Bradford they had first school, middle school and then upper school).

The language centres were an early incarnation of the way the state, in the form of the local education authority, began to assume responsibility for something that might otherwise be expected to be happening at home. Most language experts will tell you that those first pre-school years are crucial. But Bradford's inner-city wards, even in the early seventies, were an English-free zone. Children entered the school system with the most rudimentary grasp of the language of the country they lived in. You can see why the education authority did it – and it was no doubt considered an enlightened policy at the time – but its effect was to absolve parents of the obligation to prepare their children for school. There was little incentive for parents or community leaders to encourage the use of English in the home if the state was going to do the job for them.

It wasn't long before Rizwana was allocated a place at another school – Queensbury, about five miles along the road to Halifax. She would catch a bus every morning with other Asian children. Further along the route white children would start boarding the bus. Pretty soon it would look exactly as a school bus should look in a cosmopolitan city like Bradford – except, of course, that this particular bus was the product of social engineering.

'I remember the bus so well. It was the A56A. My mum would give me about twenty pence every day and before getting on the bus we used to nip into the sweet shop. We had to finish all the sweets on the journey because we weren't allowed to take anything like that into school.'

What the bus gave Rizwana, and eventually her brother as well, was the opportunity to mix with white children, something that was denied to thousands of children then and still is today.

'It was scary at first. I remember it being quite daunting. But quite quickly I made friends. You know, kids are kids.'

As a teenager Rizwana started keeping a 'memories' book, noting down, with hindsight, some of the seminal moments in her young life. On the face of it there is nothing extraordinary about the things she remembers, until you realise that the generation of children who attend Bradford's inner-city schools today couldn't even begin to comprehend what Rizwana is talking about. Here's a sample, taken from the section headed SCHOOL DAYS.

My best friends were: Gary Haylock, Shawn Holdsworth, Fiaqa Iqbal and Fatima Patel. I had the best time of my life with these four although sometimes I ended up having major fights with Fiaqa and Gary.

There are schools in Bradford now where it would be virtually impossible for any child to list both English and Asian pupils among his or her friends. In 2005 there were thirty-eight primary schools in which children from ethnic minorities made up over 75 per cent of the school roll – often the figure was as high as 98 per cent. In some schools the only English children left come from families that are so dysfunctional they are unable or unwilling to take the trouble to relocate their children. In the years since 2000 there has been a small influx of children from eastern Europe – so the only hope left of a racial mix lies not with indigenous white kids but with a new generation of immigrants whose mother tongue is not English either!

Here's another entry from Rizwana's school diary:

The best part of school was: Christmas. I loved Christmas time. Went [sic] Santa came to our party and gave us presents. I loved rubbing my face on his pretend beard. (By the way, I knew Santa wasn't for real, I just liked the presents.)

It's difficult to imagine any latter-day Santa being allowed to be that intimate with a child these days – that too has changed. More importantly, the extent to which Christmas is celebrated varies from school to school. While many of the predominantly white schools have studiously broadened their religious education to include non-Christian religions – marking Diwali and Eid-ul-Fitr is commonplace – the Asian-dominated schools have not necessarily gone the other way. They have become de facto faith schools. In some schools there are separate faith tutors. Occasionally, a local inter-faith centre provides a service which is non-denominational and which tries to look for common ground. It was only in February 2006 that leaders from the country's main faiths – the Church of England, Hinduism, Sikhism, Catholicism, Islam, Judaism and Buddhism – signed a joint statement to promote the teaching of all their religions in school. It was a voluntary agreement with no force in law.

Marking Christmas in a predominantly Muslim school is no more a capitulation to Christianity than celebrating Eid-ul-Fitr or Diwali in a school where most of the children are nominally Christian is a genuflection to Islam or Hinduism. Rizwana is no less a Muslim today for having accepted the odd present from a make-believe Santa when she was a child. What she gained was an experience she could share with millions of other children in this country, even if it had long since lost the religious force it once enjoyed.

Friendship at school spilled over after hours. She was invited to the homes of her white friends and they came to hers. Her parents' openness to this kind of experience was in stark contrast to the attitude of some of their Pakistani neighbours. 'We were looked on as sort of snooty. This wasn't just about the bussing business, I think it was also because my mum was educated and wanted us to be outgoing.'

Rizwana didn't say it in so many words, so let me do it for her – there was and still is a bias against integration within Bradford's Pakistani community. If it was understandable in those early days of immigration when the community was new, it is unconscionable now. And yet it persists – a by-product of the religious and social exclusivity of the community coupled with a failure of the state to offer any viable alternative. To be sure, not all families were as well equipped to reach out to the wider community as the Mahmoods. Rizwana's mother, in particular, was exceptional (her decision to study for a degree in education is proof enough).

In 1975, the Race Relations Board decided that bussing Bradford's Asian children into white communities contravened the Race Relations Act. The board argued that because children were only being bussed in one direction, it was being done on the basis of racial or ethnic identity rather than educational need. But surely that was the whole point! The parents of white children out in the suburbs would no doubt have objected to their children being bussed into inner-city schools, which by definition were underachieving in the most significant area – language. They would have been right, too. It wasn't their children who needed the extra help.

Bussing in Britain differed in one significant way from its more famous counterpart in America. There it was supported and pursued by liberals desperate to smash a hole through the colour bar that still survived in the South. It was opposed by the redneck racists who saw it as yet another assault on their way of life. Here it was the other way around. In Britain it was the left that opposed the policy and social conservatives who were its proponents. The fact that it was a policy designed to integrate immigrant children was lost in the whirlwind of political correctness that swept the country in the seventies and eighties.

The left's response was a kneejerk reaction to the fact that those who called for some action were always white families in areas with growing numbers of immigrants. In those early days of multiculturalism, immigrants who complained were deemed to have a grievance, but white families who voiced their fears ran the risk of being labelled racists. Some of them no doubt were, but there was a wilful refusal to accept that for many white parents the rapid recasting of their communities presented a genuine challenge for which they were ill-equipped and unprepared.

It shouldn't be so difficult to understand what these people were thinking. Immigrants need only to look back at the history of the countries from which they came to get an inkling of what it must feel like to be confronted with foreign customs and ideas. After all, what was it that our parents and grandparents most despised about the British colonialists who lorded it over vast tracts of Asia and Africa? The land-grab aside, wasn't it the way they never really bothered to learn our languages, eat our food or wear our clothes? Generations of colonial subjects were forced to accept a culture that was quite alien to them, and the resentment that bred certainly helped to fuel independence struggles across the world.

In the early sixties in places such as Southall, west London, white parents began to worry that their children would become a minority in schools with an ever-increasing number of Punjabis. And they did have some support from semi-official quarters. The same year of the notorious Smethwick by-election, 1965; the TUC produced a report in which it attributed the failure of ethnic minorities to progress in the workplace to their poor English and unfamiliarity with English customs. To top it all, the Schools Inspectorate argued that large numbers of immigrants were likely to drag standards down.

These were the pressures that led Sir Edward Boyle, Minister of Education at the time, to issue the government circular 7/65. It recommended limiting the number of immigrant children in a class to 30 per cent. Entitled *Spreading the Children*, the circular pointed to evidence which showed that when a school 'had more than a certain percentage of immigrant children then the whole character and ethos is affected'. So the department of education came up with dispersal, or bussing as it came to be known by both its supporters and detractors.

Even though the practice was effectively banned in 1975, Bradford city council continued to bus children across the city for another five years so that the education of those already in the system was not disrupted.

Rizwana's story alone is not an argument in favour of bussing, nor do I think it was the best way of dealing with the problem. Children should be able to get everything they need from an education – whether it is academic excellence or social interaction – from their local school. That is how you build cohesive communities. In any case, there were, no doubt, plenty more children who sat on those buses and hated it. What Rizwana's story does show is that it will take some other, equally radical form of social engineering to break down the separate development of children. Without reforms to the admissions system, schools will continue to replicate the social mix – or lack of it – of their catchment area.

As for Rizwana Mahmood, she considers herself lucky to have gone to school in those years. What bussing gave her was a glimpse of a world beyond the geographically separate and psychologically blinkered community she lived in. Once she'd seen what was on offer outside, she wanted more. But it wasn't the bright lights and loose ways so feared by the Pakistani community's elders that enticed her – it was the notion of opportunity. The idea that you could aspire to something more than merely repeating what the previous generation had done. 'Bussing gave me the ability to interact,' she says. 'It's given me tolerance. It's given me a bigger picture and the skills to communicate. Kids today don't have that – we're failing them.' Rizwana should know. She, in her turn, is an assistant head teacher in a Bradford school where the vast majority of children are of Pakistani origin.

The extent of that failure became obvious in devastating form on 7 July 2005 when four young men, three of whom grew up a short drive away from Bradford, in Leeds, targeted the capital's transport system. Whatever else motivated the suicide bombers, an alienation from the country in which they lived must surely have been a factor. They may have been born in Britain but they were not of Britain. This may read like semantics on the page, but on the ground it is real enough.

Salman Rushdie was the archetypal cosmopolitan man, a darling of London's chattering classes. An unabashed intellectual, upper-middle-class and Oxbridge-educated, he seemed to personify the best of both East and West. The English have always had a soft spot for immigrants like Rushdie (and me). We fulfil their fantasy of the Oriental gentleman in a way the corner-shop owners who day in, day out sell everything from tins of baked beans to scratch cards for the National Lottery could never satisfy. In 1988, the great and the good of the literary world had gathered to mark the publication of Rushdie's *The Satanic Verses*.

Born in Bombay in 1947, Rushdie had been educated there and later at Rugby, one of Britain's most traditional and expensive public schools. From that school he trod the well-worn path to King's College, Cambridge, where his creative instincts first came to the fore in the Cambridge Footlights (a university theatre company that produced such luminaries as the late Peter Cook, David

Frost, Emma Thompson and Stephen Fry). Rushdie's second novel, *Midnight's Children*, won him a clutch of accolades, not least Britain's prestigious Booker Prize. In 1993, twelve years after it was published, it was hailed the 'Booker of Bookers', the best novel to have won the award in its twenty-five-year history. While *Midnight's Children* told the story of India's independence through the life of a pickle factory worker, Rushdie's next novel, *Shame*, was seen by many as an allegory of the political situation in Pakistan. One book tackled the country in which he was born; the next dealt with the country to which his parents had moved. They were Muslims, and though Rushdie himself had parted company with Islam, he used it as a backdrop in his next novel, *The Satanic Verses*. It was the launch of this book that brought together the great and the good in publishing.

The men and women who no doubt sipped their obligatory chilled wine and nibbled their way through delicately moulded canapés could not have known and would not have believed that they were presiding over an event that would mark a seismic shift in Britain's multicultural history. The libertarian values they represented, the moral elasticity they accepted, and the religious tolerance they believed in were all anathema to some of their fellow citizens up north in places like Bradford. Indeed, they inhabited parallel and separate worlds. Though the Rushdie crowd championed cultural and racial diversity in the rarified atmosphere of London's media village, few if any would have had any real idea about what that actually meant on the ground. What they, in their expansive interpretation of freedom of expression, were celebrating as a masterpiece in cross-cultural fiction was decried as a frontal assault on Islam by those whose vision of the world was limited to the short walk from their drab terraced houses to the local mosque.

On 2 December 7,000 Muslims staged a demonstration on the streets of Bolton in Lancashire. The climax of the protest was a ritual burning of a copy of *The Satanic Verses*. About five weeks later, in nearby Bradford, there was another demonstration. Again a copy of the book was burned and this time the national media, including TV news crews, were on hand to record the event. These images, with their historical echoes of religiously inspired censorship, revealed something new about race relations in Britain. The demonstrators on the streets of Lancashire and Yorkshire had more in common with their kith and kin in the subcontinent – where the first protests against the novel had taken place – than with their fellow citizens in this country. The glee with which so many of the Muslim community here greeted the fatwa in which Iran's Ayatollah Khomeini decreed that Rushdie had blasphemed and that it was every Muslim's duty to kill him revealed the extent to which some immigrants had fallen out of the mainstream.

The Rushdie affair was largely portrayed as a battle over intellectual freedom. In fact, the violent disagreement over the book was a symptom of a far greater challenge to British values. What the crisis over *The Satanic Verses* actually showed was that some Muslims had been drawn towards an interpretation of their religion which was entirely at odds with the prevailing mood of the nation. More troubling still was the fact that under a race relations policy underpinned by multiculturalism, this drift towards social isolation and religious extremism was left largely unchallenged.

In the Channel 4 film *Yasmin*, a moving portrayal of a post-9/11 Muslim community in Bradford (first broadcast in January 2005), the central character's father is occasionally seen in dewy-eyed contemplation as he shuffles through a handful of photographs. The pictures show the home he is building back in Pakistan. An old and troubled man, at odds with both his son Nassir and his daughter, the eponymous Yasmin, he finds a kind of solace in the house that is being built many thousands of miles away. He may never actually get to live in it, but the fact that it is there, a solid pile of bricks and mortar, is what counts.

In Mirpur today there are hundreds of homes built by families who have now lived in Britain for three generations. These houses, set against the general poverty of rural Pakistani Kashmir, are grand in both scale and ambition. It is not uncommon to find five- or even ten-roomed houses in Mirpur which are owned by families living in cramped Victorian-era homes here. The reason Bradford's Mirpuris lavish so much of their hard-won savings on homes in Pakistan when they could be spending the money on better and bigger homes here offers some kind of insight into the social dynamics that drive this immigrant community.

Abdul Bary Malik says making an impression back 'home' is what counts for many people. 'You see these houses all over the place,' he told me over lunch at his home in Low Moor, a suburb of Bradford. 'Sometimes they are locked up or relatives are living in them. They are houses, but they are not really homes. The families that own them are not going to live there. The whole point of these mansions is to show the people back home how rich you are. The same people who have Pajeros and Shogun jeeps in the garage in Mirpur are driving around in old Toyota Corollas here.'

In a supreme irony, the family elders who are so keen to display to their relatives back in Pakistan the accoutrements of a life in the West are precisely the same men who have remained suspicious of Western values in their day-to-day lives here in Britain. In Bradford's Mirpuri community the wealth that has come with immigration has been used to cement kinship ties with the old country rather than foster new cross-cultural relationships in Britain. Bradford's Mirpuri community lives in a time warp in which its communal clock chimes with the practices of rural Pakistan and not with twenty-first-century Europe.

According to Malik, Bradford's Mirpuris adhere to practices which have long ago been abandoned even in much of Pakistan. 'I go there every couple of years. I can see how people are moving on. It's only here that we are still stuck in the sixties and seventies,' he says. 'Take something as simple as food. More and more families have stopped using ghee in their cooking [because they know it's not healthy], but here it's still very common for the women to use ghee.'

All immigrants, especially the elderly, look back with a fondness for the land of their forefathers, but few have managed to replicate its mores and habits quite as comprehensively as Bradford's Mirpuris. Two factors account for this – religion and marriage.

The muezzin's call, as it wafts over the wet, shiny-grey slate roofs of Bradford, is no different to the one that emanates from the mosque at the centre of London's Regent's Park and is then carried across the genteel lawns and borders that surround it. So too, a church bell that tolls in rural Wiltshire sounds much like the one that echoes around Hoxton Square in London's East End. But listen more carefully. The largely African congregation at St Monica's Roman Catholic church in Hoxton may worship the same God as the good folk at St Thomas More in Marlborough, but they do it with a vitality and abandon that would unnerve the people of that ancient Wiltshire town. Islam is the same. Some of the mosques of Bradford resound to an inter-pretation of the faith that is a product of the city's particular immigrant history. The words of the imams there may be quite dif-ferent to the sermons you're likely to hear in cosmopolitan London.

A significant number – though nothing like most – of the imams who hold sway in Bradford's mosques are themselves recent immigrants from Pakistan, where they have been shaped by a deepening intra-Muslim, sectarian intolerance over the last twenty-five years. Historically Pakistan was home to a relaxed Sufi Islam – a religion of shrines, holy men and vernacular hymns. Over the years this has been challenged and eroded by a harsh and uncompromising Saudi strand of the religion – Wahhabism. This in turn was influenced by the reformist traditionalism – Deobandi – that gave birth to the Taliban in neighbouring Afghanistan. Out of this vortex of religious fervour emerged Osama bin Laden and his terrorism. There's little doubt that the arrival of imams from Pakistan in recent years has meant that this stringent, not to say volatile, version of Islam has seeped its way into Bradford's *madrasahs* – the religious schools..

The Brussels-based International Crisis Group has accused Pakistani president Pervez Musharraf of failing to curb the extremism of the *madrasahs* as he promised in the aftermath of the 11 September attacks on America. In an article published after the terror attacks on London in July 2005 – and after it emerged that one of the bombers had visited a Pakistani *madrasah* – the Asia director of the ICG claimed that the religious schools still preach an 'insidious doctrine' that is a 'threat to the stability of Pakistan' and incubate a hatred that is 'spilling blood in western cities as well'.

Philip Lewis is a lecturer at the University of Bradford and is an adviser on inter-faith relations to the city's Anglican bishop. 'Many imams imported from Pakistan still belong to the majority Sufi tradition but they have been much slower in creating Islamic seminaries in Britain which can translate this tradition into an accessible and relevant form. This leaves the door open for the more intolerant strains of Islam, often supported by Saudi funding, to take root here.' While their firebrand interpretation of Islam leaves the vast majority of Bradford's Muslim community cold, it does strike a chord among some young men. These are the restless, angry men who turn to religion on the rebound from a bitter disenchantment with what modern Britain has to offer them. According to the Oxford Centre for Islamic Studies, for example, over a third of Muslim youth grow up in households where there are no adults in employment.

Lewis told me how, back in Pakistan, textbooks have been pumping out a hatred of the West. It's something I can attest to after a conversation with my translator in Pakistan when I went there to cover the aftermath of the earthquake in 2005. He quoted a social studies textbook in the Northwest Frontier Province which reduced the Balkan crisis of the 1990s to one in which 'European countries openly provided Serbia with weapons but slapped sanctions continuously against [Muslim] Bosnia. What happened in Bosnia has exposed the so-called civilization and progress of Europe and has proved it completely hollow and evil-natured from inside.'

As a member of the Commission on British Muslims and Islamophobia, Philip Lewis has made it his business to try to understand the segregation of Bradford's Muslim communities. 'The irony is that those who can connect to British Muslim youth are often carriers of an Islam intolerant of its own rich inner diversity, still less able to connect with wider society. In all, this amounts to a crisis in the transmission of Islam.'

So young Muslim men in Bradford are being exposed to a form of the religion that many within the faith and outside it would find hard to recognise. In *A Passage to Africa* I wrote about how I grew up watching our family driver, Al Hassan, pray every day. He was the gentlest of men and his daily ritual, laying down his prayer mat and genuflecting before his God, instilled in me a profound sense of well-being. Everything seemed right in the world when Al Hassan whispered the words of the Koran. It was a feeling of assurance that I carried through to my days as a foreign correspondent. The sight of a mosque – whether it was in the searing heat of Timbuktu or the bitter cold of Kashmir – always reminded me of the quiet intimacy with which Al Hassan seemed to relate to his God. In a mosque one would find sanctuary; among Muslims one would be safe – that was how it felt to me. Al Hassan's Islam is in stark contrast to the strident and vehement version available today inside and outside some of the mosques of Bradford.

So why do mosques in the heart of west Yorkshire have imams from Pakistan instead of recruiting someone locally? The mosques are run by committee, usually a collection of men from the community. Often they are elders. These men are conservative. It is not necessarily the militant Islam of the clerics that the committees are attracted to, but the fact that they bring with them the traditional values they are so keen to preserve in Britain. But, as we've seen, these clerics, the product of religious schools or *madrasahs* in Pakistan, are more radical in their outlook than their counterparts here.

There is also the question of money. An imam brought over from Pakistan is far less demanding than the British-born version. He is likely to work for less and accept poorer accommodation than a local. For communities that are still stuck on the bottom rung of a ladder that has enabled other immigrants to move on and up, the financial considerations are important.

These immigrant imams may be part of the reason why young Muslim men today have become radicalised to the point where they see the country in which they have been born as collectively debauched, morally decadent and theologically bankrupt. I can see how they might arrive at this conclusion even if I disagree profoundly with where it leads them. They are brought up to believe that alcohol is bad and premarital sex forbidden. It is a message that is utterly at odds with what they see around them. If they were to hang around any Yorkshire city centre on a Friday night – and they would be advised to avoid these places – they might well conclude that British youth had indeed lost its way. Above the screech of police sirens they might hear the foul-mouthed abuse hurled across the pedestrian precinct at whoever happens to be on the other side. This is the hour when jittery cab drivers and nervous kebab shop owners wonder if there isn't a better, safer way to earn some money. In a modern echo of a Hogarth print they would see the young women, as binge-drunk as their male counterparts, squatting down to urinate in the street.

For these young Asian lads Britain is no longer a land of opportunity – as it was to their parents and millions of other immigrants from other countries and faiths – but an affront to Islam. The combination of radical Islam and conservative leadership means that Bradford's Pakistani community is socially ossified in a way that other Muslim communities in the country, let alone immigrants from other faiths such as Hindus and Sikhs, are not. Nowhere is this more obvious than in the institution of marriage.

Even now, nearly fifty years after the first generation of Mirpuri immigrants arrived in west Yorkshire, marriage represents, above all, an instrument of social engineering rather than one of personal choice. Many betrothals may be successful and most couples may eventually find mutual respect, if not love, but these attributes are not necessarily the primary aim of those who arrange the marriages of their children. Strengthening and nurturing family ties remains the single most important factor governing the choice of partners for marriage. This means that the search for brides and grooms leads inevitably to rural Pakistan. According to the Ousley Report, published after the riots in west Yorkshire in 2001, there were about 1,000 marriages a year in Bradford's Pakistani immigrant community. The majority of these – at least 60 per cent – involved a spouse brought over to Britain from Kashmir. Virtually all of these marriages were to close relatives – probably first cousins, who are considered the perfect match. Across Britain, according to Home Office figures for 2000, over 10,000 Pakistani nationals obtained entry clearance to join partners who are British citizens; that's more than the figures for India and Bangladesh combined.

In a striking piece of research, the Oxford academic Alison Shaw, suggests that the proportion of marriages involving cousins may have recently increased among the children of the pioneer generation. Her own work in Oxford follows several other academic studies that have looked at what specialists call cosanguineous marriages – they too have noted an upward trend. These studies – which looked at second- and even third-generation marriages in Oxford, and to a lesser extent in west Yorkshire – suggest that cousin-marriages may now account for more than half of all marriages.

If these findings can be extrapolated, they give the lie to one of the most commonly accepted views about what happens to immigrant communities – that they become more integrated with every new generation. What the Shaw study may show is exactly the opposite. Significant parts of the Pakistani community are becoming more and more entrenched in their 'home' culture. With every imam who comes to Britain, with every marriage that is arranged with a cousin in Mirpur, the most culturally introspective aspects of the community are reinvigorated.

The reasons these cousin-marriages are still promoted so assiduously are complex but they have their roots in the ancient but powerful clans – *biradaris* – that form the social bedrock of rural communities in Pakistan. A *biradari* is a kinship group that starts with a small cluster of intermarrying relatives and widens out into a theoretically infinite extended family. The level of obligation between two members or families will depend on where exactly they are in the chain of ties that make up the *biradari*.

For minds schooled in the Western notions of individual needs and nuclear families, the idea of an all-powerful loyalty to a clan is hard to fathom, but it is really the only way to make sense of what has been going on in places like Bradford. While we probably see the union between husband and wife as the most important building block of society, the *biradari* places far greater value on cooperation within the extended family. Being a member of a clan invokes such concepts as honour and shame which are all but forgotten here. The *biradari* encompasses a system of reciprocity (*lena-dena* – literally giving-taking), in which gifts are exchanged. Crucially, a return gift is always worth slightly more than the original offering so that the 'debt' is perpetuated.

Far from being the exercise of individual enterprise and ambition that is normally associated with migration, the movement of Pakistani Mirpuris to Britain in the sixties was driven as much by the desire to enrich the *biradari*. And so it has continued in a chain of migration that has drawn in more and more members of a particular *biradari*.

With so much at stake, it is little surprise that maintaining a *biradari*'s integrity has remained such a powerful preoccupation of clan elders here in Britain. And marriage to a cousin in Pakistan is still the surest way of guaranteeing the blood purity of a clan – Shanaz Gulzar, who is now an artist working in Bradford, learned that the hard way as a teenager.

Shanaz was a year into her A levels when she noticed that her mother had started buying the kind of things that normally presage a wedding. In an upstairs room of their home in Keighley, on the outskirts of Bradford, Shanaz became aware of a steadily increasing collection of clothes, gold jewellery and other presents. 'We are going to Pakistan,' her mother would say by way of explanation. Shanaz did not need to ask why to know that her life was about to be rearranged.

The subject of her marriage had been in the air ever since she was into her teens. 'My mother would have been happy if I'd stopped school at twelve,' she told me as we walked along the lake at Lister Park on a sunny but windy late spring day. The final decision about her education was settled not in the intimacy of a family chat, but by a group of elders, all men. 'I think there were about twelve of them,' she said. Her father had told the other men that Shanaz was keen to go on to university. They were opposed to the idea, portraying university life as licentious and unsuitable for a Muslim girl. They might have found the bitter pill easier to swallow if Shanaz had wanted to study something that could be useful to the community, but she wanted to take art. Shanaz fought back. 'I used the Koran as my weapon,' is how she put it to me. 'You see, it says in the Koran that you should travel to the four corners of the world in the pursuit of education.'

It is a tribute to Shanaz's determination that the elders eventually relented. She was allowed to continue her A level course and apply for a place at university, though there was what Shanaz called an 'indirect' condition that marriage would be thrown into the bargain – no dates, just a commitment. When I first met her, Shanaz's hair was dyed red with a lightning streak of silver-grey that swept back from her forehead – a work of art in itself. To see her is to wonder why a woman of such independence, such verve, could ever have countenanced wedlock at a time other than that of her own choosing and to a man she did not know. The only way she could explain her acquiescence was simple but, as we shall see, tragic: 'I went to Pakistan because I loved my parents. I never did love my partner, but I did love my mother and father. I did it for them.'

The man chosen as her husband was a first cousin back in Mirpur. Ali Shezad (I have not used his real name because Shanaz wants to protect his privacy) was a year older than his bride-to-be but light years behind her in education, aspiration and outlook. Shanaz, even if she was brought up within the confines of a Muslim home, was a child of the city, a British city at that. She is a living embodiment of all the contradictions that swirl around the lives of so many young immigrants: Asian but British; a woman but independent; a Muslim but with secular values; above all a dutiful daughter but with a sense of her own being. Her husband-to-be had the customs and traditions of Mirpur written into his bones. 'Like chalk and cheese', they might have said in Yorkshire. If in her mind Shanaz had decided to accept her place in the family plan, the same could not be said of her heart. Within days of getting to Pakistan, she fell ill, losing all her hair and dropping down to five stone in weight. And still the wedding took place – the honour of the *biradari* apparently more important than the health of an individual.

Two weeks after the marriage, in August 1989, Shanaz returned to Keighley. Her husband was to follow later when he was able to get a visa. Shanaz went back to what she had always wanted – her education. A levels in theatre studies and art won her a place at Leeds Metropolitan University, a commutable distance from Keighley.

By the time Ali Shezad joined her in Bradford in January 1995, Shanaz was in her final year at college. At first his visa had been withheld because Shanaz, as his spouse, had to prove she was independently capable of supporting him. As a student, it was a condition she could not meet, and it was an incapacity she was happy to prolong for as long as possible. Even when she found work, the immigration authorities further delayed granting a visa. Ali Shezad had let it be known that his prime purpose for coming to Britain was not marriage, let alone love, but the financial rewards of life in this country. 'Not very bright, our Ali,' is how Shanaz puts it, with all the power of Yorkshire understatement.

Incredibly, the marriage lasted fifteen years, and produced a daughter. 'We'd stopped living as man and wife by 2002.' Ali Shezad had never really been capable of reconciling his vision of what a wife should be with the reality of the energetic woman with whom he shared a home. 'In those years with him I learned to put my life into compartments. He couldn't understand what made me tick,' Shanaz said. 'He refused to be a part of my life and work. He only ever came to one of my shows, and never again. I realised I couldn't invite my colleagues back home. That's when I worked out how to put my life into little boxes. One for home, one for work, one for being a Muslim, one for being a woman, one for being British.'

Shanaz is not alone. There are plenty of other women in Bradford who could tell stories like hers. The UK High Commission in Pakistan even has a team dedicated to rescuing young British women who find themselves forced into marriage. But we don't need to cast the net that far. A look at how Shanaz's siblings have got on is enough to convince me that she is special only in her determination to challenge the custom of first-cousin marriages. She is the second of eight children. Seven of the eight siblings went through with arranged marriages to first cousins (in Pakistan). At the time I spoke to her, six of those unions had ended in divorce or were in various stages of falling apart.

So her experience may be common but her reaction to it is quite unique: she risked a great deal in talking so openly to me, not least the opprobrium of her community. She did not take the easy way out and move away from Keighley completely. Even now she lives in the same street in which she grew up. 'Honesty has been my way through all of this,' she said. 'Whatever else people might think of me they have to know that I was honest – both to myself and to them.' It has earned her respect, if not total acceptance. Crucially, it has meant that she continues to have a relationship with her parents. 'I still love them and respect them. This was never about them as people, this was about a practice that they believed in and I didn't,' she says. 'I know that they did what they did because they thought they were protecting me, it was how they showed their love for me.' Shanaz compares talking to her father about these issues to walking on eggshells. It's an apt metaphor for the care and attention that will be needed by those who look for genuine change in these communities.

Shanaz remembers precisely the date Ali Shezad moved out – 2 July 2004. When I last spoke to her, she was well on her way to recasting her life – a single parent but infinitely happier than when she'd had a man in the house. There were commissions in England and a trip to New York. We talked as she redecorated her studio – mostly apple white, but with a strip of crimson which she called 'luxurious, like velvet'. I wondered if the use of stark contrast here and in her hairstyle reflected the sharp divisions in her own life between the self she wanted to be and the one her community demanded.

I asked her how she looked back at her marriage. Did she regard it as a forced marriage?

'It was unequivocally a forced marriage,' she said.

'But you've already said you went through with it because you loved your parents, so is it fair to call it a forced marriage?'

'There are many ways to apply force. It doesn't have to be physical force. It can be emotional pressure.'

'Are you saying that's what it was with you?' I may have been labouring the point, but with good reason. I was aware that in some quarters the direction in which this exchange was going would be seen not as a description of an individual's plight but as an attack on a whole culture.

'Yes. You know what Asian communities are like,' she said. 'The elders have a stranglehold, especially over women.'

'But surely that's the community that you belong to and those are the rules?' I asked. 'Is it anybody else's business what goes on within a particular community?'

'I don't agree. It's not just the business of a community.'

'But aren't we supposed to accept many cultures these days?'

'Cultural understanding is all very well, but human rights come first,' she said.

There it is – the heart of the matter. Are there values that we in Britain covet so dearly that they trump everything else we are trying to achieve as a society? Is there anything about being British that is more important than the many cultures that now sit side by side in the country? To put it simply, is the British whole greater than the sum of its parts? At times in the last few decades it has seemed as if there is nothing truly British, only a mishmash of ideas and customs without any real unifying creed. There has been no attempt to impose any obligation on immigrant families to conform to a British way of doing things. From the seventies onwards, even to suggest that there was a British model to conform to would have you labelled as a racist.

The same feminists and liberals who worry about the plight of women in Muslim countries or female circumcision in some African societies have chosen to turn a blind eye to some rather unsavoury practices in their own backyard. One of the justifications for going halfway around the world to attack Afghanistan in November 2001 was to liberate women from the sexist clutches of the Taliban. Speaking in the aftermath of battle, Laura Bush, America's First Lady, told a radio audience that 'the fight against terrorism is also a fight for the rights and dignity of women'. Here, Lord Bach, who was then an undersecretary of state for defence, told his fellow peers that the Taliban was a 'brutal, repressive and hypocritical regime with a particularly appalling record of abusing the human rights of the women of Afghanistan'.

To attack the Taliban was to strike a blow for women's emancipation, but to take on the elders who were making the lives of women like Shanaz miserable would have been deemed an attack on multicultural Britain, and that is something most people – particularly on the left – did not want to do.

There have been some notable exceptions. Ann Cryer, the Labour MP for Keighley, one of the constituencies in Bradford, managed to put the issue on the parliamentary agenda in 1999 with a debate on forced marriages. Since then she has not lost an opportunity to challenge the tradition of first-cousin marriages. Her pioneering stance has begun to have an effect, with others gradually becoming more willing to question the practice. In November 2005, the BBC's *Newsnight* programme aired an investigation which claimed to show that there was a higher incidence of recessive disorders among the children of first-cousin marriages.

British Pakistanis account for 30 per cent of all British children with recessive disorders such as cystic fibrosis, although they account for just 3.4 per cent of all births. In the programme Ann Cryer said the practice of first-cousin marriages could not be seen simply as a cultural issue: 'As we address problems of smoking, drinking, obesity, we say it's a public health issue, and therefore we all have to get involved with it in persuading people to adopt a different lifestyle. I think the same should be applied to this problem in the Asian community. They must adopt a different lifestyle.'

We have turned multiculturalism into a shibboleth, as if it were a national characteristic rather than a means to end. It was only ever meant to be a way of easing the relationships between races, but in the last thirty to forty years or so it has acquired a status that is nearer to a founding principle – such as habeas corpus – than the social policy that it is. It's all upside-down and inside-out. As the author and broadcaster Kenan Malik has pointed out, 'the right to practise a particular religion, speak a particular language, follow a particular cultural practice is seen as a public good rather than a private freedom'. That conflation between the public realm and private space is where multiculturalism began to go wrong.

At first it was simply a correction to the way in which immigrants had been treated after their arrival in large numbers in the 1950s. Then Britain was viewed as a monocultural nation in which 'aliens' had to be assimilated. That was a rendition of British identity that was rooted in race. There were people who were white and there was everybody else. But as immigrant numbers continued to increase (despite numerous attempts to limit them), such an interpretation of British identity became less and less credible or relevant.

That was the conundrum that multiculturalism sought to answer. Roy Jenkins, the Labour home secretary of the 1960s, could rightly claim to be its architect, though he never did so specifically. In 1966 he spoke about race relations based on 'cultural diversity, coupled with equal opportunity, in an atmosphere of mutual tolerance'. He could not have envisaged the way in which this new policy would be interpreted in council chambers around the country. Instead of providing the intellectual under-pinning for the battle against racism – Jenkins's equality of opportunity – cultural diversity became a goal in itself. As Malik has noted, there was a redefinition of racism. More than the denial of equal opportunity, it became the 'denial of the right to be dif-ferent'.

The Greater London Council, under its radical leader, Ken Livingstone (later to become the first directly elected mayor of the capital), led the way in championing this new right to be different. It poured money into ethnic community organisations. The first newspaper I ever worked on (as an internee), the *East End News*, had a dedicated page for the black and Asian communities. It was supported by the TUC and several church groups. Throughout the seventies and eighties local authorities up and down the coun-try followed suit – setting up race relations units, drawing up equal opportunity policies and, crucially, funnelling tax-payers' money towards myriad groups based on ethnicity. This flow of cash created a perverse incentive for communities to show just how different they were. Instead of encouraging the 'mutual tol-erance' the high-minded Jenkins had hoped for, multiculturalism began to encourage something entirely different – ethnic exclu-sivity. In Bradford, for example, the council entrenched religious differences by channelling funds through the Bradford Council of Mosques, the Federation of Sikh Organisations and the Vishwa Hindi Parishad. In fact, it helped to set up these organisations.

It may be that things would have been better if the country's burgeoning races had each had to find their own accommodation with its dominant culture – the one that represents over 80 per cent of its population. What multiculturalism did was to put paid to any notion of a host culture. Unlike Americans, who seem to need no excuse to fly the flag, the English (the dominant group in the UK) have been far more reticent to parade their sense of self.

Call it a post-imperial crisis of confidence, or simply a stiff upper lip, but the vast majority of English men and women have recoiled from any public display of national pride. With the notable exceptions of sport and Britain's role in the Second World War, the notion of what it is to be English has been left largely unsaid. Jeremy Paxman devoted a whole book to the topic, *The English, A Portrait of a People*, and even he seemed to accept that no single ideal appeared to sum up the national character. Instead he gave a list of characteristics: 'a quizzical detachment, tolerance, common sense, bloody-mindedness, willingness to compromise, [a] deeply political sense of themselves [and above all a] sense of "I know my rights"'.

The failure or refusal to assert a positive national rallying point has left a vacuum into which two opposing groups have poured. First came the racists, the people who turned patriotism into a narrow, sneering, often violent rejection of everyone who didn't fit their warped idea of what it was to be British, let alone English. And in response to them came the multiculturalists, with their good-to-be-different anthem. If the first group turned Britishness into a dirty word, the second made it meaningless. You couldn't assert one culture or value over any other because they were all supposed to be equal.

What multiculturalism did was to confuse the fight against racism (which undoubtedly existed and exists today) with the business of nation-building. Perhaps there was a way to isolate and punish the racists without losing sight of the need to forge an integrated community of shared values and aspirations. In the early days of modern immigration there was a form of ad hoc integration going on. It was often hit and miss, and many fell victim to racism, but through it all people began to inch their way towards a cultural middle ground. That was before the race relations industry got to work.

It's 5.30 in the morning. I'm parked outside Willis House, one of the blocks on the Will Crooks Estate in Poplar, Tower Hamlets. It's a March morning, and as I step out of the heated car I know we still have some way to go before spring kicks in. I look up to see if there's any sign of life. A hundred double-glazed windows stare back at me, dark, unblinking. All except for one. Behind this window a soft purply light flickers this way and that, bouncing off the only wall I can see from the pavement below. It's the TV. Someone couldn't get to sleep, or, perhaps they've just got back from the night shift. I'm intrigued. Behind every front door a different family, a different story to tell. The nightlights, evenly spaced above the long open corridor that runs across the front of the council flats, remind me of runway markers tapering away in the distance.

It's not long before I see Helen walking towards me. Helen Modesk and I are going shopping. We're going to buy some fish. And this is the time she always goes to Billingsgate fish market.

It isn't the real Billingsgate fish market, of course. Helen used to go the original one when it was on the north side of Lower Thames Street, near St Katharine's Dock. It had been there since 1698, when an act of parliament made it 'a free and open market for all sorts of fish whatsoever'. The only exception to this was the sale of eels, which was restricted to Dutch fishermen whose boats were moored further along the Thames. Apparently, their monopoly over eel sales was given in recognition of their sterling work during the Great Fire when they had helped to feed the people of London.

The new Billingsgate market is a five-minute drive from Helen's estate. From the outside, with its corrugated metal roof, it has all the charm of an aircraft maintenance hangar. Inside, hundreds of stallholders have tamed the industrial efficiency of the purpose-built trading hall. Their East End chatter, their cheeky-chappy humour, and above all their inherited stake in the business of shifting 25,000 tonnes of fish every year reduce the place to human proportions.

At LeLeu and Morris, Stand D10, Mark and Ryan are the fourth generation to run the business. It was founded by Thomas Morris, their great-grandfather.

'So who was LeLeu?' I ask.

'Good question, mate, but I'm buggered if I know. Bit of a mystery. Now, you here to ask questions or buy some fish?'

Helen butted in. 'Leave him alone. Don't you know who you talking to?'

'Nah, never seen him before,' he says in mock ignorance.

We walk around a few more stalls. Helen's giving me the full tour.

'Hello, darlin',' says the man from A. H. Cox at stand H5 before he spots me tagging along behind Helen. 'And who have we here? Fishing for a bit of news, are we?' It's such a bad joke we have to laugh. Pinned on the wall behind him is the Union Jack. They're not embarrassed to be patriotic here.

There's every shape and size of fish on display. They're brought in every morning. By road from Penzance, by air from Sri Lanka. Tilapia and kingfish, bonito and red snapper, Helen's favourite. I pause by the stall selling razor clams.

'Quite handy,' says the trader. 'Eat it first, have a shave later.'

By now Helen has moved off ahead of me. She's heading for John Koch's stall. It's where she does most of her buying on these monthly trips.

'Why do you keep coming to this one?' I ask.

' 'Cause we're the best-looking lads on the block. Aren't we, love?'

Helen lets it all wash over her. But I can tell she's tickled.

'Now you going to sell me some fish or what?' She pretends to scold the lad; in fact she's flirting.

Helen buys some tiger prawns. I match her kilo for kilo.

'I think I'll make some curry with these,' she says as we head out of the complex. 'I learned how to do it from the Indians. We got a lot of them back home.' She's not talking about Poplar. Helen means St Lucia in the Caribbean. That's where she came from in 1959.

Back in her flat, I ask why she keeps going to Billingsgate when these days most supermarkets offer a pretty comprehensive array of seafood.

' 'Cause it's half the price, man. I ain't got money to throw away, you know. I'm not a TV presenter. And they're very friendly there.'

As we talk, I realise that's really the point of the exercise, the friendliness, the camaraderie. Going to Billingsgate reminds her of the London she used to know, before 'everything got messed up', as she puts it.

Helen has lived in the same two-bedroom flat on Will Crooks Estate for thirty-six years. She brought up six daughters in that time, much of it single-handed. And as if that weren't enough of a handful, she adopted another girl, a Sri Lankan.

'It must have been tough,' I say.

'Well it was, but everyone got along. You know, people, your neighbours, used to help.'

'So what were your neighbours like when you first moved here?'

'They were mostly cockney or Irish. Old Mr Sharpe next door, he was like a dad to the kids.'

Her youngest daughter Carolyn, now thirty-three, practically lived next door.

'They could see how crowded we was in here. She used to get dressed here in the mornings, but the rest of the day she lived there. She had her dinner there and slept there.'

'So he didn't mind that you were black?'

'No, he didn't mind. I'm not saying we didn't have a colour problem. In those days it was very hard for some black people. When I used to go to some of the shops I had to ask permission before I went in. Sometimes they had notices saying 'No Blacks'. It was tough. But here on the estate it was different. We got along.'

'It must be better now. You can't have racism like that any more.'

'No, it's worse now. All those old people have gone. They took them out in coffins. Now it's all messed up. The Bengalis just do their own thing. They don't mix. I've got neighbours who I don't know. It was more multicultural.'

She says it, not me.

'But, Helen, there was no such thing as multiculturalism in the days when you first got here. They hadn't started the policy in the sixties. That's what we're supposed to have now – multiculturalism.'

'I don't know about the politics, but I'm telling you it was better then. When we West Indians moved in we had to learn to survive, you know, to get on with the people here. That was the only way. That was before all these laws and things. Now the Bengalis and so on don't need to do anything.'

We're sitting in Helen's front room. In fact it's the only communal room. One of her daughters, thirty-nine-year old Linda, is finishing off her coffee before heading out to work. I suggest, politely, that Helen may be falling victim to the 'good old days' syndrome, that wonderful facility the old have for reinventing their lives. Linda says I am wrong; I haven't heard the half of it.

'The Bengalis get priority over all the other people. Everything is done for them. If your name is not Begum as a woman or Mohammed as a man, you're not going to get anywhere.'

Linda has been waiting for a flat of her own since 1989. At first all she needed was a one-bedroom place. Later she applied for a flat with two rooms. In 1998 she had a daughter, Tasia, who has cerebral palsy. The two of them share a bed in Helen's spare room.

'If a flat becomes vacant, you can be ninety-nine per cent sure it will go to a Bengali family,' she says. 'It's just not fair; it's supposed to be multicultural.'

There it is, that word again. Whatever the theory, the perception of multiculturalism on the ground is that it is inherently unfair, pandering to difference not need. The more different you are, the more the state will come to your aid. Housing policy, social services policy, language and education policy, all of it has contrived to turn an area of London with a long history of interaction with wave after wave of newcomers – not all of it cordial – into what it is today: an outpost of the Bangladeshi province of Sylhet.

If you look south from the Will Crooks Estate all you can see is the steel and glass of Canary Wharf. Perfectly straight, perfectly symmetrical, the buildings rise together like an oversize bar chart displaying the relative fortunes of the banks and law firms that have turned the area into London's newest financial centre. Barclays, Citigroup, Clifford Chance, HSBC. They are all there. So too are the restaurants and penthouse suites to serve the expensive tastes of the brokers and bankers. Some of the men – and women – who look out from their lofty perches count their annual bonuses in seven figures, while below them in the red-brick council blocks the average household income is less than £10,000 a year.

If Canary Wharf is a symbol of the invisible earnings of digital transfers across the planet and futures markets in commodities produced thousands of miles away, the area around it is redolent of a time when the only way to trade was for people to move from one place to another.

Here, from what is now called Virginia Quays, is where a group of merchants set out in 1606 for the New World. Ordered to bring back gold and treasure by King James I, their four-month voyage was a precursor to the more famous *Mayflower* voyage in 1620. They established the first English colony in the New World and duly named it Jamestown.

On the other side of Helen's estate is the East India Dock Road. The Queen Victoria Seamen's Rest is still there. Established in 1843 by the Methodist Church, it is the oldest maritime charity in the country. It is here that the Lascars, the Indian sailors who once accounted for over a fifth of Britain's maritime labour force, would look for sanctuary when they had been abandoned by the ship-owners. Eventually they would seep into the city, becoming petty traders and, much later, the first cooks in curry houses that began to open up in the city. At the Queen Vic, as it was known to those who lived there, the Lascars would rub shoulders with sailors whose far-flung nationalities reflected Britain's seafaring dominance. There were Greeks, Malays, Dutch, Spaniards, French and Scandinavians.

Towards Limehouse, on West India Dock Road, was the Strangers' Home for Asiatics, Africans and South Sea Islanders. From 1857 onwards it became a home from home to various seamen, notably Chinese from the Dutch East India Company's Straits Settlements. When the promises of repatriation to the colony came to nothing, the one-time ships' launderers and porters settled in the local area. By the end of the nineteenth century they had formed a distinct, if embryonic, Chinese settlement.

At the time of George V's coronation in 1911, the district, no more than thirty or so shops and restaurants, was already being described as Chinatown. Soon the streets either side of the West India Dock Road became synonymous with vice, encouraged by the descriptions of it in some contemporary literature. Arthur Conan Doyle used the area as a seedy backdrop for *The Man with the Twisted Lip*, and Oscar Wilde used it in very much the same way for *The Picture of Dorian Gray*. In 1918, fiction seemed to turn into fact when the actress Billie Carlton was found dead from a cocaine overdose allegedly sold to her by a Chinaman. A couple of years later *The Times* reported that the 'Poplar Borough Council is seriously concerned over the problem of the increasing number of white women with Chinese men in the borough, including the greater part of Chinatown.' By the mid-twentieth century, a combination of the Blitz and slum clearance policies had ensured that this original Chinatown had all but disappeared. It would, of course, reappear phoenix-like and with new vigour in Soho in London's West End. All the same, the Chinese contribution to this part of Tower Hamlets remains in the road signs: Canton St, Ming St, Amoy Lane, and Pekin St.

Absorbing foreigners, even if it was reluctantly done, is virtually written into the DNA of this part of the East End. Its position on the Thames, with its wharfs and warehouses, meant it was always going to be one of the city's most cosmopolitan areas. Most of the people who lived in the area understood that; some even liked it.

Mandy Molyneux – does she ever stop to ask where that name

came from – grew up on the Will Crooks Estate. The family moved out in 1969, the first on the estate to buy a property of their own. Her memories of the place pre-date Bangladeshi immigration.

'It was all sorts in those days,' she said. 'It was fantastic really the way we all got along.'

'Can you remember any of the nationalities?'

'Let's see. The Lorenzos, I think they were Afro-Caribbean. The Lewises as well. Mr Lee was Chinese. Al Dorino, I think that's how you say it, they were Spanish, and the Webbs were Irish.'

'So it was quite multicultural then.'

'We didn't call it multicultural. I don't think we knew what that meant in those days. They were just friends and neighbours.'

Even after the family moved round the corner to Woodstock Terrace, Mandy would come back to the estate to play with her friends.

'One of our favourite games was "knock down ginger". I don't know why it was called that, but what you had to do was knock on someone's door and run. I remember there was this Chinese man on the ground floor. When we did it to him he used to come running out with an axe, laughing his head off.'

'So when did things start to change, then?'

'I don't know if I can put a date on it,' she said. 'I remember when the first Bangladeshi family moved in. The man's name was Arub Ali. That was about twenty-five years ago. That was fine, it was just another family. It happens slowly. You don't realise it. One day you wake up and you think, "Where's everybody gone?".'

They've gone their separate ways. That is the short answer. Much of the available evidence – empirical as well as anecdotal – suggests that Mandy's experience may be widespread. She sees a far smaller range of people from different ethnic groups now than she did when she was a child growing up on the Will Crooks Estate.

In 2004 the Commission for Racial Equality carried out a survey in which they asked people to say how many of their friends came from a different ethnic background. The results were worrying. Fewer than one in ten could name two. Even in London, where nearly one in three people comes from an immigrant background, only a tiny proportion of white people could name a good friend who was non-white. And if whites were sticking together, so too were their immigrant counterparts. Young people from the ethnic minorities were more likely to socialise with friends from their own group than their parents were.

The trend continued in 2005, when the CRE carried out another survey. The proportion of white people who said that all or most of their friends were white went up by one per cent – from 94 to 95 per cent. More than half of those questioned couldn't even name a single friend who was non-white. It didn't matter whether they were working-class or middle-class, whether they lived in Brighton or Bradford, whether they were young or old – the answer was the same.

In the 2005 survey, the number of ethnic minority Britons who said that their friends were mainly or exclusively from the same background had gone up from 31 per cent in 2004 to 37 per cent the following year. This time, too, the CRE found that the younger generation formed more ethnically exclusive relationships than their older relatives. That is certainly the case in Bradford, where, once again, the council has had to resort to transporting children across the city in order to encourage contact between the races. This is not bussing as Rizwana Mahmood once knew it, but it is a form of social engineering that should be unnecessary if multi-culturalism had delivered the goods.

Nasser Hussain shares a name with the one-time captain of English cricket, but that is about all he has in common with his namesake. While the cricketer attended the fee-paying Forest School in Essex, where he honed his sporting skills on its extensive playing fields and mixed with some of the brightest and best from north London, the opportunities for the Nasser Hussain that I met on one of my trips to Bradford are altogether more limited.

It was one of those drizzle-mizzle days that west Yorkshire specialises in. The weather outside was in stark contrast to the chirpy enthusiasm of the group of 10-year-olds I'd come to see at Keighley's St Andrew's Church of England Primary School. Despite its Anglican status, 96 per cent of the pupils are Muslim. The school is part of Bradford's Linking Project, a council-funded attempt to bridge the racial divide in the city. St Andrew's had been paired with the predominantly white Burley and Woodhead Church of England Primary School a few miles across the city.

While we sat in one of the classrooms waiting for their counterparts to arrive, I asked Sophia Ahmed, Umay-Laila Bukhari (who told me she wished she had a shorter name), Aneesa Saeed, Zulfiqar Ali Bhutto (who shared a name with a former prime minister of Pakistan) and Nasser what they thought the Linking Project was meant to do.

'It's about meeting people that you haven't met before.' Zulfiqar was the first to volunteer an answer.

'What's the point of meeting the children from Burley and Woodhead?'

'It's so that we can make friends,' said Sophia.

'It's good to meet other people,' said Laila. We'd agreed I could call her that. 'You know, if your normal friends are not there, you can still have someone to talk to.'

'So who are your normal friends, then?'

'The people at this school,' Sophia said.

'So what kind of children are they, the ones you meet from the other school?'

'They're different.' Zulfiqar again. 'Their religion is different.'

'Is that it, or is there anything else that's different?'

'They've got different skin colour. They're white,' said Nasser

It was a conversation that took me all the way back to my family's time in South Africa, when I was the BBC's correspondent there. Frances and I had enrolled our children, Adam and

Matthew, at the local state school. Over the four years our children attended Saxonwold Primary School in Johannesburg, it went from being a predominantly white school to a predominantly black one. These were the heady days of transition, and Marion Wheater and her staff knew they were in the vanguard when it came to forging a new identity for a nation once divided by the most systematic policy of racial discrimination ever seen in the modern world.

Many, if not most, of the black children came from the townships that surrounded Johannesburg. The rest of the children – mostly white, but including a few mixed-race pupils like Adam and Matthew – lived locally and comfortably in vast houses surrounded by manicured gardens and shimmering swimming pools. Children who sat next to each other in the classroom walked out of the playground in the afternoons and into lives that were a world apart. The children were united in their common future but still divided by their history. In an attempt to break down this barrier, staff and parents instituted a homework club where children from the townships could spend time in the homes of their more privileged classmates. It was, in effect, a 'linking project'.

If such a venture was necessary in a country trying to undo nearly 250 years of institutionalised racism, what are we to make of the need for a similar venture in a country which prides itself on its racial harmony? Bradford's Linking Project is proof that multiculturalism has fallen short of its ideals. The staff who run it for the city council are having to make up for a social policy that has delivered an outcome entirely at odds with its stated aims. The conversation I was having with the children from St Andrew's was one I might easily have had with the pupils of Saxonwold in the mid-1990s.

And what would it be like if the number of faith-based schools in England is increased, as substantial parts of both the Labour and Conservative parties want? Only the Liberal Democrats oppose an expansion of religiously grounded schools for fear that it will lead to segregation.

In 2005 there were about 7,000 state-maintained religious schools, overwhelmingly Christian. They account for about a third of all primary schools and less than one-fifth of the secondary sector. Together they cater for 1.7 million of the five million-plus school-age children whose parents say they are Christian, though as with St Andrew's in Bradford, some of the places are taken by non-Christian pupils.

Any expansion in the number of faith schools is likely to be in the non-Christian sector. There are some 371,000 Muslim school-age children in Britain, and only five state-maintained Muslim schools, with just over 1,000 places. There are only two Sikh schools, with places for about 600 children. The Sikh school-age population is 64,000. There are places for 13,000 children in state-maintained Jewish schools. That caters for a larger proportion of the Jewish school-age population (33,000) than is the case with any of the other minority religions. There is one Seventh Day Adventist school and one Greek Orthodox school.

The assumption is that faith schools – of whatever denomination – will attract substantial numbers of children of other faiths though attempts to set a target have failed in parliament. Without some form of incentive, it's difficult to see large numbers of parents willing to cross the religious divide. Indeed, the head of the Catholic Church in England and Wales, Cardinal Cormac Murphy O'Connor, has said he would not want to see Catholic children educated in Muslim schools because 'the creed of Islam is totally diverse from the creed of Christianity'. Though many Muslims, Sikhs and Hindus go to Christian schools at the moment, it is not clear whether that would continue if the parents of those children had their own-faith options.

Back in Bradford, Tom, Danielle, Katie, Lucy and Max trooped in – five of the thirty children that were involved in the linking programme at the time. This was the tenth time the two sets of children had met through the project. On previous occasions they had celebrated Eid-ul-Fitr (the Muslim festival that marks the end of Ramadan), played games at a leisure centre, gone to a local museum and travelled to Liverpool together. Now it was time for the children from Burley and Woodhead to answer my questions.

'What's the Linking Project all about?'

Tom had the textbook answer: 'It's to help us to work with people and understand people from another culture.'

'Can anyone tell me what it means to be from another culture?' Silence.

'It's quite difficult, isn't it?'

Lucy said she'd have a stab at an answer: 'Well, it sort of means that I'm from England and, like, I don't really know where Aneesa is from.'

'So what do you think Aneesa is?'

'Aneesa could be English, but I'm not sure,' said Lucy.

'Why do you need a Linking Project?'

'Well, because Burley is separate to Keighley,' said Katie. 'So all the people like me live in Burley.'

'And what kind of people are they?'

'People whose skin colour is white,' said Tom.

'So what was it like the first time you all met up?'

'We were quite nervous,' said Katie. 'We hadn't really met any Muslims before.'

'My grandad's friend is a Muslim.' This was Tom. 'But I'd never had a Muslim friend.'

Bradford's Linking Project was established in January 2002, when the carnage of 11 September in New York and Washington was still fresh in the memory. The shock waves from those events reverberated across the world, not least in places like Bradford, where people began to look more closely at communal relations. What they found was a form of social apartheid. Across the Bradford district, 59 per cent of primary school children (that's 30,717 out of a total of 51,335) attend classes in which one culture is dominant. In an evaluation of the project researchers found that, in October 2004, only 5 per cent of children who attended schools serving a community of predominantly one culture (essentially Asian and Muslim or white and Christian) were able to say they had a friend in the other group.

Under a year later, by July 2005, 64 per cent of the children involved in the project could boast two or more friends from another culture. Such progress was neither guaranteed nor expected. In fact when the project's director, Angie Kotler, first mooted the possibility of a programme to bring children together she encountered considerable reluctance in official circles. 'Don't go there, that was the early reaction,' she says. It was a pioneering concept and there were fears in some quarters that white parents might simply vote with their feet and leave schools that looked as if they might join the scheme. Such a response reflects the extent to which local bureaucrats had come to accept that separation was inevitable. That the project exists at all is a tribute to her refusal to take no for an answer. By 2006, the linking programme was an entrenched part of the council's work, with plenty of support from officials in local and national government. Indeed, the lessons of the project have not been lost on Asian parents themselves. Those that can afford to have started to taxi their children out of the city centre and into predominantly white schools on the outskirts.

To see the two sets of children mixing as I did (even if it was only for a couple of hours) is to know that in a child's world there are no limits to friendship. To watch them pore over photographs of their days together is to understand the potential for genuine multiculturalism. But in Bradford it seems as if these contacts are but brief encounters across an all too entrenched pattern of housing and education. Very few of these fleeting friendships develop beyond the structure of the Linking Project. I asked both sets of children how often they had met outside the organised trips. Not a murmur: not one child had been in contact with their new-found friends. At last Nasser offered a glimmer of hope. 'Once I played a game on-line with my friend from Burley.' Perhaps a virtual friendship is worth more than no friendship at all.

It's hardly surprising that the Cantle Report into the causes of the 2001 riots in west Yorkshire came to the conclusion that it did:

'Separate educational arrangements, community and voluntary bodies, employment, places of worship, language, social and cultural networks, means that many communities operate on the basis of a series of parallel lives.' Since those words were written, we have had the 7 July bombings in London, the attempted bombings just a couple of weeks later and the communal violence in Birmingham – all of them in 2005, an *annus horribilis* if ever there was one. In each case the individuals concerned will have had complex reasons for doing what they did, but, equally, they must all have had one thing in common – one assumes their antipathy to mainstream British life and their sense of alienation from it was powerful enough to drive them towards violence.

The riots in the run-down Lozells area of Birmingham in 2005 exposed a fault line that has always been there but which rarely gets the attention it deserves – the mutual mistrust between some Asian and some African-Caribbean immigrant communities. Several nights of violence were fuelled by no more than a rumour that a black teenager who had been caught shoplifting in a Pakistani-run shop had been gang-raped as a punishment. The girl never came forward and whether the story was true or not was irrelevant. Deep-seated and simmering tensions between the two communities meant that on the streets it was as good an excuse as any.

The unrest in Lozells was reminiscent of the riots in Los Angeles in 1992 when Korean businesses bore the brunt of African-American anger. The actual cause of the riots, in which more than fifty people were killed – the acquittal of four police officers who had been filmed brutally attacking a black motorist, Rodney King – was forgotten as black youth went on the rampage. Some 2,000 Korean-owned businesses were destroyed. The grievance in Los Angeles was much the same as it was in Lozells. Koreans, like the Pakistani shopkeepers in the Birmingham district, were accused of exploiting their black customers. In neither case have the allegations been borne out by the facts.

What is certainly true is that in Birmingham the Asian families have outworked and outflanked the African-Caribbean community when it comes to running local businesses. The fact that the Pakistanis are more recent immigrants has been particularly galling for the black community. It's also true that there is a strong and visceral strain of racism amongst some Asians that is rarely, if ever, confronted with the same vigour that is reserved for white racism.

But the more fundamental problem thrown up by Lozells and, years before that, the riots in Bradford, Burnley and Oldham is the uneven integration of Britain's ethnic communities. We have to confront some awkward but telling comparisons. Why, for example, have the Gujaratis of Leicester and the Punjabis in Southall fared so much better than the Mirpuris in Bradford or the Sylhetis in Poplar? Why do Sri Lankan and Chinese children do well at school while their African-Caribbean counterparts (especially boys) trail behind? And how do we explain the success of the Jews?

Above all, is there a danger that all these communities might simply drift apart, their successes or failures barely impinging on the body of the nation except for periodic eruptions of violence?

In the opening decade of the twenty-first century, there appears to be a growing understanding among policy-makers that the emphasis placed on difference must give way to a new concentration on a common identity. Policies which actively encouraged communities to think of themselves as separate are being ditched. The most significant changes are in the way in which cities and regions get access to public money – whether it is for housing, education or job creation. For the past thirty years or so too many schemes – including those backed by the European Union through its regional funding policies – have had an inbuilt bias in favour of race or culture. Inner-city regeneration grants have all too often encouraged competition between communities for limited resources. Those who lose out are left resentful.

Perception is everything. Even the most laudable projects can seem divisive. During my research in Tower Hamlets I came across the case of the Sonali Gardens Day Centre. When it opened in 2004 it caused uproar locally because it was targeted at the Bangladeshi and Asian community. The council insisted it was not exclusive, but all the available literature about the centre – with its emphasis on 'culturally appropriate' care – gave a contrary impression. And it is not just elderly white people who feel left out. Some of the most strident criticism comes from other immigrant groups, such as the older African-Caribbean community, who feel they were never offered such tailor-made services.

Much the same applies to social housing. The growth of housing associations in the 1980s was a direct result of the inefficient and often racist management of council housing stock. The most recent immigrants were almost always dumped in the worst council estates. According to John Brewster, director of a local housing association, there was an unofficial policy of social engineering. 'It was pretty crude but effective. If someone was called Jones they went into one block, if someone was called Ali they were put into another block, usually the one with the biggest problems. These were the people the associations were set up to help.' John Brewster grew up in Brixton, south London, and has worked in local government since the 1990s.

But, again, what started as a laudable attempt to counter racism began to acquire an altogether different purpose: the separation of tenants by ethnicity. The housing associations themselves fell into the trap of allocating resources according to where prospective tenants had come from. Today there is a housing association for virtually every ethnic or religious group. Thirty-two housing associations around the country replied to my enquiries about who their tenants were. Whether it was the Ashiana Association in Rochdale or the Zebra HA in London, they all catered for a disproportionate number of people from ethnic minorities. In some cases, such as the Ebony Sistren HA in London, all its tenants were black or Asian. Gharana in Northants is for elderly Asian people only, while the Imani Housing Cooperative is open only to black African or African-Caribbean tenants. A sample of just over

thirty associations out of over 1,500 in England is hardly repre-
sentative, but it begins to tell a story about how housing policy
may – even inadvertently – have played its part in the separate
development of communities.

The persistence of separate communities may be the result of
well-intentioned but ultimately counterproductive thinking. 'I
think we have been guilty of political correctness,' says John
Brewster. 'As a black man I have been able to turn down a request
by my tenants for a mosque in one of our blocks – nobody can
accuse me of being racist. I simply felt there were plenty of places
for worship in the area and to have installed a prayer room in a
Portakabin would have smacked of ghettoising. But plenty of
white people would have found that kind of decision very difficult. They have been cowed by political correctness.'

Indeed it may be true that much of this division is by default
rather than design. That certainly appears to be the case in higher
education. The Labour government's push to enrol at least 50 per
cent of those eligible in colleges and universities appears to be
bearing fruit. The number of full- and part-time students has
certainly increased since 1997 when Tony Blair came to power.
Many of these new entrants to higher education come from ethnic
minorities, but their growing numbers tell only half the story.
Their concentration in certain urban institutions points to a two-
tier system based as much on ethnicity as it is on acumen. While
the old polytechnics, rebranded as universities, draw their students from a largely state-educated pool of students from low- to
middle-income families, the older universities cream off the most
able students from the best state schools and top up their numbers
with large numbers of privately educated students from more
privileged backgrounds.

Figures published by the Higher Education Statistics Agency
show that in 2004 one new university alone, London Metropolitan
(a merger between two former polytechnics) had more black students from African-Caribbean backgrounds than all the
universities that make up the elite Russell Group. In nine of the

nineteen universities that make up the group there were fewer
than 30 students who described themselves as black Caribbean.
Conversely, there were eleven institutions where white students
were in the minority. All of them are in London and seven of them
were former polytechnics

I first became aware of what some have called a 'colour-coded'
higher education system when I attended a graduation ceremony
at Middlesex University to collect an honorary doctorate. It was
an entirely different experience from the one I remembered at
Durham University where I had studied. Instead of the restraint
and decorum with which we had collected our degrees, at
Middlesex every name in the roll-call of graduates was greeted
with a shameless hollering from sundry relatives and friends. It
was a thoroughly un-English occasion and all the more jubilant
for it.

It was not just a matter of tone, but composition as well.
Virtually every graduate was from a British ethnic minority with
a sprinkling of foreign students. In 2004, the year I received my
honorary degree, 527 students completed courses in the School of
Computing Sciences, achieving BSc status. Between Ahmad
Jamin Bin Ab Aziz at the top of the list and Nikolaos Zografakis
at the bottom, I counted just 52 names which suggested they
were of white English or north European origin. Whenever I was
in doubt I assumed they were white, though, of course, they
might have been African-Caribbean students with English-
sounding names.

Looking through the whole list of graduates for that year, other,
more subtle, patterns emerge. The vast majority of vocational
degrees leading to careers in the health service, such as nursing
(but not doctors), were apparently awarded to ethnic minority
students. But in courses such as art and design there was a bias
towards white English students. If it's a picture of the future, it's
a telling one, in which the public services are disproportionately
staffed by people of immigrant origin while in the private sector
the reverse may be the case. There are already enough tensions

between the public and private sectors – not least over pay differentials – without adding the combustible issue of race.

So at school, at university, at home, and possibly at work, there are a number of young people, whether black, white or Asian, who have little real contact with people from other backgrounds. And yet in town halls and social services offices across Britain the myth of multiculturalism runs deep. But that is what it is – a case of collective make-believe. When you see posters advertising leisure centres, admissions brochures for schools, and on-line adverts for council services, the designers are always careful to make sure there is a racial mix in the photographs. You have to wonder how many of the people who talk about the benefits of multiculturalism actually live anywhere that is racially mixed. While some resolutely live on in the inner city and try to build bridges between classes and communities, many have bought their way out of the areas where different ethnic groups live cheek by jowl. Multiculturalism, with its emphasis on difference, suits the latter. Separateness works for the chattering classes, the advertising executives, the media types, the policy wonks and the estate agents. It allows them to talk the talk of racial harmony without ever having to test it in their personal lives.

The people for whom it manifestly doesn't work are the very people for whom it was designed. They are the ones whose lives are governed by public policy. They do not have the option of going private. If the state gets it wrong, their lives go wrong. It is the nexus between poverty, race and religion that has proved so pernicious. Multiculturalism, with its emphasis on diversity and cultural retention, has been a poor medium through which to tackle economic disadvantage. Segregation alone is bad enough, but when it is coupled with poverty its effect can be truly poisonous, as we are beginning to find out. For those people caught between the twin evils of racism and penury, marginalised socially and geographically, multiculturalism is failing to deliver what it promised all those years ago.

There will be some who will leap on my analysis of multiculturalism as proof that mass immigration to Britain has been a bad thing. That is emphatically not what these pages have been about. If I have been critical about multiculturalism it is because I want to get the best out of immigrants, not prevent them from coming here at all. The argument is not about whether immigration is a good thing or not, but whether those people – and they are a minority – who are locked away or who lock themselves away into an enclave can play a meaningful part in national life.

I could have written a book about the sheer exuberance, vitality and creativity that flows from the parts of Britain where the presence of diverse peoples has created something new and better than what was there before. In my own corner of London, Stoke Newington, in Brixton, in Leicester, in Liverpool and yes, even in Bradford, there are places that point the way to what genuine multiculturalism should look like. But my concern is with the places where it is not working. These are also places assailed by other problems – the social conservatism of the communities themselves and an entrenched poverty. The communal dissonance that is bubbling away in these places has a capacity to undermine much of the progress I believe we have made as a country.

Where they have been able to join the mainstream of British life, immigrants have consistently shown a capacity for hard work and a desire to contribute to national life. They have enriched our country, both body and soul. Much of what we take for granted in day-to-day life would be impossible without them. You can see this growing reliance on immigrants in the institutions that promote our physical and spiritual well-being – the National Health Service and the Christian churches.

5

Body and Soul

It really shouldn't have mattered, but there was an imperceptible, but genuine, sigh of relief when we heard that the consultant haematologist was an Asian. It was in the spring of 2003 that we – my sisters and I – were forced to confront the fact that our father's leukaemia could no longer be treated with pills. The original diagnosis had been made many years earlier, but now the condition had become close to debilitating. After his latest check-up at the Royal Free Hospital in north London, the consultant, Atul Mehta, had told my father it was time to consider chemotherapy. It wasn't that we thought an Asian doctor would be better than anyone else, but we knew my father would feel more comfortable in the hands of someone with whom he could feel a sense of affinity. Above all, we assumed that an Asian doctor would understand the subtle nuances of respect for age and patience with the elderly that one cannot always take for granted in modern British culture, least of all from the kind of men most likely to have climbed to the top rung of the medical ladder.

There comes a moment when the roles between parent and offspring are reversed. This was one such moment. The announcement about my father's health brought us up short. Suddenly this man who had helped to raise us, this husband who had nursed his wife through a long illness to a dignified end, seemed to diminish in stature. Where once we had seen strength we were confronted with frailty; the carer had become the cared for. We were in charge of him and not the other way around. It had probably been that way for some time, but now we were forced to acknowledge it.

I imagine Atul Mehta is the sort of person who would hate the idea of a 'dress-down' Friday. Some people wear a suit in a way that suggests they are bursting to put on something different. It's usually the tie or the socks, or even the handkerchief, that give away a hidden sartorial flamboyance. Not so Atul Mehta. Proper is how I would describe him. I'd add reserved too. A full head of jet-black hair belied his fifty years. The thick-framed glasses gave him a more severe look than his face deserved. There wasn't any small talk when we first met at the Royal Free Hospital, not even the Asian-to-Asian recognition of mutual achievement that I had become accustomed to. Perhaps an English consultant would have been fine after all! Still, all I needed to know was whether the chemotherapy was absolutely essential. On that he had no doubt. The alternative was for my father to end the year so weak that leaving his flat would become difficult. With the chemo he could look forward to a few more years of being out and about, including the all-too-important trips to Geneva and Florida where my other sisters lived, and, of course, Sri Lanka, towards which my father was increasingly drawn in his old age. So it was settled.

My father was given the first dose as an outpatient. Two days later, back at his flat, he was so weak he could hardly walk. The chemotherapy had delivered a knock-out punch and he was admitted to hospital. So began a period of several months during which my father suffered various complications. For weeks at a time he was in the Royal Free's Compston Ward. It was during this time that I developed a profound respect for what the NHS does day in and day out and a realisation that very little of it would be possible without the work of an army of immigrants.

The Royal Free Hospital began life in the early nineteenth century with the then revolutionary concept of treating the infirm regardless of their ability to pay. One December evening in 1827 a newly qualified surgeon called William Marsden was on his way home when he noticed a young woman lying on the steps of St Andrew's church in Holborn. The medic took the woman to three different hospitals, only to be turned away at each one. In those days you either paid or had what was called a 'subscriber's letter' – effectively an IOU for treatment handed out to those who had donated money to hospitals, which were all then run as charitable organisations. These benefactors often passed on their subscribers' letters to poor relatives or their domestic staff. For everyone else there was the dreaded workhouse infirmary. Marsden took care of the woman himself, but she died two days later 'unrecognised by any human being'. The event so shocked the young surgeon that he resolved to set up a hospital committed to the principle that 'while it has accommodation, it takes in all it can, and the more wretched they are, and the more diseased, the greater is their claim on this charity'. The fledgling hospital opened its doors in Hatton Garden in February 1928. Today, after several moves, it is situated in Hampstead – one of London's teaching hospitals. It could not live up to its historic mission in the modern age (albeit now under the aegis of the NHS) without the help of workers from virtually every corner of the globe.

A breakdown of the hospital's employees in 2005 showed that 46 per cent of its non-medical workforce and 40 per cent of its medical staff came from ethnic minorities. Over the summer and autumn of 2003 I got to know some of them. From the most senior consultants to the most junior ward staff my father's carers had invariably started out in life somewhere else. In their dedication and expertise they provide a powerful antidote to the hoary old image of the immigrant as a sponger. Those who shout loudest about being swamped by immigrants had better stay well, for if they ever fall ill they will have to swallow their words along with their pills. The National Health Service is as eloquent an argument as any in defence of immigration. Behind each one of the staff who treated my father is a story that helps to join the dots in the great tale of migration. From the epic impulses of history to the personal search for fulfilment and freedom, they reflect the varied motives of millions of travellers through the ages.

Atul Mehta's mother brought him and his elder sister to Britain from Kenya in 1959. He was five years old. Two other children, both boys, joined them three years later. Their father remained in Kenya, only joining the rest of the family in 1970.

Atul Mehta's arrival in Britain was, in a sense, the end of a cycle begun under British colonialism in the late nineteenth century. His great-grandfather, a Gujarati, was one of the 30,000 or so Indian indentured labourers taken to east Africa by the colonial administration. Between 1896 and 1901 they built the rail line that still links Mombasa on the coast with Kampala in the east African hinterland. It was an epic task for which the British took credit and the Indians shed blood. Nearly 2,500 Indians were killed, one for every four miles of track. Another 6,000 were injured. The line ran through some of the most challenging territory imaginable – much of it is now the Tsavo National Park – and it is said that some of the labourers were killed by lions.

In fact the Indians who were taken to east Africa were the last in a system of contract labour devised largely to fill the plantation labour shortage left by the abolition of slavery in the 1830s. Indeed the indentured labour system bore a remarkable resemblance to the slavery it purported to replace, though its iniquities are not nearly as well known. Drawn from the poorest sections of the populations around the port cities of Madras and Calcutta, thousands were hoodwinked into cramped ships by agents, only to be offloaded in a strange land and forced to work under the most brutal of conditions. In his comprehensive and still authoritative study of indentured labour, *A New System of Slavery*, Hugh Tinker found that the vast majority would return penniless and sick after five-, sometimes ten-year contracts. The first of these labourers were transported to Mauritius in 1834. Over the next sixty years they were taken as far afield as British Guiana and Trinidad in the Caribbean, Fiji, and the Natal coast of South Africa.

By the time Atul Mehta's great-grandfather made the journey to east Africa, conditions had improved somewhat. Thousands of labourers had chosen to stay on and take their chances as artisans and employees of the railway company. The railway they'd helped to build became the conduit for their penetration as traders into the remotest corners of Africa's interior. The *dukawallahs* who once sold everything from paraffin to perfume in the provincial towns of east Africa are the descendants of the railway workers. By the late sixties there were thought to be nearly 200,000 Indians in Kenya alone. As I wrote in *A Passage to Africa*, their history on the continent after that is an unhappy one.

The Mehtas' journey to Britain in 1959 pre-dated the expulsion of Asians from east Africa (brought about partly because of their own unwillingness to integrate fully in African life) but their progress once here was a precursor of the hard-won success enjoyed by so many of the African-Indian diaspora in Britain. Atul and one brother both went into medicine. While Atul studied at Cambridge and later specialised in malignant haemotology, his brother runs a nephrology practice in the United States. The third brother works for the European Commission in Brussels. His sister is married to an architect. 'I think we were all driven by the knowledge that my parents had sacrificed so much to get us educated here,' says Atul. 'They put up with years of separation and we were conscious of that.'

Atul Mehta's home on a leafy north London street speaks of the solid professional success he and his wife Kokila (who is a GP), enjoy. To walk into their home is to walk into a vision of what the vast majority of British people aspire to. Theirs was an arranged marriage, the kind that makes you wonder if there isn't, after all, something to be said for that way of doing things. Crucially, and quite unlike the practice of the Asians in Bradford, who go back to the home village for marriage partners, Kokila too is part of the African-Indian diaspora. Her family also came from Kenya. The couple have a shared history, not the first-world–third-world clash of habits and aspiration that so often leads to an unequal and unhappy union. Their relationship epitomises the cross-cultural juggling act that goes on in so many immigrant homes. Kokila, who studied medicine in India, says she doesn't feel as rooted in Britain as Atul. 'Whenever he wants to say something important, he says it in English,' she remarks, with the mischievous eyes that tell you that if the sparks ever fly in this relationship, it's mostly from her corner. 'Whenever I want to say something important, I resort to Gujarati.' In a sign of the way immigrant aspirations change with the generations their daughter, Avani, had her sights set on a career in journalism.

If Atul Mehta took the lead in the diagnosis of my father's leukaemia, it was left to others to implement the treatment and deal with its enervating consequences.

Among them was a young staff nurse named Zuber Mohabeer. In the hospital's hierarchy he might be at the opposite end to Atul Mehta, but the two of them do have something in common, even if they never acknowledge it. Zuber is from Mauritius, an island off the south-east coast of Africa that is populated almost entirely by descendants of Indians taken there through the indentured labour system. Like me he is a Tamil, though few in Mauritius acknowledge that part of their heritage. They are what they are famous for – an elegant, enchanting mix of Asian looks and French habits.

His first recollection of England was watching premiership football back home in Mauritius. 'I used to see players from every country on the TV and I used to think that was great,' he says with an accent that still echoes the Creole he'd be speaking if he were back in Mauritius. 'I thought it was great that all those Africans and so on had made their home there. I was about eighteen at the time and it was like my dream to come here.' Zuber arrived in Britain in July 1998 to do a course in business studies. The fees turned out to be more than he could afford and he switched to nursing.

I met Zuber at his bedsit on the top floor of a three-storey Victorian pile in London's Golders Green. As we headed up the stairs, Zuber pointed to each door we passed, reciting the names and nationalities of the other tenants. There were two Italian guys, a British couple, another from New Zealand, a Greek woman and a man from South Africa – all of them playing their part in the world's most cosmopolitan city.

If you can judge a man by the state of his room, then Zuber is a man with his life in order. In fact it may only prove that the smaller the space you live in, the more organised you have to be. The nine different bottles of perfume I counted on his dresser-cum-desk – Hugo Boss, Chanel, Versace among others – put my own habitual reliance on a couple of old favourites to shame. The 14-inch TV is linked up to a PlayStation. 'Last night I played some games with friends while we listened to "Dark Side of the Moon".' That Pink Floyd number is just one of the seventies tunes he can play on his guitar. 'I play every day. It's a way of relaxing after a shift at the hospital. Usually I play some Clapton or Jimi Hendrix. I like that era.'

When he goes into Compston Ward at the Royal Free Hospital he is one of about twenty nurses. He says all but one are foreigners. And the unit manager is English. 'For us, foreigners, nursing is a big opportunity. We make a lot more money than we would at home. It doesn't matter where you come from – whether it is the Philippines or Mauritius.' The work is tough. 'There are so many opportunities here so English people don't look at nursing. They don't really want to do this kind of thing, they don't want to clean people up. It's not glamorous enough for them. They think it is dirty work.'

Dirty it may be, but it is certainly essential work. The Royal Free Hospital's reliance on people like Atul Mehta and Zuber Mohabeer is mirrored across the NHS as a whole. In 2003, nearly a third of all the doctors (29.4 per cent) employed by the NHS were foreign-born. The vast majority of these were educated outside the European Economic Area (the twenty EU countries plus a few more such as Switzerland). Consultants in the difficult-to fill-specialities are disproportionately foreign-educated.

In dentistry, the number of overseas-educated staff in 2003 was over 5,000 – a little less than a fifth of all dentists. But according to the General Dental Council, the figure for new admissions on to its register shot up to over 40 per cent in 2003.

The number of foreign-trained staff on the register of the Nursing and Midwifery Council is about 65,000, or 10 per cent of the total. But if you look at new entrants on the register since 1999, over 40 per cent are foreign. As in the case of doctors, the vast majority (over 90 per cent) were from non-EEA countries. The Department of Health's recruitment website for overseas nurses (www.nursinguk.nhs.uk) features the 'real-life' stories of Spanish, Filipino and Indian nurses. One of them is Rani Jose from Kerala in India, who, according to the website, began nursing in Worcester in April 2002. She paints an enticing picture of life in an NHS hospital: 'I usually come in 15 minutes before my shift starts, and have a cup of tea in the canteen while I do my emails on the free computer . . . My lunch break starts at 1 p.m., and I usually go to the canteen. A coffee costs 50p (about 35 rupees), but when you compare your salary with that cost, it's OK. Sometimes I bring my food from home and heat it up in the kitchen – it's easy to find all the ingredients we have in India.'

The trend is clear: an ever-growing dependency on the skills of foreign workers, many of whom may go on to become immigrants. This reliance on foreigners began quite early in the NHS's unique history.

The NHS was the first health system outside the Soviet Union to offer free medical care to the entire population. Unlike in other European countries, it was not based on the insurance principle, with entitlement following contributions, but on the national provision of services available to everyone at any time. At its ten-year-anniversary celebrations, Aneurin Bevan, its founder, said the service was 'the most civilised achievement of modern government' anywhere in the world. In Britain, at a time when other institutions like parliament and even the monarchy have lost public support, the NHS retains a central place in people's loyalty. With the election of David Cameron as leader of the Conservative Party in 2005, and his avowed belief in the public services, the NHS's future appeared to be beyond party politics.

From the 1950s onwards, thousands of doctors from Pakistan, India, Bangladesh and Sri Lanka came to the UK to fill NHS vacancies, particularly in the more deprived areas of the country. The sixties saw a considerable expansion of the service by the Tories, who, under their 1962 National Hospital Plan, created district-run hospitals for areas with populations of around 125,000. The plan would not have been possible without a new injection of staff from abroad. As I pointed out earlier it was none other than Enoch Powell (who became famous for his anti-immigration views) who sought to address the staff shortage with recruitment abroad. The NHS was relentlessly marketed to Indian medical students during this period. The sixties also saw the emergence of the 'Cinderella' specialities – chronic illness, psychiatry and geriatrics, specialities which overseas doctors were often forced to take up on arrival.

But this early dependency on foreign nationals has created what some have called the NHS's 'retirement timebomb' as increasing numbers of the doctors who came in that first wave of recruitment reach the age of sixty-five. It's thought that about two-thirds of the doctors who qualified abroad, mostly of south Asian origin, will be retiring around 2007. They are concentrated in some of the country's most deprived areas. Over half the GPs in Barking and Havering in east London are Asians. This was the generation of foreign doctors who replaced the disillusioned English doctors who had emigrated in their hundreds in the sixties and seventies to the United States, Canada and Australia. The English GPs who stayed on also migrated, but to the suburbs, or they specialised in disciplines such as gynaecology and paediatrics. This left Asian GPs in the run-down inner-city practices. In places like Manchester's Moss Side or Hackney in London they make up the majority of doctors. Some of these areas will soon lose up to a quarter of their family doctors.

Whether it's medicine, dentistry or nursing, most of these foreign workers have come from a handful of countries which have the capacity to train staff and where English is spoken or taught in schools. The British government has a code of practice which bans the NHS from recruiting medical staff trained in a number of poor countries. In December 2004 the ban was extended to include recruitment by private agencies. But the code does not have the force of law and is widely recognised to be unworkable. In 2004, for example, the NMC registered 3,301 nurses (including some midwives) who came from sixteen countries on the banned list, among them some of the poorest countries in the world and where Britain has substantial aid programmes. It really is a case of giving with one hand and taking with the other. Tiny Nepal provided 73 nurses. Twenty-four nurses came here from Sierra Leone, which languishes somewhere near the bottom of the list of the world's most wretched countries. Even Zimbabwe, where appalling governance has contributed to one of the continent's worst health crises, lost 311 nurses to Britain.

Many of these people start work in private nursing homes and care centres before transferring to the NHS. As Britain's population continues to age, the demand for care workers in nursing homes will continue to grow. This country, and the rich world in general, is not producing enough home-grown medical staff to fill the gap. Taking retirement and natural wastage into account, Britain will need 25,000 more doctors and some 250,000 extra nurses by the end of the decade. America will need a staggering 800,000 more nurses by 2015. Countries where tens of thousands of children still die before they reach the age of five will be supplying medical staff so that more of us can live into our dotage with our dignity more or less intact.

What represents a gain for Britain is a loss for these nations, which can ill afford to be subsidising our health service. According to the Institute for Public Policy Research, more than one in ten Indian-trained doctors works in the UK! In Ghana, the cost of training all its health professionals who work abroad is thought to have been about £40 million. Between 2003 and 2004, the southern African kingdom of Swaziland lost three-quarters of the 200 nurses it trained to the UK. In South Africa, over a quarter of the annual vacancies for doctors and nurses in state-funded hospitals remain unfilled. An article in *The Economist* on Africa's brain drain put the cost to South Africa of training the healthcare professionals who now work abroad at US$1 billion.

Here in Britain there are thought to be about 7,000 South African-trained doctors on the General Medical Council's permanent register. One of them is Geoff Dusheiko, an honorary consultant at the Centre for Hepatology at the Royal Free Hospital. He joined the team of people treating my father when he developed liver problems in the aftermath of the chemotherapy. Professor Dusheiko came to Britain on 2 January 1988. If Atul and Zuber share a history that goes back to the British Empire's thirst for cheap labour, Geoff Dusheiko's life is inextricably linked with the disastrous fate of European Jewry.

Professor Dusheiko's grandfather left Lithuania for South Africa in 1902, part of a massive Jewish exodus. He was one of thousands of Lithuanian Jews – Litvaks, as they called themselves – who were escaping the repression, the anti-Semitism, the pogroms and conscription into the Tsarist army in the late nineteenth century and the early years of the twentieth. The Bolshevik revolution did little to improve their prospects. The Second World War and the Holocaust finally put paid to what had once been an important centre of Jewish thought and culture. It is thought that about 90 per cent of the pre-war Litvak population of over 200,000 perished in the Holocaust.

In fact the very first Litvaks to head for South Africa were drawn by the prospect of making money – diamonds were discovered in Kimberley in 1867. The founder of De Beers, now synonymous with the glamour and glitz of the precious stone, was the Litvak Barney Barnato.

At its height, the Litvak population in South Africa numbered some 70,000. They brought much more than their business acumen. South Africa's progressive politics is replete with the names of Lithuanian Jews. Helen Suzman, who for over a decade in the eighties was the lone voice of opposition in the apartheid parliament, was a Litvak. But perhaps the most famous of them all, at least to the oppressed black population, was Joe Slovo. He was head of the South African Communist Party and led the African National Congress's military wing in exile. Long before Nelson Mandela was released, years before the ANC was un-banned and its leaders allowed to return in triumph, Slovo's name was painted on township walls. He was a white hero for a black people.

Geoff Dusheiko was aware of this proud history as he contemplated a move to Britain in the late eighties. South Africa seemed to be going nowhere. President P. W. Botha's 'rubicon' speech in August 1985 had promised so much but delivered so little. Geoff was genuinely torn between the prospect of a new life in Britain and staying on in the hope that something, anything might change. He was not a political animal but he tried to take a stand. He refused to make segregated ward rounds, saying that black doctors had to accompany him to see white patients or there would be no ward round at all. His was the kind of protest that went unnoticed but was, nonetheless, one of the million little blows that would eventually bring down the walls that separated black from white.

The offer from the Royal Free Hospital was tempting: the chance to do research on hepatitis, a condition on which he had already published research. 'Fifty-one per cent of me wanted to leave and forty-nine per cent wanted to stay. It was that close,' he says wistfully, as if he were having to make the decision all over again. 'I was happy to leave apartheid but unhappy to leave the country of my birth. To this day I have a sense of guilt.'

Where once he lived in a country where a white doctor was not allowed to make a ward round with black staff, he now finds himself in a country where it would simply be impossible to insist on such a rule. 'I can often do a ward round where there are no English graduates at all,' he says with just a touch of irony.

While the opportunity to further his research into liver disease, with all the facilities that the Royal Free Hospital had to offer, prompted Geoff Dusheiko's move to Britain, one suspects he might not have made the journey had it not been for his quiet revulsion with apartheid. For others, though, the move to Britain is driven by more personal motives.

'When I left Hong Kong, being gay was difficult, at least as far as my family was concerned,' says Chun, an intensive care unit nurse who also treated my father. 'They would have had a big difficulty if I had come out when I was with them. That was one of the main reasons I decided to get away from Hong Kong.' Chun came to Britain in 1992 when he was in his late teens. 'Here it is different. And the men are gorgeous which is a bonus,' he says playfully, even now relishing the freedom to be what he is.

For Chun, nursing has become a passion, though it is not what he thought he would do when he began looking for work. First he studied computing at a college in south London. 'I was going out with someone who worked in computing,' he says as if that were reason enough to start a career in the field. In between his work at the Royal Free Hospital and extra shifts through a private agency, he is taking a part-time degree in history at Birkbeck College and has reached stage two in his accountancy studies. 'I like learning,' he told me.

We meet in his upper-floor bedsit in Ornan Court, a block for the hospital's nursing staff. The room reflects a man who finds it hard to choose between his many enthusiasms. His books and magazines (everything from *Nursing Standard* to Matthew Parris's autobiography, *Chance Witness*, and the Harry Potter series) compete for space with cooking utensils and clothes. His rice cooker rests somewhat precariously across two unequal stacks of books, while many of the clothes are stuffed into those huge blue and yellow IKEA bags. Predictably, his PC is parked on the Amazon home page.

Ornan Court, all five floors of it, is packed with foreign nurses. 'No one wants to be a nurse in this country,' says Chun. 'It's got the two things English people hate most. Low pay and lots of responsibility.' It is as acute an observation as I've heard to explain Britain's continuing failure to find native-born nursing and medical staff. 'You know, it's all funny hours and hard work and they just want to go to work, get paid and go out and spend it all.'

You'd have thought that safety of numbers would protect all these foreign workers from the petty racism that still seeps into their daily life – not from other staff but largely from the patients. Both Chun and Zuber, who I had met earlier, told me that clearcut zero-tolerance policies on racism in the NHS mean the problem rarely escalates beyond being an irritant. But the irony of abuse from patients whose very lives often depend on the attention and care of these foreign nurses is not lost on Ernest. 'Bloody foreigners! I just love that,' he says. 'Finish. The end. That's what would happen if we all walked out.'

But they are not going to do that. They are here because, in each case, life in Britain gives them something they could not get at home, even if some of them no longer think of anywhere else as home. We have something they want – a stable future in a largely tolerant country. In return, with their intelligence and labour, they bring something we need. There are other immigrants, though, who have come to these islands because they think they have something which we have lost. They come to Britain with a vocation, a calling to help us rediscover our forgotten faith.

Elizabeth Jane Jarvis lay in her father's arms, blissfully unaware of what was happening to her. Steve Jarvis, his wife Karen and their relatives had gathered at the Church of the Holy Ghost in Yeovil for the baptism of the latest addition to their family. In a neat historical echo of a time when white hands were laid on dark skins, four-and-a-half-month-old Elizabeth was brought into the Catholic faith with the delicate anointing of her forehead by

Father Sunny Paul, a priest from India. Nearly 2,000 years after St Thomas the Apostle first took Christianity to the Indian state of Kerala, a descendant of one of his original converts had made the journey west, bringing with him a religious conviction that has all but faded in Britain but which still beats strong in the hearts of hundreds of millions in Asia, Africa and South America. It was an unseasonably warm November day in 2005 and Father Sunny Paul was living up to his name, bringing some spiritual sunshine into the lives of his parishioners. He is one of a growing procession of foreign priests who are reinvigorating, and sometimes changing, the Christian faith in all its guises – Catholic, Anglican and Evangelical. He is a reverse missionary.

Earlier in the day I had sat in a pew at the back of the church as a small congregation gathered for the ten o'clock mass. There were not many of us, twenty to thirty at most. That in itself was a commentary on what is happening to the Catholic Church, but it was the race and age of the congregation that was most telling. All the white worshippers, except for a mother with her two children, looked as if they were of retirement age. The only young adults there were workers from the nearby hospital – Indians, Sri Lankans and Filipinos. In front of us Father Sunny brought life to an ancient ritual, assisted by two altar boys. They too were Indian; Royston, whose parents came from Goa, and Jittu whose family came to Britain from Kerala. Among the congregation were the foreigners who administer to our bodies, up on the altar those who care for our souls.

I had first met Father Sunny Paul four years earlier while on a family holiday in south-west England. It was just after Christmas and before the New Year. A couple of my sisters and their children were with us. We are not regular churchgoers but my father, a devout Catholic, was with us, and only in the most extreme of circumstances does he miss Sunday mass. In fact I rather like accompanying him to church. In the same way our teenage sons continued to put their stockings out on Christmas Eve long after they knew just who was nibbling the mince pie and swigging the sherry, I too cling to the idea of our family at prayer. I still look along the pew, as I did all those years ago, and wonder what my father is thinking behind those closed eyes. There is something comforting about knowing that while so much has changed in our lives, this particular aspect of it stays the same.

We sat in the ancient chill of Our Lady of the Assumption on the southern edge of Tavistock. We were among the first to arrive. That, too, has not changed. Our Yuletide twittering disappeared into the emptiness of a vaulted roof. Slowly, like a gentle tide that laps its way into a cove, people began to drift in. You sensed the church was never going to fill up, but it did begin to look less empty. The gritty scrape of a leather shoe on cold stone, the genteel cough of a tweedy old dear and the sturdy thump of a hymn book as it fell on an oak bench – all these reminded me that I was in an English church and not in one of the mosques, temples, chapels or shrines that I had visited on my travels. Those places in which, even in the most desolate of times, I had watched people seek some solace, some relief from war and pestilence.

The mass began. We rose to our feet. 'In the name of the Father, and of the Son . . .' I had heard those words a hundred times before, but that day in Tavistock they struck me as odd. I looked up and peered across the congregation to where the priest was standing. I realised then that it was not the words that were unusual, but the way they were spoken. In this old stannary town, in this Victorian church, from the altar where a priest once lectured miners in their Sunday best, I now heard the unmistakable tones of Indian English. It was like finding out that one of Enid Blyton's Famous Five was a black child. It dawned on me that Sunday that there was something profound happening in the Catholic Church. Our paths crossed once or twice after that, but it was only when I began research for this book that I found Father Sunny Paul again, this time in his new parish in Yeovil, Somerset.

Father Sunny is a Fransalian, a member of the Missionaries of Francis de Sales. The order began life in India in 1845 after its founder, a French priest called Peter Mernier, failed to establish a mission in Africa. Sunny Paul's first contact with the order was in the late fifties, when a cousin who had already been ordained would visit the family home with a French priest. 'I remember it because my parents used to get very excited that a European was coming to their home,' he told me. 'All I remember is that the French priests looked so tall, so huge.' His cousin's parting gifts were always the same – pictures of saints, 'holy pictures' they used to call them. By the time Sunny was fourteen, in 1968, he had entered a seminary and twelve years later emerged as a priest.

His first assignment was what you would expect from a mission order. He was sent to the north-east of India, to the state of Meghalaya. 'We lived in a hut deep in the jungle. It was very remote. There was no electricity, no running water. Even the local people lived in isolated communities. Every hill had its own language.' As his French predecessors had once done, the young priest helped to open dispensaries and schools. He was responsible for about forty villages spread out across an area that stretched over a hundred miles from end to end. He told me the only food they had was what they managed to grow or hunt. 'We'd go out on a full moon and sit in a tree near a waterhole. Around midnight the animals would start to gather. You could tell the difference between the animals by the way their eyes reflected the light of the moon. Mostly we were after the deer; they gave off a reddish reflection.' Father Sunny, one of the mission workers and a couple of the older boys would gut and skin the animals in the bush before carrying the carcasses to the mission station.

It all seemed such a far cry from where we sat in the comfort of his dining room. In Yeovil he has an English housekeeper. Bridget Fox had just treated us to roast beef, potatoes and all the trimmings, with a trifle to follow. No more hunting now, just a bit of washing up and an affectionate hug for Bridget. It certainly wasn't what he'd had in mind when he joined the priesthood in India, but he thought there was a certain logic to it. 'History goes in cycles,' he said. 'The greatest gift the English gave us was their language. And that is precisely why I am able to come here and work. I regard England now as mission territory.' With us at lunch was Father Andrew (himself the son of Polish immigrants) and the retired Father Allan. It was Father Allan who saw the funny side of what was happening around that table: 'It's not the US cavalry that's rescued us,' he quipped. 'It's the Indians! As a congregation we would have been wound up if it had not been for people like Father Sunny.'

It was back in 1990 when the head of the Southwest Province in India received an SOS from the order's provincial in England. In the letter the provincial spoke of how the order was in danger of losing its parishes because it no longer had enough priests. Father Sunny Paul was on his way. He embarked on a journey that is reshaping the story of the Christian faith. What he is doing is to turn the notion of what it means to be a missionary on its head.

Some four centuries ago the first Catholic missionaries set out from Europe in the wake of the Spanish and Portuguese colonisation of Central and South America. By 1622 the Church even had a committee of cardinals – the Sacred Congregation for the Propagation of the Faith – devoted to disseminating Catholic teaching across newly colonised territories. It even produced a sort of operating manual for missions known as the Propaganda. There were missions in the Americas, China and India, although early attempts to take the faith to Africa were a failure. The heyday of the African mission did not come until the nineteenth century. This was the period when the great Catholic orders dedicated to spreading the religion abroad were founded. The White Fathers and then the White Sisters were established just a year apart in 1868 and 1869.

The first Protestant missions began in the seventeenth century, piggy-backing on the Dutch commercial ventures into Indonesia, Taiwan and Sri Lanka. By the end of the eighteenth century both the London Missionary Society and the Church Missionary Society had been founded.

Historically, nothing in the world of ideas can match the spread of Christianity. By the time of the Edinburgh Missionary Conference in 1910 it was far easier to cite the countries which remained closed to the missionary effort – places such as Afghanistan, Tibet and Nepal – than to try to add up all those places where men and women in white habits roamed more or less at will.

Missionaries played a huge role in my own family. Both my maternal grandparents were Catholic, while my paternal grandfather was a Methodist. His wife was a Hindu but converted to Methodism after marriage. These young men in white cassocks occupied a rather surreal space in the social hierarchy. A mixture of religious authority, white-skinned novelty and an easy-going American charm meant they could be both holy and hot, celibate and celebrated. My father tells me how one priest, Father Del Mamo, would speed around the eastern town of Batticaloa on his scooter leaving a trail of admiring looks in his dusty wake. Another, Father Harold Weber, was so good at sports that when they built a stadium in the city years later it was called the Weber Stadium. In the late forties, when their incompatible castes appeared to stymie a relationship between my parents, it was the Catholic Church they both turned to for advice. I am named after Father George Hamilton, a Jesuit who had grown up in New York and arrived in Sri Lanka in 1942. In retrospect, it is certainly true that our Christianity has played a pivotal role in my family's integration into a Western society.

Eventually, though, the sight of educated white people ministering to their dark-skinned and uneducated flock added to the notion that Christianity and colonialism (along with that other 'c', commerce) were inextricably linked. As Archbishop Desmond Tutu once put it in his impish way, 'When the missionaries came to Africa, they had the bibles and we had the land. They said "Let us pray." We closed our eyes to pray, and when we opened them they had the land and we had the bibles.' Acute though his observation is, it isn't entirely fair. Church men and women were among those most strongly opposed to the slave trade and other forms of exploitation. Practically the whole generation of leaders who took Africa to independence gained whatever education they had under the tutelage of the missions. Some, like Robert Mugabe of Zimbabwe, prove that they did not always go on to practise what they had been taught.

Few of the delegates at that 1910 Edinburgh conference would have believed it at the time, but that was a high-water mark for the missions. After the Great War, the rate of expansion of the missions would slow down as the local branches of the churches became self-sustaining. In 1914, the Catholic Church did not have a single non-white bishop outside the four created specially for India late in the previous century. In the decades that followed, it was impossible for the Church to ignore the birth of modern nationalism in the colonies, and the idea that only white people could 'carry the weight of the episcopate' began to look increasingly anachronistic.

But it was developments at home that put paid first to the missions, and then to the faith itself. The formal Christian churches have withered in the face of the growing secularisation of Britain that began after the Second World War. Like a disease that eats away at a body from the inside, the buildings and institutions of the churches have remained intact, but the people, their lifeblood, have seeped away in astonishing numbers.

For those who care about the fate of the Christian churches, the *Religious Trends Handbook* makes for some very depressing reading. It is the most comprehensive snapshot of what's happening to Christianity in Britain. Though 72 per cent of the population regarded itself as Christian in 2000, just 8 per cent said they were regular churchgoers. (These figures had fallen from 76 per cent and 11 per cent in 1980.) In 1998 the average Anglican congregation in more remote rural areas (as opposed to commuter areas) was fourteen people. By 2010 the average congregation in these churches is projected to be just three ageing people. Ten years later, by 2020, church attendance across all the Christian faiths will be down to just 4 per cent of the population. The England of village churches, choir boys and Sunday schools has all but disappeared. It retains a hold on the collective imagination, periodically conjured up by some politician eager to evoke a forgotten past. But in reality that's all it is, a forgotten past. In the relatively short time I have spent in this country, I have seen Sunday transformed from a day of rest, if not necessarily a day of worship, to a day of consumerism, when millions genuflect at that altar of modern life, the out-of-town shopping mall.

In the final section of their handbook for 2005, the researchers try to paint a picture of what the UK might look like by 2020. By then only half the population will even bother to describe itself as Christian. No section of the Christian faith will escape the seemingly remorseless spread of secularism. The number of Presbyterian church members is forecast to drop by 42 per cent, Methodists by 37 per cent, Anglicans by 31 per cent, Catholics by 28 per cent, independents by 22 per cent and the Baptists by 17 per cent. The TV programme *Songs of Praise*, which in the nineties had an average audience of nearly five million viewers, will long since have been taken off the schedules, and the small number of Christian radio stations in London and other big cities will struggle to survive. Some 2,000 rural churches will have been shut down, and nearly half of what's left of the churchgoers will be over sixty-five years old.

Late in 2005 Christian Research were in the process of analysing another survey. Their preliminary findings appear to show that the picture for the Church of England may not be as bleak as forecast in the previous study, although the numbers will continue to decline. In remoter rural areas, in particular, the size of congregations, though they will decline, may not fall as low as three worshippers. It's thought this may be due to a shift in rural demographics, with a growing number of urban professionals moving into the countryside, a move assisted by the flexibility that the internet has brought to working practices. The overarching trend remains the same, however. As Christian Research's director, Peter Brierley, says, 'unquestionably the numbers are still decreasing at an unacceptably quick rate'.

But there is another story to tell about the Christian faith, both here in Britain and globally. There is one part of Britain's Christian community that is still managing to keep its collective head above water. Like the urban buddleia that you see growing in the most improbable terrain, sprouting out from the cracked brickwork of some derelict building, the evangelical movement, especially its Pentecostal branches, is putting up a more robust fight against the spread of secularism. Its numbers in Britain may also have diminished but nothing like as disastrously as the mainstream churches – indeed, some ministries, in some places, are still growing. Many are imports from Africa, serving that continent's diaspora.

Nana Acheampong from Ghana is a driver for one of the cab companies on contract to the BBC. Over the years I have sat in the back of his Mercedes Benz on a number of occasions, and our common interest in Ghana (I was at primary school there) has been the springboard for many a conversation. It was during one of these chats that I discovered that Nana the chauffeur is also Nana the pastor. He is a leading light in the Elim Church of Pentecost, founded in Ghana but now with some sixty congregations in this country. The church in the UK is led by what Nana calls 'the resident missionary'. His name is Nene Amegatcher, his official title, Apostle.

For Christmas 2005 Apostle Nene Amegatcher decided to try something new. In the past the Christmas service had always been on 24 December because it was assumed that the streamlined public transport services on Christmas Day itself would make it difficult for his members to get to his church in Dagenham, Essex. But his congregation has changed. Many Ghanaians have established themselves in Britain, they are more prosperous than they once were and can afford to own cars. There was only one way to find out if enough of them were in that happy position to make a service on Christmas Day viable – try it out.

So it was that my wife Frances, our son Matthew and I set out on the A13 to Essex for a Christmas service like no other we had ever been to before. The route carves its way through some of the most dispiriting urban landscape imaginable. Tower blocks clad in multicoloured façades that some seventies architect thought looked modern jut out like concrete watchtowers from a flat, lifeless plain of social housing. London's many suburbs have soul because each of them has a centre; they are places that were absorbed into the capital as it grew towards the outlying villages. Finchley, Dulwich, Stoke Newington, all of them still retain a sense of being rooted in their long history. It's different out east. Places like Becton still look as if they have been built rather than evolved. The hand of the postwar town planner, with his penchant for uniformity and mediocrity, is all too evident. Here it felt as if the buildings defined the people rather than the other way round. This sense of life subdued by architecture, rather than released by it, was heightened by the empty pavements and boarded shops we sped past as we hurried to make the service that Christmas morning.

We found Green Lane in Dagenham. The house numbers had four digits. We were looking for 746, the address Nana had given me. We didn't need to check the number; we knew we had arrived when we saw a black man outside what looked like a converted bingo hall or cinema. He was dressed in an immaculate cream suit, striped tie and two-tone shoes. In one hand he had a bucket of water, in the other a broom. It was as if he were trying to feed and cleanse this jungle of bricks and mortar, trying to find something beneath the accretion of urban life, the discarded packets of yesterday's takeaway meals and wasted cigarette butts, that would make the place fit for the spiritual.

We were a bit early. Like father, like son! Inside, it felt like people were preparing for a rock concert, not a church service. Instead of white-haired women in sensible shoes putting the final touches to the flower arrangements, there were young men in sharp suits testing out the sound system. Up on a raised stage where the bingo caller might once have sung out someone's lucky numbers, there was a set of drums, two electronic keyboards and couple of guitars. Halfway up the gentle slope of the hall a man at the sound desk checked his faders and pushed an array of buttons. A video projection screen flickered into life. I watched it run through the different phases of the Microsoft Windows start-up sequence before settling on a page with the slogan 'God Richly Bless You'. Who needs a wooden board with hymn numbers hanging from brass hooks when you have Mr Gates's software at your disposal? Their faith may belong to an era hardly any of us can remember, but the evangelical movement is very much of the twenty-first century.

The hall could hold hundreds, and many a time it had been full to overflowing. I knew that because on one of my journeys home Nana had played a DVD in the car which showed the congregation in all its glory. There you go, the technology thing again. How many Church of England parishes or Roman Catholic congregations do you know that have compiled a DVD of their activities? But on this Christmas morning, as the minutes ticked towards ten o'clock, there were no more than about fifty people. What the congregation lacked in numbers it made up for in sartorial elegance. There were men in African printed tunics or the high-collared long jacket and trouser combination that is Africa's take on the two-piece suit. There were older women in hats that would have held their own at Ascot and younger women in long pencil skirts and blouses that stayed tight to the skin till they hit the waist and flared out in a frill. Oranges and greens. Some of the women wore the trademark wraparound headgear of west Africa in which one starch-stiff end would be splayed like a peacock in full cry. Their children darted from one row to another. Little boys with clip-on ties and waistcoats and the girls like ladies-in-waiting with their shiny little handbags and matching court shoes. Their braided hair, pulled away from the scalp, looked like sculpted bark on rich mahogany.

'Why didn't you tell me they'd all be dressed up?' Matt shot an anxious look at me. Back home when we were getting dressed and he'd asked me what to wear, I'd told him to put on whatever he felt comfortable in. I hadn't meant the jeans with the carefully torn knees and frayed hems but I'd let it pass. I'd forgotten that in Africa, and in much of the poor world, church is still somewhere you dress up for. Now, as he tried to pull his military green hooded jacket below his knees, I told him not to worry. In Africa, unlike some places in England, I have never been judged by what I have worn, only by what I have said,

A minute to ten and I heard a voice from the aisle. It was Nene Amegatcher; dark suit, grey shirt and a matching tie knotted to perfection. 'You're welcome,' he said. 'Nana told me you would be coming.' I told him we couldn't stay that long, perhaps an hour. 'That's a pity, our services usually last about three hours. It will be a little difficult to get a proper feel for what we're doing in such a short time.' I wondered when the service would start. I'll admit I half expected the Elim Church of Pentecost to be on 'African time', to start the service when they were ready and not as advertised. I was wrong. 'We'll start in a couple of minutes,' Nene said, and with that he walked down the aisle and found his place in a small row of seats at the front which, unlike the others, had high backs and armrests.

It wasn't Nene but one of his trainee church officials, one of the 'brothers', who double-stepped his way on to the stage for the opening prayers. 'Praise the Lord,' said Joshua Hodo. 'Hallelujah,' they shouted back. He began with a litany of disasters that had afflicted others but which had left his congregation unscathed. The tsunami had killed tens of thousands but they had been saved. 'Not one strand of our hair is missing.' The bombs of 7 July had exploded but they had been saved. Again, 'Not one strand of our hair is missing.' You could hear it happening, you could feel it happening. Pace and repetition. He strode across the stage, microphone in one hand, gesticulating with the other. The earthquake in Pakistan had robbed many lives and 'Not one strand of our hair is missing.' Each time Joshua said this there would be a rejoinder from another official on the floor. 'Thanks, Jesus.' Over and over until some in the crowd joined in. 'Be in our midst, Jesus,' I heard the woman to our right say.

Slowly the congregation, which had continued to grow, was being brought together. And then, seamlessly, we were singing. The words flashed up on the screen. 'Excellent is thy name/ Excellent is thy power/ God you are so wonderful/ My God you are excellent.' I looked from side to side; there were twice as many people around us. Up on the stage the musicians had taken up their instruments. Four women and two men provided backing vocals. We felt the vibrations of the bass guitar ripple through the floorboards beneath us. 'Holy Spirit, move me now/ Make my life whole again/Spirit move over me/ Spirit move over me.' The congregation began to sway with the music. We shifted uneasily from foot to foot. We must have looked like the guy at the disco, and there always is one, who's going up when everybody else is coming down.

It was time for another sermon. This time, as the pastor spoke, the man at the keyboard underlaid the words with music. Deftly, like a member of an orchestra following the conductor, he matched the rhetorical phases of the pastor with his fingertips. Every now and then the drummer would strike the cymbals. And then suddenly, as if this was a play-list they had rehearsed a hundred times, it all stopped. Quiet. Just quiet. It takes nerve to do this, I thought. How long will he risk it? I realised I was holding my breath, counting off the seconds. And then, just as you thought somebody would break the silence, the brother lifted his microphone and cut in: 'What have I done to deserve your coming, Jesus? Why me? Why ME? Why? Why? Why? Thank you, Jesus.'

I can't say it's my kind of worship. But I will say this. I saw more joy, more fervour, more power, more togetherness in that one hour than I have ever seen at any mass except for the services in my childhood in Ghana. We edged our way out of the hall, past even more people coming in. Outside, the street that had been empty just an hour before was now lined with cars, and 200 yards up the road you could see where more were pulling in. Nene Amegatcher's experiment had been a success. There will be more Christmas Day services to shake this tatty corner of England out of its apathy.

If immigrants in Britain show a greater inclination to go to church than their native-born co-religionists, their kith and kin in the developing world are leading the way. The latter half of the twentieth century saw an historic shift in the shape of Christian worship across the world. In 1970, Christians in the rich world were in the majority, but by 1990 they had been overtaken by Christians in the poor world. The number of Christians as a proportion of the world population is expected to remain more or less the same over the next few decades (about a third), but projections show that by 2050 there will nearly three times as many Christians from the developing world as there are from the developed world.

The evangelical movement (or the Pentecostals, as they are sometimes referred to) is growing as a proportion of all Christian churches in the UK, and this too is mirrored in the world at large. By 2050, just under half (46 per cent) of the world's Christian community will be made up of evangelicals. Crucially, the number of evangelicals in the developing world is growing because of conversions, not simply because more children are being born into families from these denominations. There is only one other religious group in the world that is growing as rapidly as this – Islam. In Britain alone there is likely to be a threefold increase in the number of Muslims by 2040.

What does all this mean? Increasingly the nature of faith in this country may be defined by immigrants. While they are only beginning to understand their power within the Christian churches, they dominate Britain's other religions. In 2005 there were about a million and a half Muslims, around half a million Sikhs and a similar number of Hindus. The Jewish population of Britain was about 300,000 but with an influence that belies its numbers. To a greater or lesser degree they are all affected by their respective global congregations, but none more so than the Christians.

Who would have thought that in 2005 the Church of Henry VIII should appoint as its second most important cleric a man born and raised in Uganda? When John Sentamu was installed as the ninety-seventh Archbishop of York on 30 November 2005 it was as if Africa had come to the north of England. There was a lion and a buffalo embroidered into his inaugural vestments. Bare-bodied drummers in leopardskin loincloths struck up a rhythm that reverberated off Gothic walls and pillars more accustomed to echoing the sounds of organ music. His message was as striking as the visual display that accompanied it:

Having shed an empire, has this great nation, and mother of parliamentary democracy also lost a noble vision for the future? We are getting richer and richer as a nation, but less and less happy. The Church in England must rediscover her self-confidence and self-esteem

Having diagnosed the nation's spiritual ailment in such stark terms, he went on to remind the great and the good assembled before him of the words of a previous incumbent of the great office he was about to assume. In a series of lectures in 1960, Archbishop Michael Ramsay had spoken of the religious fervour of the missionaries and, in words that would turn out to be prophetic, had longed for the day when the Church in England might relearn its faith from those converts in the colonies. 'Well here I am!' proclaimed John Sentamu that November morning, laying claim to an historic task.

His is only the most spectacular example of the reverse mission. In the course of researching this book I spoke to several others.

Patrick Mukholi, ordained into the Anglican Church of Kenya in 1998, now lives on the Blackbird Leys estate in Oxford with his wife, Helen, and their fifteen-year-old son. His own Christian faith is the product of the great east African revival of the 1930s when he watched people like his grandparents reform the mission church, moulding it into an institution that reflected their own experiences and heritage. Now the couple are trying to do something similar – except today they are trying to reform the 'complacent' Church that the Archbishop of York had spoken about into something more relevant to the nearly 15,000 people who live on the estate. 'We are trying to reach out to young people,' he told me. 'Trying to deal with the issues of life as they see it. Many of them don't have any adult friends, in some cases no adult family to speak of. They are troubled and troublesome at the same time.'

The Mukholis are called 'mission partners', who were brought over to this country by the Church Mission Society. Patrick believes that Christians in England have lost some of the moral certainty they had when the Society was founded in 1799 by men such as William Wilberforce, who played such a powerful part in the abolition of slavery. 'It seems to me as if the Church and many Christians here have almost lost their nerve. They somehow feel guilty for the mistakes of the Church, they still feel hounded by them and they have decided to keep quiet.' Reverend Mukholi argues that Christians in the old colonies are not burdened in a such a way. 'We in Africa still appreciate the role and authority of Christianity. People here are reserved. We speak out – some with more exuberance than others.'

But speaking out may involve speaking in tones that would embarrass the modern Church in England. Some, maybe most, of these reverse missionaries bring with them a social and moral conservatism that is at odds with the liberal atmosphere of the Church at the beginning of the twenty-first century. 'Our conservative thinking on issues such as family, marriage, sex and morality comes with the package. People can call it backward if they want to but I have to tell them that in my mother tongue, Luhyia, I would not know what to call a gay or lesbian person.' Factor these views into the already schism-threatening debates on gay priests in the Anglican Church and you begin to see how revolutionary the influence of these reverse missionaries could be.

In the heart of London's West End, at St Patrick's church in Soho, I met Father Kidane Lebasi. He shares the priests' quarters with Father Pat Davies, who baptised our son, Adam. Father Kidane has come a long way from the boy who worked on his father's farm on the outskirts of the village of Ambadarho in Eritrea. Born in 1946, from the age of six he helped till the land. The plough was pulled by a pair of oxen. In the winter he would take the farm animals to the eastern region for five or six weeks. His best memories are of returning home once the winter had passed. The crops would be lush and the valleys sprinkled with *gel-gele meskele*, spring flowers. Father Kidane remembers how one of the Comboni missionaries who worked in the area, Father Miguetti, would cycle the eleven kilometres to his village from the capital, Asmara. He would sit with them in their house and drink *shahi*. This was in the 1950s. Years later Father Miguetti would be one those missionaries slaughtered in the political violence in Congo.

Father Kidane was sent to London primarily to serve the growing Eritrean community here. He, too, has noticed what Christianity is up against in modern Britain. 'Secularism is swallowing our spiritual values. There's too much wealth or searching for wealth. People's minds are distracted all the time,' he told me. He believes Britain's relative wealth is part of the reason the Catholic Church is struggling to attract young men into the priesthood. The conditions that continue to push so many towards the Church in Africa simply don't exist here. 'I don't want to make too crude a connection, but vocations go side by side with material need. For young people that material need no longer exists.'

Time and time again the foreign priests that I spoke to returned to this idea that the Western world's wealth was itself a problem. It was what Father Sunny Paul had told me back in Yeovil. 'When people's physical needs are so well looked after, the need for God becomes less and less evident. I envy those early missionaries in Asia and Africa. They arrived and looked out and what they saw was a landscape of physical deprivation. It was obvious where they had to start,' he told me. 'When we, the reverse missionaries, look out, we see a land of spiritual deprivation. It's much less obvious how we are to go about our work. Some days I still feel as if I am discovering what it means to be a missionary in England.'

Thinking out loud, he began to put his finger on what he thought was the problem. He believes there is a paradox at the heart of modern, Western life. As wealth gives us so much more control over our 'outer' lives – we can buy bigger houses, more luxuries, go out more often, eat better and drink more – we have lost control of our 'inner' lives. The juxtaposition of outer and inner lives is mine, but the general point is Father Sunny's. 'When I visit schools or go to see people in their homes, I see kids who have to be entertained constantly – whether it's the TV or computer games. The capacity for sitting still has gone. We need to rediscover the quietness in our hearts.'

I asked him whether anything in his experience in north-east India was relevant to what he had to do in south-west England. 'I learnt in Meghalaya that it was no good just preaching the Ten Commandments, and the same is true here.' In those early years as a missionary, he very quickly realised that the Catholic Church's teachings on sexual morality were meaningless in a society in which sex was not taboo. 'It was normal for thirteen- and fourteen-year-olds to live together.' Similarly, he has learned that wandering around the parish talking about right and wrong is less useful than simply offering something that has all but disappeared in modern life – a friend to talk to. With home visits from a local doctor carrying a battered old leather holdall now replaced with on-line services and walk-in centres, there is little personal contact for many who need just that. On most evenings Father Sunny does his rounds. He has about forty people on his 'visiting list'. 'What we find is that there is hardly anyone out there who is simply listening to people. That is what we can offer.'

So whether it is doctors in the NHS or priests in the Catholic Church, whether it is Geoff Dusheiko from South Africa or Father Sunny Paul from Kerala, whether they have come to treat our bodies or our souls, these people have one thing in common – they have reversed an old trend. It is simply no longer true that it is the rich world that must send out its doctors and missionaries to a deprived and heathen world. In crucial and civilising areas of our life – health and spirituality – we are more dependent than ever before on outsiders. They prove one thing about the modern world of work – it is more fluid than at any time in history.

The movement of people across borders for work makes the borders themselves seem less relevant. The great cities of the world are beginning to look more and more like little versions of the planet. Over 300 languages and dialects are spoken by the children of London's schools. According to the 2001 census, 30 per cent of Londoners had been born outside England; that's 2.2 million people. Melbourne in Australia is home to the largest Greek community outside Greece. Over 40 per cent of the population of Toronto, Canada's commercial heart, is from what the country's official statistician calls a 'visible minority'. About half the population of Los Angeles is of Hispanic origin.

These immigrant communities comprise what can only be described as a supra-national community. There are thought to be about 200 million immigrants around the world. They have their feet firmly planted in one city or country but continue to have significant emotional and physical links with the countries from which they or their parents came. One way you can measure their attachment is to look at the amount of money they send back to their relatives. In 2005, India alone received over US$20 billion. For Sri Lanka, the amount sent by its diaspora was worth more than the country's tea exports.

These massive flows of money and people have even spawned their own business niche. The on-line consumer analysts, trend-watching.com, have dubbed it 'immi-merce'. Cathay Pacific, the Hong Kong-based airline that flies from three US cities, credits growing demand from Chinese, Filipinos, Indians and Vietnamese living in America for the 28 per cent growth in its revenue in 2004. That same year Pakistan's national carrier, PIA, launched a dedicated service to Houston largely on the back of the number of immigrants travelling home every year. The German airline Lufthansa has a special website, WeFlyHome.com, aimed specifically at the immigrant market in America. It offers fares to places as predictable as India and as unpredictable as Kazakhstan.

The people who use these new services are rewriting old notions of home and abroad. Where exactly is home? In the case of one of my relatives, a second cousin, London represented a 'home' some months before she even got here.

6

The Homecoming

'I'm not up to it, son. You do it.' It sounded as if my father were asking me to do some little chore, some piffling thing that didn't matter. Nothing could have been further from the truth. The economy of his words belied the weight of the task he was asking me to perform. It was the traditional homecoming ceremony for Rukshini, the orphaned daughter of one of my cousins. As Rukshini's most senior surviving relative – in both age and status – it was my father's job to say something on behalf of her side of the family. The ceremony was not long after my father's chemotherapy, which had left him physically weak and, more to the point, lacking in confidence. To stand in his place meant accepting a role, a place within a web of relationships that I had only just begun to acknowledge – let alone accept – on my trip to Sri Lanka a couple of years previously. Simply to stand in front of that audience on that occasion would be more telling than any of the words that I began to juggle with in my mind.

There's always an assumption that because I 'talk' to millions of people every night on TV I must be completely relaxed about public speaking. Not a bit of it. There is a part of the newsreading job that is about performance. Once I hear the programme's sig-nature tune, once the red light comes on, it is George Alagiah the news presenter who starts talking. The role itself offers a certain protection. You have to earn the audience's trust over many years – in my case as a foreign correspondent – but the authority, part of that, comes with the desk. On my own, however, without the aura of the BBC studio to bolster me, I'll confess to being assailed by the same butterflies that play havoc with the nerves of every best man who has ever had to stand up in front of a crowd of wedding guests.

But any misgivings I had were insignificant compared with what must have been going through Rukshini's mind. If I was bat-tling with the idea of standing *in loco parentis*, as it were, this young bride had to deal with the idea of coming 'home' to a place she had only ever dreamed about. This was not Sri Lanka; this was Harrow, north London. Ten months earlier, in Sri Lanka, she had not even met the young man with whom she was now plan-ning to spend the rest of her life.

The homecoming, which was originally a Hindu ritual, has worked its way into Sri Lankan culture regardless of religion. I was brought up a Catholic and Frances an Anglican, but after we got married we too had a homecoming. The ceremony has its roots in the tradition that a bride throws in her lot with the groom's family, often living under the same roof. In our case my parents' insistence on a homecoming – especially as our decision to have a small, no-frills wedding meant the guest list had been tiny – led to some tortured logistical arrangements.

My mother was over in London for some weeks before and after our marriage but my father could only manage a week away from his job with the World Health Organisation in Zimbabwe. So we had to have a wedding and a homecoming in the space of a few days. The problem was what to do in the days between these two events. As far as Frances and I were concerned, a couple of days with my parents and two sisters in the house they kept for us here was the answer.

'But what about your honeymoon?' I can't remember if that was my mother or father. The honeymoon was an entirely foreign concept to Sri Lankans until the British arrived on the island, but it was one colonial habit that they were happy to adopt. We'd actually planned for a week walking in the Black Mountains after my father left.

'We'll go off after the homecoming,' I said.

'No, no, no. You must go somewhere before that,' my father countered.

'Dad, that's madness. We'll only have two days before we'd have to come back.' There was also the question of money, largely the lack of it in our yet-to-be-joined accounts.

'That's all right. Two days is better than nothing.'

Suddenly the penny dropped. It wasn't so much that he was worried about us having a honeymoon; rather that he was concerned about what we were supposed to be doing while on honeymoon! Traditionally a homecoming is also supposed to mark the consummation of a marriage and satisfaction all round that the bride was everything she said she was. In more traditional homes the groom's mother is expected to inspect the marital sheets. Years later my father would tell me how some couples would be forced to arrange to have the blood of some unfortunate mouse or lizard to hand to provide the proof the mother-in-law would be looking for.

This was delicate. Let's just say that my father's assumptions about our courtship and the reality did not match – we were skating on thin ice. We decided to make a weekend dash up to Durham where we'd met at university.

We returned two days later to a house full of 'aunties' and 'uncles' who no doubt searched Frances's demeanour for the blooming signs of marital, not to mention bedroom, bliss. And, as it happened, Frances did seem suitably flushed, though she's always quick to remind me it was because of the Asian habit of having the central heating turned up too high rather than anything I could take credit for.

Thirty years later, it was Rukshini's turn to play the demure and contented bride. We had first met Rukshini during our family visit to Sri Lanka in 2002. She was at one of those gatherings. I remember her sitting next to Frances. They had taken to each other. Rukshini had sung alone that night, her voice trembling with nerves yet expressing a deep yearning for love. She did not know then that before long her wishes would be fulfilled. We didn't know then that our paths would cross again in such unexpected circumstances.

It was early in the summer of 2004, one of those balmy June days that fools you into thinking it will be a hot, dry season, and which almost always turns out to be the one you look back on through a curtain of July rain. We were in a school hall in Harrow which, for the afternoon, had been transformed into a little corner of Sri Lanka. From the kitchen that usually served up portions of bland, institutional food came the vapours of south Asian cuisine. Instead of the greys and creams and pastel pinks that are the hallmark of English wedding attire, this gathering was a riot of crimsons, greens and blues. Delicate wrists weighed down with bangles struck the refectory tables with the satisfying jingle-jangle of gold on wood.

At the front of the hall Rukshini and her new husband, Jude Anton, sat in nervous isolation. I marvelled at the way migration had brought them, on separate journeys, from the northern town of Jaffna in Sri Lanka's Tamil heartland to this English suburb. They had grown up streets away from each other but never met. Yet here they were in London, man and wife, embarking on a new life and making their mark on the changing face of Britain. Theirs is a story that started in war and has ended in love.

The eighth of August 1990 was a baking hot day in Jaffna, a town built on a flat, sandy, curved peninsula in the north of Sri Lanka. On an atlas the peninsula looks like a hook that has broken free of India, allowing the whole island to drift into the welcoming tropical ocean. If Tamils ever get a state of their own, which some of them crave, this town would almost certainly be its capital. That is one of the reasons why Jaffna, and the surrounding countryside, has been the scene of some of the most vicious fighting in Sri Lanka's on-off civil war. If the thousands of civilians who have been killed in the conflict attest to its inhumanity, the burning, in 1981, of the Jaffna public library – with its precious collection of Tamil literature – must surely be evidence of its senselessness.

At the age of thirteen Jude Ṣusivan Anton had developed a keen ear for impending disaster. Like so many people in Jaffna he knew which sounds to ignore and which should send him scurrying to the bunker most families had dug in their gardens. It was the drone of a distant aircraft that alerted him that day. Was this a dummy run, a reconnaissance flight, or the real thing – a bombing raid?

The answer to that question came with the first explosion. The street went quiet; you could almost hear the swish of palmyra palms. Jude began a silent, fearful countdown. The people of Jaffna had learned through bitter experience that there were eight bombs on every plane and it was rare for the Chinese-built Y8s of the Sri Lankan Air Force to depart without disgorging all their vicious cargo. One. Two. The noise got louder and Jude knew that the plane might be coming in his direction, that his home might be under the plane's murderous flight path. Three. After a while he could even see the fat-bellied bombs tumbling out of the plane like lazy acrobats in a slow-motion circus. Four. There was something very familiar about Jude's description. I remembered how, in other parts of the world, I had seen planes drop bundles of food to the starving. Same technique. Different consequences. Five. Six. As a child I too used to look up at the sky and count. In Ghana's rainy season I used to calculate the seconds between a flash of lightning across a steel-grey sky and the thunder that followed. As the gap between the two got shorter I would know with skin-tingling anticipation that the storm was coming our way. I would marvel at the power of nature; that August day Jude feared the power of man. Seven. The silence in the street gave way to screams of panic. Mothers grabbed their children. Dogs howled and barked. Fistfuls of money were pulled out from under mattresses. Fathers cursed. Jude and his mother went one way, his father another. They ducked into a neighbour's bunker; Jude shut his eyes and covered his ears. Eight. The mud walls of the bunker shook. Heat and dust. Rubble rained down on the looted railway sleepers that now served as the roof of the bunker. Up above, in a clear blue sky, the plane banked perfectly and turned for base.

When they emerged into daylight, Jude and his mother looked across the road. There was one thought on both their minds. Where is *appa*, where is father? Leo Anton Savermuthu crawled out of his own bunker. He too was safe. The family stood together in what used to be their front garden and looked at where their house should have been. Number 4 Mount Carmel Road had taken a direct hit. The 750 kg bomb had crashed through the terracotta-tiled roof and landed in a bedroom. They could see a hot, twisted part of the shell casing; it was like an obscene calling card left behind by an intruder. The eighth of August 1990, the day Jude's life changed.

About half an hour's walk across Jaffna, on Hospital Road, an eleven-year-old girl was going about her chores. Perhaps Rukshini Fontgalau had heard the same plane, watched its destructive path across the sky. It's certainly likely. In Jaffna no one ever ignored the Y8s. She may even have rushed into her family's bunker. 'I was always the first to go into the bunker,' she told me. 'I used to sweep the bunker every day. Try to keep it clean. I would light the *kumamjam*, the incense, and touch the statue.' It was an image of the Virgin Mary of Vellankami which the family had brought back from a pilgrimage to that holy shrine. That day faith and fate kept her and her family safe. They were left unscathed by the raid on 8 August, but the war would change her life too. It would turn her first into a refugee, and later a migrant. In the years in between she would lose both her parents to untreated illness, victims of the war in a different way. As she sprinkled holy water around the bunker in thanksgiving, Rukshini could not have known that across town the Anton family had already begun to think about the first steps in a journey that would lead to their lives together.

While most of their relatives had fled to Sri Lanka's capital, Colombo, and further afield to Toronto in Canada and London, Jude's parents, Leema and Anton, had resolutely tried to make a go of it in Jaffna. But the bombing raid had changed everything. It was decided that Jude and his mother would leave for Colombo, while his father would stay on and try to run the 'fancy goods' shop that he owned on 'KKS' Road.

Their reasoning was simple. Jude was their only child. His safety was paramount, both for his own sake but also because, as a boy, he represented the couple's security. At the time the fears of Tamil parents who had boys were split almost evenly between the chances of death at the hands of the Sri Lankan army and recruitment by the Tamil Tigers, the rebel group fighting for a state independent of the country's Sinhalese majority. Many Tamils had a love-hate relationship with the Tigers. They were proud that at last there were Tamils who would stand up to what they saw as Sinhalese oppression but appalled by the near-messianic devotion they expected of their cadres. It was the Liberation Tigers of Tamil Eelam who, after all, had introduced the suicide bomber into modern guerrilla warfare.

Once in Colombo, where they stayed with one of Jude's aunts, their journey seemed to take on a momentum of its own. The advice from the family's web of relatives abroad was that it was time to get out altogether. As a Tamil boy, prospects in Colombo were bleak and their future back in Jaffna would be as fractured as the pile of bricks and mortar that had once been their home. Jude's mother Leema – who was one of ten siblings – had three sisters and a brother in London, where his father also had a brother and sister.

The first step was to see an agent who could organise the trip to Britain. It was a decision Leema had to take on her own. There was no way to reach her husband, Jude's father, by phone. Letters still got through, but how long they took was anybody's guess. The fee was £3,000 each, an amount they did not have but which was generously paid by the relatives abroad.

In October that year, just weeks after fleeing Jaffna and without the chance of a family reunion, Leema and Jude boarded a plane at Katunayake airport. It was the first time either of them had ever set foot on an aircraft. I have tried to tease out the details of the journey from Jude, but he says all he really remembers is the overriding sense of fear. Besides, the agent had told them that the less they knew, the better it would be for them. 'We were so scared,' he says. 'We didn't want to remember anything. We didn't want to see anything. We were just frightened.' For those of us who plot and plan our trips on-line, ensuring that no part of the journey, from check-in and seat number to car hire and hotel reservation, is left to chance, it's difficult to imagine how faithfully Jude and his mother handed over this life-changing trip to an agent they had never actually met.

They remember two stops. Jude says one was in Africa but he doesn't know which country they were in, despite the fact that they were taken to a hostel in the city. On the next leg of the journey, to Europe, Jude was given a jigsaw puzzle by the air hostess. 'I wanted to keep it but we had been told that we mustn't pick anything up on the journey, so *amma* said I had to leave it.' Another change of plane and they were on the final stretch of the journey. It was on this flight that they destroyed their passports as they had been told to do. When they landed in London, there were officials waiting at the plane before they even got to the immigration desks. And so they joined the list of those seeking asylum in Britain.

When I first heard Jude's story I'll admit to a sense of shock. Oh so comfortable in my Britishness, it hadn't occurred to me that I could be connected in any personal way with someone who had

had to do what he did to get here. I had met refugees before, many of them, but they were either people I had encountered through my reporting or exiles linked to causes that I had become interested in. South Africans, Chileans, Palestinians, Rwandese and Congolese. The one nationality that was not on that list was Sri Lankans, despite the fact that the country has been one of the biggest exporters of refugees since the mid 1980s. It was a telling omission, a measure of the extent to which I had become estranged from the country of my birth. If I'm honest, I know it wasn't an accident. In *A Passage to Africa* I wrote about how, as a child, I tried to cut Sri Lanka out of my life story, preferring my family's association with Africa and all its apparent bounty. By the time I arrived in England, it was, as I have said, a case of 'sink or swim', with little room for my Sri Lankan past.

Jude and his mother, and then his father, all went on to receive their papers to stay in Britain. They became a part of the Sri Lankan community in London, one that I would have continued to have little to do with if Jude's parents hadn't chosen for his bride a young woman who turned out to be related to me.

In 1995 it was the death of Rukshini's mother, my cousin, that had prompted her own journey out of Jaffna. She too left a father and a brother there. 'I didn't want to leave them. I threw myself on the sand shouting and crying, begging them to let me stay.' She had always been a bright student, and it was thought she stood a better chance of sitting her A levels in Colombo, where her mother's sister had already settled. She'd had to get an exit pass from the Tamil Tiger administration in the northern town of Kilinochi. Her first few nights there were in a church, after which the priests had moved her to a nearby village, Amathipuram. The whole business took about six weeks. Finally she remembers walking through the 'no-man's land' that divided the Tamil Tiger-controlled north from the rest of the country.

In Colombo she proved every bit as hardworking as her family had expected, passing A levels and then taking a series of diplomas in computer studies. In time-honoured fashion her studies were paid for by friends and relatives, including my father. By October 1999 she'd got her first paycheque as a trainee programmer for John Keelles Computer Services, a branch of one of the country's most reputable companies. Her father lived to see her vocational success but not long enough to supervise that other duty every Tamil father has – to ensure that his daughters are married off. He died in 2001.

It was around this time that the search for a husband had begun. She told me it started the way these things always do: 'My aunt and others would tease me. They made it all look like a joke but you know it is serious.' She was an attractive young woman with good career prospects, but she was hobbled by something she had no control over – she was an orphan, and that accident of nature placed her near the bottom of the league table of desirable brides-to-be.

For the vast majority of people in Sri Lanka, as in much of Asia, marriage remains more than the union of two individuals. It is the coming together of two families. A big part of the equation is what the bride's side is going to bring to the union, not least in terms of a dowry. Once, the dowry may have been a way of assuring that a woman had something to fall back on, some independent means, should a marriage break down. Certainly there is some historical evidence to support such an interpretation. But over the centuries it has become corrupted and is today little more than a piece of social engineering which ensures that marriage between rich and poor remains almost impossible. The size of the dowry is almost always related to the social status of the groom, making it virtually impossible for poor families to find the means to attract a husband from a wealthier background – at least without ruinous financial consequences. Add the continued influence of the caste system (which had so nearly stifled my parents' romance) and you have one of the most socially claustrophobic societies I have ever come across.

A glance at Sri Lanka's *Sunday Observer* marriage proposals page is revealing. In this entry from early 2005 religion and caste come first in the list of requirements:

> Catholic *govigama* parents seek an educated professional partner below 30 years for their elder daughter 23 years, 5' 7" height, dowry coconut land of one acre worth over 15 million rupees.

> Buddhist *govi* Sinhalese parents ... seek a professionally qualified son from a similar family ... for their fair and pretty graduate daughter. Inherits property and other assets.

There is, of course, an on-line version of the proposals page now, but new technology has done little to reform old habits. Take this from 2006:

> Affluent, well-connected *govi* Buddhist parents seek a tall, very handsome, well-established professional with assets, or an educated businessman, teetotaller, non-smoker under 36, for fair very beautiful daughter, just 29, foreign-qualified graduate, highly qualified in English. Substantial assets including house, land, car, jewellery. Separated after a very brief unfortunate marriage. Very innocent girl. Differences immaterial. Similar background important.

Religion, caste, assets, education, looks and even complexion – all part of an odious sales pitch designed to attract the right sort of partner. Note that the assets are listed and quantified. Whatever its origins, the system ensures that wealth and influence remain concentrated with those who already have so much more than their fellow Sri Lankans. The dowry remains a powerful tradition even within the Sri Lankan diaspora. There's little wrong with the arrangement of marriage in this way – after all, we have our dating agencies – but it's the conditions that apply that make it so pernicious.

In such a milieu Rukshini was supposed to curb her ambitions and accept that as an orphan she could not hope for a marriage other than to someone in similar circumstances. And sure enough, the first proposal came from the brother of another orphan. 'I didn't like him. It didn't feel like he was the one for me. But I couldn't say no. I knew my position. I knew that not many people are going to be interested in me.' It was the intervention of her own brother that eventually put paid to that proposal.

It was a brave thing to do, especially as the young man had had permanent residence in Australia. She had not turned down simply a marriage but an opportunity to get out of the country too. But she did get another chance. This time her Cupid came in the form of a Catholic priest back in Jaffna, a man who had, coincidentally, baptised both Rukshini and the young man whose name he was now proffering – Jude. He had maintained an interest in Rukshini's welfare, and the first step was to send some photos and a video to Jude's mother.

Back in London, Jude's mother played a subtle game. It was the spring of 2003. One Sunday, after mass, Leema and one of her sisters sat down to watch the TV. With studied nonchalance they played a cassette of a wedding in Sri Lanka. It was not the happy couple they watched, but someone who appeared in the background, one of the bridesmaids. 'They didn't actually call me over,' says Jude, 'but they kept watching and pointing. In the end I just got curious and sat down with them.' Leema's little ploy had worked. Jude wasn't instantly smitten, but there was enough there for his mother to work on – which she did assiduously.

If Rukshini's lack of a family would have prompted an aboutturn from most men, it had the opposite effect on Jude. When he heard she had been orphaned, that was when he began to get interested. 'I suppose that touched a soft spot in me,' he said as they sat together, telling me their story. 'I wanted someone who knew about hard work. We had to work hard in Britain, we owed people money. We had to work for everything we had. I wanted someone who would understand all of that.'

In August 2003 Jude flew back to Sri Lanka. The priest turned matchmaker, Father Selvarajah, organised a meeting with Rukshini at her aunt's house. The story of their first meeting is charming in its naïvety and refreshing in its innocence. In our world of love-at-first-sight and sex-before-marriage, it's hard to imagine such arrangements being accepted. But with around two marriages out of every five in the UK ending in failure, who's to say whether we have got it right? They were together in their north London home as they described that first meeting back in Sri Lanka. It reads like the script of some Bollywood movie, a corny one at that, but it is true and all the more remarkable for that. Rukshini was told she'd be called into the sitting room when the time was right.

'I couldn't wait till they called me, so I was trying to get a look at him. There was a curtain across the door from the kitchen so I peeped through.'

'Well I saw her peeping,' says Jude, still able to recall the frisson of first sight. 'But I pretended not to notice.'

'I could tell that he was quite confident. I wanted someone who was forward. Somebody who would stand up for me.'

After a few pleasantries between Father Selvarajah and Rukshini's brother-in-law, she was asked to come in.

'You were wearing that black skirt and green blouse.'

'We were not sure whether I should wear a sari or not but I did not want it to be like a fashion show,' says Rukshini, exhibiting the streak of independence which lies hidden behind a retiring façade.

'She was beautiful. I just thought to myself, "Why me?"'

'He said hello almost like an Englishman. I wanted to laugh. It seemed funny coming from him.'

There followed an excruciating half an hour or so where they sat with the others.

'I was trying to make eye contact with her,' says Jude. 'But I was nervous. But just a couple of times our eyes would meet and she would give me a little smile. I knew she was the one for me.'

And that was it really. They were allowed to spend a little while on the veranda together. They exchanged telephone numbers. Arranged their first date – a cappuccino at Deli France. There were meals with the family, some outings together, even a little row. On 12 September, just thirteen days after they first met, Jude and Rukshini were engaged. A week later Jude flew back to London. They spoke to each other every Sunday; Jude from his home, Rukshini from a cubicle at an internet café in Welawatte, the Tamil quarter of Colombo. Rukshini sent Jude a birthday card in October and the following February he posted her a Valentine's card, the first he'd ever sent.

Behind the scenes the arrangements were put in place for the wedding. The speed with which it all proceeded was certainly helped by the fact that the dowry was not an issue. In Britain, where even the tradition that the bride's family stumps up for the wedding party is beginning to die away, it's hard to imagine that in places such as India (where the dowry is supposed to be banned) and Sri Lanka a groom's family will see marriage as something of a money-spinner.

One of my first reports for the BBC was from India, where we filmed a story about how some relatives of poor brides (usually a brother) would 'sell' one of their kidneys to make up the money for a dowry. The beneficiaries were often rich patients from the Gulf states who were treated in some of Mumbai's many fine private clinics. There was little after-care for the 'donors', many of whom went on to live blighted lives.

In 2003 an Indian woman, Nisha Sharma, gained fame (or notoriety, depending on where you stand on the dowry system) when she had her husband-to-be arrested when his family demanded US$25,000 on the wedding day. She called their bluff but her story is very much the exception. According to official statistics in India, some 7,000 women have been murdered over dowry disagreements.

To his credit, Jude had told his parents that he was not interested in a dowry. 'I didn't want a penny. I hate the dowry system, it's like buying a person. Anyway, I didn't want my future wife to feel obliged to anyone – she would have had to borrow the money for the dowry.'

Jude and his parents travelled to Sri Lanka for the wedding on 24 April 2004.

Three weeks later the family, now expanded by one, returned to Britain. Rukshini came to London, she came home.

'I just want to say a few words on behalf of Rukshini's family . . .' The first hesitant words of a man unaccustomed to the role. Till then the only family I had really cared about was Frances and the boys, my parents and four sisters. In our peripatetic life from Sri Lanka to Ghana, Ghana to Britain, we had become self-reliant, perhaps even insular. Yet here I was, standing in front of about 200 people, laying claim to something much bigger. A couple of hours earlier I hadn't even known that I would be making the speech. I had been looking forward to an afternoon full of colour and fun but free of responsibility. Virtually every single one of the people in that hall – except for one white English family (Jude's neighbours) – was related. A part of me felt fraudulent. I was related by blood but not by habit.

My sense of dislocation was heightened as I waited to be called up to the front. The previous speaker, Newton *athan* (a term of respect reserved for male relatives), had praised the way Jude continued to believe in Tamil customs. In particular he pointed out that Jude would still use all the honorific titles that lace Tamil conversation. The wife of an elder brother, for example, would be called *anni*; an elderly female relative *peri-amma*. Newton *athan* listed quite a few. He drew a somewhat unflattering comparison with those in the community who had begun to forget such etiquette. He mentioned the 'youngsters' but he could have been talking about me.

Why couldn't Dad have done this? I thought to myself. I looked across the hall. Rukshini sat there garlanded in red and white flowers, carnations and jasmine set off against the traditional red homecoming sari. She was radiant. She was looking at me, expectant. What is Uncle George (which is what she had called me from the day we had first met back in Sri Lanka) going to say? It occurs to me now that the awkwardness I was feeling had much more to do with my own tussle with identity rather than any obvious disapproval from those around me that afternoon. On the contrary, just as I had found on that flight back to Sri Lanka, I was one of them whether I liked it or not!

All I had to do was to look at myself the way Rukshini saw me. There was no reproach in those eyes. No muttering under her breath, 'He's ignored me and my family for most of my life; now he wants to stand up and speak for us.' If anything, there was pride. She had accepted my new role in her life with the same equanimity she seemed to accept her new home in Britain. That afternoon I took my cue from her. There was no need to feel 'out of place', as Edward Said once described his own predicament, an identity stretched uncomfortably between the various influences on his life – an Arab Christian whose early education was in the British tradition. I went on to deliver a short but heartfelt tribute to Rukshini's many virtues.

As I took my seat next to my father and sisters I knew – even then – that this was where my book (of which not a page had been written) would end. Looking around, I realised that there, in that west London hall, was a distillation of all the versions of home that now exist in a world where migration is happening more often and more easily than ever before. For my father, as he approaches his twilight years, Sri Lanka is home. In the insecurity of old age he is drawn back to the place where life seemed simpler. But he also feels at home in England because this is where his children live. We, his children, call England home because this is the place where we grew up (albeit in the trammelled version of England you get in boarding school) and where we are now most comfortable. Rukshini called it home because this was where her husband had settled. And all the other guests? I can't be sure, of course, but judging by the way they clung to the old traditions, seeing how singularly Tamil the gathering was, my guess is that they still thought of England as the place they lived in and Sri Lanka as their home. Judging by the dress and savoir-faire of their children, it would not remain that way for much longer. A home from home – one phrase, many meanings.

Each of us in that room had a different relationship with this country, and any notion of what it is to be British has to encompass all of them. The alternative would be to say there are different levels of Britishness, in which someone like me is the full-blown version while someone like Rukshini is a half-baked one. That doesn't work, because in law we are both the same, both with the same right to live in this country. The old definitions simply don't apply any more.

The temptation, of course, is to ask the old questions about race and identity. It's particularly strong at those times when we, as a country, are feeling vulnerable to the threat of terrorism. Years ago the former Tory party chairman Norman Tebbit reduced it all to his infamous question about which cricket team you support when England is playing an international game. You would have thought that we'd moved on since those days, but in August 2004, while researching for this book, I was aghast when an interviewer on a radio station which prides itself on being cosmopolitan offered his own version of the Tebbit test.

It was a Saturday, the day before Amir Khan from Bolton was due to fight for gold in the Olympic Games. The young boxer, the son of Pakistani immigrants, had caught the imagination of the whole country and was being compared to another immigrant fighter, Prince Naseem, whose flamboyance and skill had brought him many accolades. The fact that Khan's father would turn up at ringside wearing a Union Jack waistcoat while waving a Pakistani flag spoke volumes for how far Britain seemed to have come since Tebbit's ludicrous suggestion that you couldn't be truly British if you didn't support England. The station's producers had tracked down Prince Naseem on holiday in Portugal and he was asked for his thoughts on Khan's prospects. At least I assume that was the plan. But halfway through the interview, the presenter reminded Prince Naseem that his own supporters used to wave both the Union Jack and the Yemeni flag. 'Which flag did you most relate to – the British or the Yemeni one?' he asked.

For a man who had earned his reputation with the speed of his fists, Prince Naseem showed he could be equally agile with his words. Even so, his answer illustrates the contortions immigrants have to go through as they try to explain their hybrid lives.

Well, you're putting me in a bit of a situation there – but I'm born in Britain and I owe a lot in my heart to my roots and where my parents come from but I live in Sheffield. I'm from, I'm born and bred in Sheffield, mate, I'm a Yorkshireman through and through . . . I can't sit here and say that, yeah, I lift the British flag up and that's the only one that I hold allegiance to and all that and all those things. I'd be lying to you. I'm proud of the both and I am so happy that, you know, that I'm British and born in Britain and then again I'm so happy that I'm Arab, I've got the culture that I've got. I'm a Muslim.

During its winter tour of India in 2006 it was the England cricket team itself that provided the most fitting riposte to Tebbit's hackneyed notions of allegiance. In his debut game for England in the first test it was the British Sikh Mudhsuden 'Monty' Singh Panesar who trapped the great Sachin Tendulkar leg-before. Monty's victory dance, which included leaping into the air like a kangaroo high on amphetamines, and the way his team mates embraced him, spoke volumes for how far both the sport and the country had come. If he is dropped from the team it will be because of his comical fielding, not his colour.

In writing this book, I have realised the extent to which even I have unwittingly been stuck in the past. It's the reason I felt out of kilter at Rukshini's homecoming ceremony. Though I left boarding school over thirty years ago, I have allowed its harsh test of what it takes to fit in to dominate the rest of my life. Both my trip to Sri Lanka and the subsequent rekindling of old family ties have taught me that I do not have to choose between identities any more than a Yorkshireman or a Scot does. It doesn't have to be Sri Lanka or Britain. It can be both. They are linked, tied together in a migrant's journey. Only bigots ask you which one you like best. To ask someone that question is to ask him to deny his past. No man can do that, at least not honestly. Migration is not a test of loyalty, it is a test of character. If the racists and Little Englanders worried more about character and less about whose side the immigrant is on they would see how much richer their beloved country has become. It takes guts and vision to do what my parents did. No nation can afford to turn away such people. I have come to realise how privileged I am. To be comfortable, to be welcomed in two such different places as Sri Lanka and the UK is a rare inheritance.

Perhaps we need to come up with a new question. Instead of trying to work out where people belong, we should ask what they are doing now that they are here. This is a question about citizenship rather than ethnicity, religion or culture. It takes us beyond multiculturalism, described by the commentator Yasmin Alibhai-Brown as 'a non-interference pact between groups', and into an examination of the contribution immigrants make. This way we can couple the rights that flow from gaining British nationality with the duties and obligations that come with it.

If this was the test, then the insularity I have described among some people in Bradford and Tower Hamlets would fail to meet the standard. But the failure is not the fact that the Mirpuris or Sylhetis are living segregated lives, but that in doing so it is harder for them to make a contribution to the wider nation. The Tamil community in west London is a close-knit one but it is outward-looking. Every speech made at Rukshini's homecoming ceremony was in English. These are people who have an eye to what it takes to make good in wider society. The answer to race relations in Britain is not less immigration, but better immigration.

The old test was about where you came from, which always worked against Britain's 'visible minorities' – the West Indians and Africans, the Asians and Chinese. They were the ones who stood out as foreigners even when they were trying hard to become good citizens. But if we judge people by their contribution, we might deduce that we would rather have the quiet diligence of the Asian corner-shop owner who serves his community than the flashy extravagance of the Russian oligarch whose berth in Britain owes more to pragmatism than patriotism. Equally we might feel that the hundreds of thousands of immigrants who strive hard to better themselves, who hold down one job while training for another, are as worthy of citizenship as the millions who have it by birthright but never fully live up to the responsibilities that go with it. The test of contribution is colour-blind.

Being a patriot ought to mean more than simply waving a flag about. Ours is not a flag of convenience, like the ones flying above the armada of Liberian-registered boats that ply the world's oceans, but a flag of conviction, of commitment. We should move away from the concept of Britishness as something we can buy into off the peg, a ready-made identity kit. We should accept that there is no classic design of Britishness that has remained unchanged through the ages and which can be replicated like some garment in a Far Eastern sweatshop.

Instead we ought to see that it has evolved and is evolving. The flag that Kelly Holmes and Linford Christie wrapped around themselves in victory cannot be the same flag my father and mother might have noticed fluttering in an imperial wind over the governor's residence in Colombo. It may look the same, but its meaning has changed entirely, redefined by the people who hold it now. A country in which John Sentamu helps to run the Church of England and where Shami Chakrabati is one of the most eloquent defenders of our hard-won liberties is vastly different from the one I came to in 1967.

To get from where we were then to where we are now has been a huge collective achievement. Certainly it is one that millions of immigrants have contributed towards, but it is also one that would have been impossible were it not for the good grace of the vast majority of white men and women whose ancestry in this country is as rooted as a yew tree in an ancient forest. They too have been on this journey. They have migrated from the old country to another country. They too have walked the distance. We are rightly quick to condemn the racist minority, but far too slow to congratulate the many who have gone along with change and quite often embraced it.

As I look back at what I have achieved since I came to Britain, I can see how it has been influenced by all those I have met on the way. Whenever I visit schools and universities I am always asked how I have managed to get where I am now – a senior journalist at the BBC. More often than not, the question comes from a young immigrant. It's as if they are looking for a magic formula. I'm not so modest that I ignore talent and hard work, but I always talk about opportunity too. I remind them that that is why I am here and why their parents brought them here. I tell them my achievements are not mine alone but those of the country we all live in. When these students look at me, it is not an immigrant success story they see but a British one. It is what is possible when Britain is true to its principles, something never written down in a single document or constitution but which beats strong in the hearts of so many – a sense of fair play. That is why a life that might have shrivelled in Sri Lanka has blossomed in Britain. It is the difference between the country that has taken my family in and the one that abandoned us. And that is why, in the end, I know that this is my home and that Sri Lanka is now a home from home.

Bibliography

Alagiah, George, 'Exclusion Zones', *Guardian*, May 2003

Alibhai-Brown, Yasmin, *After Multiculturalism*, London: Foreign Policy Centre, 2000

Ali, Monica, *Brick Lane*, London: Doubleday, 2003

Amidon, Lynne A., *An Illustrated History of the Royal Free Hospital*, London: The Special Trustees for the Royal Free Hospital, 1996

Andrews, Peter, and Snyder, Timothy, *The Wall Around the West: State Borders and Immigration Control in North America and Europe*, Oxford: Rowman and Littlefield, 2000

Bade, Klaus J., *Migration in European History*, Oxford: Blackwell, 2003

Balachin, Paul, and Rhoden, Maureen, *Housing Policy: An Introduction*, London: Routledge, 2002

Baldwin, James, *The Fire Next Time*, Harmondsworth: Penguin, 1963

Brown, Andrew, *Trials of Honeyford*, London: Centre for Policy Studies, 1985

Brierley, Peter (ed.), *Religious Trends 5*, London: Christian Research, 2005

Burgess, Simon, and Wilson, Deborah, *Ethnic Segregation in England's Schools*, London: Centre for Analysis of Social Exclusion, 2004

Butler, L. J., *Britain and Europe: Adjusting to a Post-Imperial World*, London: I. B. Tauris, 2002

Cantle, Ted (chair), *Community Cohesion: A Report of the Independent Review Team*, 2001

Castles, Stephen, and Miller, Mark J., *The Age of Migration*, Basingstoke: Palgrave Macmillan, 2003

Cunningham, John, *Immigration's Shining Centre*, Chicago: Arcadia Publishing, 2003

Dalrymple, William, *The Age of Kali*, London: Flamingo, 1999

Dean, Dennis, 'Race Relations and the Making of Educational Policy:

The View from the Centre in the 1960s', *Cambridge Journal of Education*, Vol 32, 2002

Dench, Geoff, Gavron, Kate, and Young, Michael, *The New East End: Kinship, Race and Conflict*, London: Profile, 2006

Dimbleby, Jonathan (foreword), *Cultural Breakthrough Essays*, London: VSO, 2003

Firth, Gary, *A History of Bradford*, Phillimore & Co Ltd, 1997

Geddes, Andrew, *The Politics of Migration and Immigration in Europe*, London: Sage, 2003

Goldberg, David Theo (ed.), *Multiculturalism: A Critical Reader*, Oxford: Blackwell, 1994

Goodhart, David, 'Too Diverse?', *Prospect*, February 2004

Green, Andrew (chairman), *Migrants: Do They Bring Economic Benefit?*, Migration Watch UK, London, 2005

Grosvenor, Ian, *Assimilating Identities: Racism and Educational Policy in Post-1945 Britain*, London: Lawrence & Wishart, 1997

Hansen, Randall, *Citizenship and Immigration in Post-War Britain*, Oxford: Oxford University Press, 2000

Harris, Nigel (chairman), *Migration: A Welcome Opportunity*, London: RSA Migration Commission, 2005

Hoffman, Eva, *Lost in Translation*, London: Vintage, 1998

James, David, *Bradford*, Halifax: Ryburn, 1990

Jones, Maldwyn Allen, *Destination America*, Glasgow: Fontana/Collins, 1977

Killian, Lewis M., 'School Bussing in Britain', *Harvard Educational Review*, Vol 49, No. 2, 1979

Klein, Naomi, *No Logo*, London: Flamingo, 2000

Klein, Rudolf, *The New Politics of the NHS*, Harlow: Prentice Hall, 2001

Kureishi, Hanif, *The Buddha of Suburbia*, London: Faber and Faber, 1991

Levy, Andrea, *Small Island*, London: Headline, 2004

Lichtenstein, Rachel, and Sinclair, Iain, *Rodinsky's Room*, London: Granta, 1999

Lupton, Ruth, and Power, Anne, *Minority Ethnic Groups in Britain*, Centre for Analysis of Social Exclusion, 2004

Maimbo, Samuel, and Dilip, Ratha (eds), *Remittances: Development Impact and Future Prospects*, World Bank, 2005

Malik, Kenan, 'Against Multiculturalism', *New Humanist*, Vol 118, No. 2, London, 2002

Marsh, Alex, and Sangster, Azra, *Paving the Way: Supporting Black and Minority Ethnic Housing Associations*, Bristol: Policy Press, 1998

Morgan, Kenneth O., *Britain Since 1945: The People's Peace*, Oxford: Oxford University Press, 2001

Neill, Stephen, *A History of Christian Missions*, Harmondsworth: Penguin, 1964

Ouseley, Herman (chair), *Community Pride not Prejudice: Making Diversity Work in Bradford*, 2001

Palmer, Alan, *The East End: Four Centuries of London Life*, London: John Murray, 1989

Parekh, Bhikhu (chair), *Report of the Commission on the Future of Multi-Ethnic Britain*, London: Profile, 2000

Paul, Kathleen, *Whitewashing Britain: Race and Citizenship in the Post-War Era*, Ithaca: Cornell University Press, 1997

Paxman, Jeremy, *The English: A Portrait of a People*, London: Penguin, 1999

Phillips, Mike, and Phillips, Trevor, *Windrush: The Irresistible Rise of Multi-Racial Britain*, London: HarperCollins, 1999

Poulsen, Mike, 'The New Geography of Ethnicity in Britain', Lecture at Royal Geographic Society, London, 2005

Ratcliffe, Peter, *Race and Housing in Bradford*, Bradford: Bradford Housing Forum, 1996

Richardson, C., *The Bradford Region: Studies in its Human Geography*, Bradford Libraries: Archives and Informational Service, 2002

Rivett, Geoffrey, *From Cradle to Grave: Fifty years of the NHS*, London: King's Fund, 1998

Royal College of Nursing, *More Nurses, Working Differently: A Review of the UK Nursing Labour Market in 2002*, London: Royal College of Nursing, 2002

Royce, Caroline, *et al.*, *Set Up to Fail? The Experience of Black Housing Associations*, London: YPS, 1996

Said, Edward, *Out of Place*, London: Granta Books, 2000

Samuel, Raphael (ed.), *Patriotism: The Making and Unmaking of British National Identity*, London: Routledge, 1989

Sanders, Ronald, *The Lower East Side*, New York: Dover Publications Inc., 1994

Sellick, Patricia, *Muslim Housing Experiences: A Research Report for the Housing Corporation*, Oxford: Oxford Centre for Islamic Studies, 2003

Sentamu, John, Archbishop for York, Inaugural Sermon, York Minster, November 2005

Shaw, Alison, *Kinship and Continuity: Pakistani Families in Britain*, Amsterdam: Harwood Academic, 2000

Sheinman, Mort (ed.), *A Tenement Story*, New York: Lower East Side Tenement Museum, 2004

Simpson, Ludi, *Measuring Residential Segregation*, University of Manchester, web report, www.ccsr.ac.uk/research/migseg.htm

Sivanayagam, S., *Sri Lanka: Witness to History*, London: Sivayogam, 2005

Smith, Susan J., *The Politics of Race and Residence*, Cambridge: Polity, 1989

Smith, Zadie, *White Teeth*, London: Hamish Hamilton, 2000

Spittles, Brian, *Britain Since 1960: An Introduction*, Basingstoke: Macmillan, 1995

Sriskandarajah, Dhananjayan, Cooley, Lawrence, and Reed, Howard, *Paying Their Way: The Fiscal Contributions of Immigrants to the UK*, London: IPPR, 2005

Sunkler, Bengt, and Steed, Christopher, *A History of the Church in Africa*, Cambridge: Cambridge University Press, 2000

Swamy, Narayan, *Inside an Elusive Mind: Prabhakaran*, Colombo: Vijitha Yapa Publications, 2004

Tomlinson, Sally, *Ethnic Minorities in British Schools*, Aldershot: Gower, 1987

Walvin, James, *Passage to Britain: Immigration in British History and Politics*, Harmondsworth: Pelican, 2004

Wilson, Deborah, 'Parallel Lives? Ethnic Segregation in Schools and Neighbourhoods', *Urban Studies*, Vol 42, Issue 7

Winder, Robert, *Bloody Foreigners*, London: Little, Brown, 2004

Index